MEMOIRS OF THE LIFE OF SIR SAMUEL ROMILLY

The Development of Industrial Society Series

MEMOIRS OF THE LIFE OF SIR SAMUEL ROMILLY

with a Selection from His Correspondence

Edited by His Sons

Volume 2

IRISH UNIVERSITY PRESS
Shannon Ireland

First edition London 1840

Second edition London 1840

This I U P reprint is a photolithographic facsimile of the second edition and is unabridged, retaining the original printer's imprint.

ISBN 0 7165 1784 1 Three volumes

ISBN 0 7165 1785 X Volume 1

ISBN 0 7165 1786 8 Volume 2

ISBN 0 7165 2062 1 Volume 3

T M MacGlinchey Publisher

Irish University Press Shannon Ireland

PRINTED IN THE REPUBLIC OF IRELAND BY
ROBERT HOGG PRINTER TO IRISH UNIVERSITY PRESS

MEMOIRS

OF

THE LIFE

OF

SIR SAMUEL ROMILLY,

WRITTEN BY HIMSELF;

WITH A SELECTION FROM

HIS CORRESPONDENCE.

EDITED BY HIS SONS.

IN THREE VOLUMES.

VOL. II.

Second Edition.

LONDON:
JOHN MURRAY, ALBEMARLE STREET.
MDCCCXL.

London:
Printed by A. Spottiswoode,
New-Street-Square.

CONTENTS

OF

THE SECOND VOLUME.

CORRESPONDENCE.

1792.

LETTER

LXXXVIII. — *To* MADAME G. The French revolution; conduct of the assembly. Slave-trade abolition; resolution rejected by the lords; feeling in favour of the bill. Lotteries - - - - Page 1

LXXXIX. — *To* M. DUMONT. Arrival of young D——. On the September massacres at Paris - - 3

XC. — *From* M. DUMONT. Death of M. de la Rochefoucauld. September massacres; how far provoked. Cabanis - - - - - - 5

XCI. — *To* M. DUMONT. On the September massacres. Union of political proscription, and religious persecution - - - - - - - 9

XCII. — *From* M. DUMONT. Parisian mob. Passports. Conduct of Catherine II. Louis XIV. Effect of the Prussian and Austrian alliance - 11

XCIII. — *From* THE MARQUIS OF LANSDOWNE. Country gentlemen. Reform in parliament. French clergy; persecution - - - - - - - 13

XCIV. — *From* MADAME G. The French republic. Trial of Louis XVI. Conduct of the convention. England and its institutions - - - - 15

1793.

LETTER

XCV.—*From* MADAME G. War with England; consolations. State of Paris - - Page 19

XCVI.—*To* M. DUMONT. Edinburgh. Dugald Stewart's account of Adam Smith. Administration of justice in Scotland. Scotch scenery; Loch Lomond. The Rev. Mr. Stuart - - - - - 21

XCVII.—*To* THE SAME. M. Guyot. Paris massacres. Manuel; anecdotes - - - - 26

XCVIII.—*To* THE SAME. On literary composition - 30

XCIX.—*From* M. DUMONT. The Gironde. Brissot - 31

C.—*To* M. DUMONT. Profession of the law. State of France. The Queen's trial. Kentucky. American writers - - - - - 36

1794.

CI.—*To* MADAME G. Anxiety for the safety of her family. State of France; of England - 38

CII.—*To* MR. DUGALD STEWART. Adam Smith. Imprisonment of Mr. D—— - - 40

CIII.—*To* MADAME G. Congratulations on the release of Mr. D——. Profession of the law. State of the country. Volunteers - - 42

1795.

CIV.—*To* MR. DUGALD STEWART. Expedition into Britany. Memoirs of the Girondistes. Madame Roland. Louvet - - - - - 46

CV.—*From* M. DUMONT. Garat's apology, and Mad. Roland's memoirs. Destruction of the Girondistes. The convention - - - - - 49

CVI.—*To* M. DUMONT. Garat. French character. French pamphlets; spies; prisons. Tronson du Coudray - - - - - - 52

1796.

CVII.—*To* THE SAME. London. Mitford's Greece. Literary composition. Charlotte Smith's novels. Drouet's escape - - - - - 55

LETTER

CVIII.—*From* M. DUMONT. Worthing. Literary composition - - - - Page 57

CIX.—*To* M. DUMONT. Proposed Visit to Bowood 60

1797.

CX.—*To* HIS NEPHEW. Friendship. Advice against too close an application to study. Hastings - 61

1798.

CXI.—*From* M. DUMONT. Congratulations on Mr. R.'s marriage - - - - - 63

CXII.—*From* MR. MANNERS SUTTON. Same subject 65

CXIII.—*To* MADAME G. Announcing his marriage - 65

CXIV.—*To* THE SAME. M. Corancez' book; Rousseau. Coxe's Memoirs of Sir Robert Walpole - 66

1799.

CXV.—*From* M. DUMONT. Education; Sandford and Merton - - - - - 68

CXVI.—*To* MADAME G. Criticisms on La Harpe - 70

1800.

CXVII.—*To* THE SAME. Riots; cause of them; mistaken expedients to check them; resolutions - 72

1802.

CXVIII.—*To* M. DUMONT. Bentham. *Traités de Législation civile et pénale.* Dugald Stewart's Life of Robertson. Hume - - - - 75

DIARY OF A JOURNEY TO PARIS.

Abbeville; beggars—improvement in the condition of the people and land.—Paris; Place de la Concorde.—Original MS. of Dr. Franklin's Life.—Talleyrand; England and France.—Picture by Girodet.—Gallois; Tribunal criminel; juries;

witnesses; frequent acquittals. Other courts; special juries; examination of the accused by the judges.—*Place de Grève;* the guillotine; execution.—Inscriptions on public buildings; monuments; Le Brun.—The opera.—Talleyrand; dinner at Neuilly.—St. Cloud; pictures.—Lotteries.—Madlle. Duchesnois.—Bonaparte.—Hall of the legislative body.—Palais Bourbon.—National Institute.—Galvanism.—Anniversary of the republic; illuminations.—Dinner at Talleyrand's.—Infernal machine.—Inscriptions in the Hôtel des Invalides.—Gallery of the Museum; West; pictures; Versailles.—Houses of the Bonaparte family; levee at St. Cloud.—National library; manuscripts.—Leaves Paris.—Abundance of specie; assignats; bank notes; high rates of interest; despotism in France; police; restraints upon the press; English newspapers prohibited; spies; Bonaparte. State prisoners.—Fouché; *Liberté* and *Egalité;* Tuileries; Bonaparte; cause of his power.—French opinion of Pitt; disposition to refine - - - - - - Pages 78—101

LETTER

CXIX.—*To* MADAME G. Friendship. Bonaparte's proclamation against the Swiss. Paley's Natural Theology - - - - - - - - 102

1803.

CXX.—*To* M. DUMONT. Edinburgh Review. Lord King. War with France. Influence of Pitt. Fox; Tierney. Bonaparte's detention of English travellers. Bentham - - - - - - - - 104

CXXI.—*To* MADAME G. Domestic happiness. Profession of the law. Bowood - - - - - - 107

NARRATIVE OF EVENTS IN 1805.

Romilly appointed Chancellor of Durham; circumstances which led to the appointment; Mr. Bernard; duties of the office; limited number of causes; reception at Durham.—Offer of a seat in parliament from the Prince of Wales; Creevey; Miss Seymour; Mrs. Fitzherbert; answer to Creevey's letter; Princess of Wales; Lady Douglas; Lord Thurlow - - - - - - - - Pages 109—132

DIARY OF HIS PARLIAMENTARY LIFE.

1806.

Romilly appointed Solicitor-General; Lord Erskine, Lord Chancellor. — R. sworn into office and knighted. — Chief Justice of the King's Bench a member of the cabinet. — R. elected member for Queenborough. — Took his seat and appointed one of the committee to manage Lord Melville's trial. — Cruel punishment in the navy; Rutherford. — Slave trade, Wilberforce. — Severity of military punishments, Mr. Grey, Mr. Windham. — Lotteries, Lord Henry Petty. — Law of Evidence, Master of the Rolls. — Liberty of the press, Sergeant Best. — Law of evidence. — Sheridan. — Lord Melville's trial; advice of Mr. Fox. — Slave trade; division in the House of Lords. — Princess of Wales, Lord Thurlow. — Mr. Forster, practice of the Court of Chancery, planting church lands. — Princess of Wales, Lord Grenville, Lady Douglas, Sir John Douglas. — Army enlisting for a limited time; Speech in favour of it. — Princess of Wales, witnesses, Sophia Austin. — Case of Miss Seymour. — Speech on slave trade. — Acquittal of Lord Melville. — Case of Miss Seymour. — Mr. Justice Fox. — Princess of Wales. — The King's power to legislate for conquered colonies, opposite opinions of the attorney and solicitor general. — Amendment of bankrupt laws. — Princess of Wales. — Applications to R. respecting the bankrupt laws. — Charges against Lord Wellesley. — Princess of Wales, report of the Commissioners. — Amendment of the bankrupt law, Lord Redesdale. — Parliament prorogued. — Fox, conduct of the Opposition. — Journey to Durham. — Fees in the Court of Chancery of Durham. — Journey to Edinburgh. — Reform of the Courts of Justice in Scotland. — Death of Fox. — Funeral. — Parliament dissolved. — Election at Queenborough. — Letter of Princess of Wales; (note) injunction to restrain the publication of it. — Cause of Purcell *v.* M'Namara; report of it in the newspapers; application to court to commit the author of it; Lord Erskine. — Meeting of parliament.
133—178

1807.

Whether real estates should be made assets to pay simple contract debts. — Welsh Judges, Lord Grenville. — General register of deeds. — Bill to make freehold estates assets to pay simple contract debts. — Judges, how far to be consulted before alterations are proposed in the law.—Princess of Wales. — Bill for the abolition of the slave trade. — Second reading of the bill to make freehold estates assets &c. — Second reading of the bill to abolish the slave trade. — An innocent man executed for a mutiny, of which he was convicted by a court-martial. — Bill to make freehold estates assets &c., Col. Eyre. — Probable change of administration. — Rejection of bill to make freehold estates assets. — Sir William Grant &c. — Conversation of Lord Erskine and George III. —Letter from Master of Rolls. — Change of administration. — Reflections on leaving office. — New ministry. — Lord Melville. — Lord Erskine. — Lord Melville. — The cry of No Popery. — Mr. Brand's motion. — Speech. — Plumer, Solicitor-General. — Debate in the House of Lords on the change of administration. — Bill to make freehold estates of *traders* assets &c. Dissolution of Parliament, speech of Lords Commissioners. — Sale of seats in Parliament. — Election for Horsham. — Imprisonment for debt, letter. — Meeting of new Parliament. — Bill to make freehold estates of *traders* assets &c. — Committee to inquire into the public expenditure. — Pension to Lord Cullen. — Education of the poor, Whitbread's bill. — Bill to abolish a privilege of members of Parliament, defendants in equity, injurious to other suitors. — Lord Cochrane's motion for an account of the places and pensions held by members of Parliament, their wives or children. — Public opinion respecting public men. — Cobbett. — Irish Insurrection Bill. — Bill to abolish a privilege of members, &c. — Education of the poor, Whitbread's bill. — Windham, Irish Arms Bill. — Bill to prevent the Crown from granting offices in reversion. — Ireland, resolution of Sheridan. — Parliament prorogued. — Bill to make freehold estates of *traders* assets &c. Lord Eldon. — Answering cases professionally. — Vacation in the Isle of Wight. — Letter to Dumont. — Criminal law, compensation to persons wrongfully accused, severity of punishment. — Court at Durham. Pp. 179—238

1808.

Meeting of Parliament. — Dinner at Lord Erskine's. — Criminal law. — George Wilson. — Lord Wellesley. — Decision of Horsham election petition. — Election for Wareham, terms of seat. — Criminal law, Scarlett. — Bill to repeal 8 Eliz. c. 4. — Bill for granting compensation to persons wrongfully accused. — Poor laws, settlements. — Too great frequency of oaths. — Pensions to Scotch judges who retire. — Criminal law, privately stealing from the person; Burton, Plumer, Abercromby. — Preamble of the bill to repeal the stat. of Eliz. — Letter of Lord Ellenborough, effect of the French Revolution, anecdote. — Tax on the alienation of property. — Tax on law proceedings. — Affairs of the Carnatic, conduct of Lord Wellesley. — Scotch judicature bill, appeals to the House of Lords. — Oyster-stealing made felony. — Parliament prorogued. — Privately stealing bill. — Vacation. — Bentham's treatise on punishments. — (Note) letter from Dr. Parr. — Bankrupt laws. — Duke of Sussex. — Duke of Kent; letters. Pages 239 — 266

1809.

Meeting of Parliament. — The Lords' Act extended to prisoners committed by courts of equity. — Bankrupt laws; object of bill. — Inquiry into the conduct of the Duke of York; Wardle; Mrs. Clarke; Captain Huxley Sandon. — Speech; (note) letter of Sir James Mackintosh. — Votes of the House of Commons. — Parliamentary reform; Major Cartwright; letters. — Votes of thanks in popular meetings. — Dinner of liverymen of London; letter to Mr. Waithman. — Bill to amend bankrupt law; law of evidence as to releasing a witness. — Sale of seats in Parliament (note), Cobbett. — Lotteries. — Criminal law returns. — Seditious meetings bill. — Welsh judges not to be members of Parliament. — Sale of seats in Parliament; bill to prevent. — Cruelty to animals. — Fees on pleading not guilty and on acquittal. — Bill to amend bankrupt laws; Lord Chancellor; alteration in bill. — Vacation. — Duel between Lord Castlereagh and Mr. Canning (note). — Resignation of two of the secretaries of state. — Perceval's proposal of a coalition. — Durham; the jubilee; sermon at Durham. — Sermon of Dr. Sparke. — Causes of the King's popularity; (note) Wilkes - - 267 — 307

1810.

Expedition to the Scheldt. — Offices in reversion. — Three bills to amend the criminal laws. — (Note) letters from Dr. Parr. — Pamphlet, observations on the criminal law, &c. — (Note) letter from Dugald Stewart. — Complaint of breach of privilege by John Gale Jones — Sir Francis Burdett. — Expedition to the Scheldt. — Sir Francis Burdett; privilege of parliament. — Popular disturbances. — Burdett's letter to the Speaker. — Motion for the discharge of John Gale Jones. — (Note) letter from Dr. Parr. — Petition from the inhabitants of Westminster. — Report of bills to amend the criminal law; Windham, (note) character of, by Mackintosh. — Master of the Rolls. — Returns of convicts. — City of London's petition to the House of Commons. — Penitentiary houses, and transportation to New South Wales. — Sir Francis Burdett, actions against the Speaker, &c. — Privilege of Parliament; course adopted by the House of Commons. — Reform of Parliament. — Thanks of the livery of London. — Criminal law. — Bill to repeal Shop-lifting Act. — Conduct of seven bishops; Lord Ellenborough's speech. — Cases before Mr. Justice Heath. — Lord Lauderdale, case before Lord Ellenborough. — Penitentiary houses. — Berkshire petition. — Irish arms bill. — Criminal law. — Business in Parliament towards the close of a session. — Criminal law. — Answer to Lord Ellenborough. — Bill to regulate the office of registrar of the Admiralty Court. — Office of deputy-remembrancer of the Exchequer. — Poor laws. — Reform in the practice of the chancery of Durham. — Reform of Parliament. — Parliament prorogued. — Sir F. Burdett released. — Vacation. — (Note) letter to M. Dumont. — Parliament met. — The King's illness. — Examination of the King's physicians. — Proceedings of the House of Commons on the King's illness - Pages 308—354

1811.

Pitt's reputation as a statesman. — Canning's attack; answer. — (Note) letter from Dr. Parr. — Parliament opened. — Objectionable clauses in the Regency Bill. — Question whether the Regent will be a responsible officer. — Joseph Lancaster's schools. — The Regency Bill passed. — The Regent sworn in. — The ministers continued in their offices. — Slave trade. — Returns of the number of convicts ordered. — Cruel military punishments, Lord Hutchinson. — Three bills to reform criminal law. — Pamphlet of criminal law. — (Note) letter of Dr. Parr. — Petitions of the owners of bleaching grounds against capital punishments. — Penitentiary houses. — Delay in the hearing of causes in the House of Lords and Court of Chancery, Lord Chancellor Eldon. — Parish apprentices. — Military punishments. — Spilsby poor bill. — Abuses in charitable institutions. — Lord Folkestone's motion respecting informations for libel. — Criminal law. — Law relating to printers. — Criminal law. — Bentham's work on punishments. — Delays in Chancery and House of Lords. — The poor laws. — Criminal law. — Delays in the Court of Chancery. — The Duke of York's restoration to office. — Parish apprentices. — Returns of convicts. — Delays in Court of Chancery. — Observations on proposed appointment of a third judge in Court of Chancery. — The Regent's festival. — Insolvent debtor's bill. — Lord Stanhope's bill to prevent the sale of bank notes for less than their nominal value. — Lord Chancellor. — Prospect of an approaching election; Lord Grenville's letter respecting Bristol; answer. — Letters respecting Middlesex election. — Major Cartwright's letter. Resolutions of the Middlesex freeholders' club. — Letter from Major Cartwright. — Case submitted. — Lord Chancellor and Master of the Rolls. — Bristol election; Mr. Harris's letter; answer - - - - Pages 355—433

MEMOIRS

OF

SIR SAMUEL ROMILLY.

CORRESPONDENCE WITH M. DUMONT AND OTHERS.

1792—1794.

LETTER LXXXVIII.

TO MADAME G——.

Madam, Lincoln's Inn, May 15. 1792.

I could willingly persuade myself that I am ill, merely that I might take the remedy which Mr. G—— recommends, and make a visit this summer to Paris. By much the strongest temptation I could have to adopt his prescription would be, to have the pleasure of seeing you both, and your excellent family. Indeed, I see little else to tempt me at Paris; and I have not the smallest wish to be present at the debates of your Assembly: to read them is more than sufficient. My opinion, however, is not in the least altered with respect to your revolution. Even the conduct of the present Assembly has not been able to shake my conviction that it is the most glorious event, and the happiest for mankind, that has ever taken place since human affairs have been recorded; and though I lament sincerely the miseries which have happened, and which still are to happen, I console myself with thinking that the evils of the revolution are transitory, and all the good of it is permanent.

You have heard, I suppose, what has passed here on the subject of the slave trade since Mr. G—— wrote; that the House of Commons came to a resolution that the trade should be abolished on the first of January, 1796, and carried that resolution up to the House of Lords; and that the Lords have determined to examine witnesses upon the subject, which must take up so much time, that there is little prospect of any Bill passing in the present session. This, however, will be no great misfortune; and, strange as it may appear, will probably accelerate the abolition. It is very likely that the House of Commons will, in the next session, pass a Bill for an immediate abolition; and, though the Lords may at first reject it, they will hardly venture to do so a second time, and they will certainly have a second Bill sent to them. However sincere the Lords are in their zeal for slavery, they will hardly carry their sincerity so far as to endanger their own authority; and the cause of the negro slaves is at present taken up with as much warmth in almost every part of the kingdom as could be found in any matter in which the people were personally and immediately interested. Innumerable petitions for the abolition have been presented to Parliament, and (what proves men's zeal more strongly than petitions) great numbers have entirely discontinued the use of sugar. All persons, and even the West India planters and merchants, seem to agree that it is impossible the trade should last many years longer.

We are likely, too, to get rid of another evil, the mischievous effects of which are felt every day among ourselves, that of lotteries. There has been a debate on the subject in the House of Commons; and it seems understood that, after the present year, there are to be no more lotteries. In these two instances, the Parliament has followed the opinion of the public, though it must be owned that it has been the speeches of members of the Parliament which has greatly contributed to form the public opinion.

I remain, &c. &c.,

SAML. ROMILLY.

LETTER LXXXIX.

TO M. DUMONT.

Dear Dumont, Lincoln's Inn, Sept. 10. 1792.

I hoped by this time to have been at Bowood, but several things have happened unexpectedly to prevent me; one of the principal has been the arrival here of the eldest of the young D——s. His whole family, you know, are accused of being aristocrats, though their only *aristocratism* consists in wishing to defend a constitution which all France has sworn to maintain. He was himself particularly obnoxious, for he was in the castle on the 10th of August, commanding a battalion of the National Guard. He has accordingly been *denounced* by the Jacobins, and he got away with great difficulty, and without any passport. He has come, as might be supposed, without letters, and has scarce any acquaintance here. I have been endeavouring to be as useful to him as I could. You know how much I am, and how much reason I have to be, attached to his family. I had not seen much of him till now; but I find him very sensible, well informed, and amiable.

I observe that, in your letter, you say nothing about France, and I wish I could do so too, and forget the affairs of that wretched country altogether; but that is so impossible, that I can scarcely think of any thing else. How could we ever be so deceived in the character of the French nation as to think them capable of liberty! wretches, who, after all their professions and boasts about liberty, and patriotism, and courage, and dying, and after taking oath after oath, at the very moment when their country is invaded and an enemy is marching through it unresisted, employ whole days in murdering women, and priests, and prisoners![1] Others, who can deliberately load whole waggons full of victims, and bring them like beasts to be butchered in the metropolis; and then (who are worse even than these) the cold instigators of these murders, who, while blood is stream-

[1] The massacres at Paris took place on the 2d, 3d, and 4th of September.

ing round them on every side, permit this carnage to go on, and reason about it, and defend it, nay, even applaud it, and talk about the example they are setting to all nations. One might as well think of establishing a republic of tigers in some forest in Africa, as of maintaining a free government among such monsters.

My plan, at present, if nothing should happen to derange it, is to be with you in the middle of the next week, and to go from Bowood to Warwick to the sessions, where I must be at the beginning of October. I have seen the Duke de Liancourt twice, and am to dine with him to-day at Bentham's: I like him extremely.

Yours, &c.

S. R.

Letter XC.

FROM M. DUMONT.

Bowood, Sept. 11. 1792.

Je vous réponds tout de suite, mon cher Romilly, pour vous prier d'écarter autant qu'il vous sera possible tous les obstacles, et de venir à Bowood au temps marqué ou plutôt.

Letter XC.

Bowood, Sept. 11. 1792.

I answer your letter at once, my dear Romilly, to beg that you will do what you possibly can to remove all impediments, and come to Bowood at the appointed time, or sooner.

Vous deviez être à diner chez Bentham quand on a appris à M. de Liancourt la mort horrible de M. de la Rochefoucauld. Nous avons cherché à croire que c'étoit le Cardinal et non pas le Duc; quoique ces bêtes féroces n'aient pas plus de droit à tuer l'un que l'autre: cependant les vertus, les services, le patriotisme du dernier, aggraveroient bien l'horreur de ce massacre.

Je me promène la moitié du jour dans une agitation extrême, et par l'impossibilité de rester en place, en pensant à tous les événemens malheureux qui découlent d'une source d'où nous nous sommes flattés de voir sortir le bonheur du genre humain. Brûlons tous les livres, cessons de penser et de rêver au meilleur système de législation, puisque les hommes font un abus infernal de toutes les vérités et de tous les principes. Qui croiroit qu'avec de si belles maximes on pût se livrer à de tels excès, et que la constitution, la plus extravagante en fait de liberté, paroîtroit à ces sauvages le code de la tyrannie! Le passé est affreux, mais ce qu'il y a

---

You must have been dining at Bentham's when M. de Liancourt received the news of the horrible death of M. de la Rochefoucauld. We tried to persuade ourselves that it was the Cardinal and not the Duke; for although those wild beasts had no more right to kill the one than the other, yet the virtues, the services, the patriotism of the latter would add much to the horror of this butchery. I walk about half the day in a state of the greatest agitation, from the impossibility of remaining still, with my thoughts fixed upon all the sad events which are flowing from a source whence we had flattered ourselves human happiness was to arise. Let us burn all our books, let us cease to think and dream of the best system of legislation, since men make so diabolical a use of every truth and every principle.

Who would believe that with such noble maxims it would be possible for men to give themselves over to such excesses, and that a constitution, the most extravagant in point of freedom, should appear to these savages the code of tyranny! The past is hideous; but what

de plus affreux encore, c'est qu'on ne peut rien attendre, rien espérer pour l'avenir. Nous ne verrons que déchiremens et massacres. A moins que la France ne se divise en un grand nombre d'états indépendans, il est impossible de se former une idée du rétablissement de l'ordre.

Je cherche pourtant à balancer ces idées par d'autres : je sens bien que le peuple est jeté dans cet état de fièvre par l'approche des ennemis ; je me rappelle l'état de colère et de douleur frénétique où j'ai été moi-même, quand j'ai vu trois armées environner Genève pour nous soumettre à un gouvernement odieux. Je comprends que dans une grande ville comme Paris où tant de passions fermentent, elles ont dû s'exalter jusqu'à la fureur contre les aristocrates, qui ont attiré ces fléaux d'Autriche et de Prusse sur leur patrie ; et comme la déclaration sanguinaire de l'Attila[1] Prussien a

---

is still more frightful is, that there is nothing to expect, nothing to hope, from the future. We shall see nothing but destruction and massacre. Unless France should separate into a great number of independent states, it is impossible to form an idea in what way order is to be re-established.

I endeavour, however, to find some counterpoise for these thoughts. I know that it is the approach of a hostile army which has thrown the people into this fever : I have not forgotten the rage and frantic grief which I myself endured, when I saw Geneva surrounded by three armies, united to enforce our submission to a government we detested. I can conceive that, in a great city like Paris, where so many passions are in constant ferment, they must have risen to a pitch of madness against the aristocrats, who have drawn down upon their country the scourges of Austria and Prussia ; and that when the people found that the sanguinary manifesto of the Prussian Attila [1] threatened to destroy

---

[1] The manifesto of the Duke of Brunswick, who was afterwards mortally wounded at the battle of Jena, in 1806.

menacé de tout mettre à feu et à sang, de faire périr dans les flammes ceux qui auroient échappé au fer, ils se seront dit à eux-mêmes qu'avant de périr, il falloit ôter aux conspirateurs la joie du triomphe. Dans le dernier accès ils ont égorgé les prisonniers, parce qu'il s'est répandu un bruit qu'à l'approche du Duc de Brunswick, les prisons seroient ouvertes, et que tous les prisonniers acheteroient leur grace en servant leur Roi, et en se tournant contre les patriotes.

Je reçois une lettre de Paris de l'homme le plus doux et le plus humain que je connoisse, et il paroît croire que tout ce qui est arrivé est nécessaire, que c'est le dénouement d'une conspiration, et que, sans cela, Paris étoit certainement livré aux troupes étrangères. C'est M. Cabanis[1] qui m'écrit ainsi. Il n'a nul intérêt dans la révolution ; il est égaré par l'esprit de parti : mais quand l'esprit de parti égare les hommes bons et éclairés,

---

all with fire and sword, that those who should escape the one might perish by the other, so they may have said to themselves, "Before we die, at least let us snatch from the conspirators the joy of their triumph." In their last paroxysm they murdered the prisoners, because a report had been spread that, at the approach of the Duke of Brunswick, the prisons would be thrown open, and that the prisoners would purchase their pardon by serving their king, and turning against the patriots.

I have just received a letter from Paris, written by the mildest, the most humane man I am acquainted with, and he seems to think that all that has taken place was necessary ; that it was the subversion of a conspiracy, and that without it Paris would undoubtedly have been given up to foreign troops. It is M. Cabanis[1], who writes to me thus. He has no interest in the success of the revolution ; he is misled by party-spirit : but when party-spirit misleads good and enlightened men,

---

[1] The author of *Rapports du Physique et du Moral de l'Homme*, and several other works. He was Mirabeau's physician in his last illness, and published an account of that illness.

il faut bien qu'il ait quelque couleur spécieuse. On n'a aucun doute des trahisons de la Cour. Beaucoup de Feuillants qui croyoient servir la constitution sont revenus à l'Assemblée, et sont les plus indignés contre le Roi, parcequ'ils ont été les dupes d'un parti qui s'étoit servi, pour les tromper, de leur bonne foi même. Voilà comme on parle. Mille choses de ma part à nos amis communs.

Adieu! tout à vous, &c.

Et. D.

Letter XCI.

TO M. DUMONT.

Dear Dumont, Sept. 15. 1792.

I am exceedingly obliged to Lord Lansdowne for his invitation of my friend D——. I have mentioned it to him, and he begs you would return Lord Lansdowne a great many thanks for his goodness. He seems, however, afraid of going so far from London, and of receiving news from his relations at this alarming time twenty-four hours later than he would if he stayed here. But still

---

it must surely have assumed some specious form. No doubt is entertained of the treachery of the Court. Many Feuillants, who hoped to do service to the constitution, have returned to the Assembly, and are the more indignant against the King, inasmuch as they have been the dupes of a party who have made their very honesty an instrument in deceiving them. This is what is said.

A thousand kind messages to our common friends. Adieu.

Yours, &c.

Et. D.

if I can persuade him to go, I shall; for solitude in his situation, with a thousand ideal dangers continually present to his mind, is terrible.

You know undoubtedly that it is the Duke de la Rochefoucauld who has been murdered. His own tenants, it is said, were among his assassins. The Cardinal had been murdered before at the Carmes; and M. Chabot Rohan, the brother of Mad[e]. de la Rochefoucauld, and the grandson of Mad[e]. d'Anville, was among those who were killed at the Abbaye. He was a very young man: perhaps you do not recollect him, but we dined with him at the Duke de la R.'s, in '88. There seems to be no doubt that all these assassinations were planned and directed by the persons who have now the power in their hands. Manuel sent an order to the Abbaye to release M. de Jaucourt on the morning of the massacre, but before there was any talk among the mob of attacking any of the prisons.

I don't think the observations you make afford the smallest extenuation of the guilt of the murderers. Observe that, at the time of these massacres, though the Duke of Brunswick was marching towards Paris, yet all the Parisians, with their stupid confidence, were very sure he could never reach the capital; and that the fury of these wretches has been directed, not against aristocrats, who would triumph at the Duke of Brunswick's victories, but against the persons who have, during the revolution, always acted the most conspicuous part on the side of the people, and who would be proscribed, and their estates confiscated,

if the revolution should be overturned. It is impossible to walk a hundred yards in any public street here in the middle of the day, without meeting two or three French priests. Who would have conceived that, at the close of the eighteenth century, we should see, in the most civilized country in Europe, all the horrors of political proscriptions and religious persecution united?

I hope to be with you by the middle of next week.

Yours sincerely,

S. R.

LETTER XCII.

FROM M. DUMONT.

Bowood, Sept. 16. 1792.

Tâchez d'amener M. D——; nous avons les lettres le matin à 9 heures, il n'y a que douze heures de différence pour la plupart.

Le meurtre du Duc de la Rochefoucauld n'est que trop vrai. Garat en parle avec un sang-froid atroce, " M. de la Rochefoucauld, qui se laissoit toujours appeler Duc, a été tué." Il y a dix à

LETTER XCII.

Bowood, Sept. 16. 1792.

Try to bring M. D—— with you. We get our letters at nine in the morning, generally, not more than twelve hours later than in London.

The murder of the Duke de la Rochefoucauld is but too true. Garat speaks of it with a cold-blooded indifference, which is atrocious. " M. de la Rochefoucauld," he says, " who always permitted himself to be styled Duke, has been killed." There are some ten or twelve men,

douze hommes, plus noirs que tous les assassins de la terre, qui seront la cause que l'Europe entière devient insensible au sort des François, et les verra passer avec plaisir sous le joug.

Je ne sais si l'histoire de Manuel est vraie. Je sais seulement que l'Assemblée Nationale est atrocement coupable des tous les meutres qui se feront encore, en n'ayant pas immédiatement aboli le décret sur les passeports. Fermer les portes d'un empire, où le peuple furieux massacre sur un soupçon tous ceux qui ne pensent pas comme lui, c'est être responsable de tous les assassinats qui se commettent.

Je ne veux pas exténuer des horreurs qui font chanceler tous mes principes, mais je cherche à voir ce qui est; c'est que, si les peuples sont féroces, les despotes ne le sont pas moins. Comptez les personnes qui ont été en Pologne les victimes d'une seule femme.[1] Pensez que cette seule femme, sans provocation, sans cause quelconque, peut

---

blacker than all the assassins of the earth, who will be the cause that all Europe will become careless as to the fate of the French people, and will look on with satisfaction while they pass under the yoke.

I do not know whether the story of Manuel is true. I only know this, that the National Assembly is atrociously guilty of all the murders which may yet be committed, in not having immediately repealed the decree on passports. To shut the gates of a kingdom, in which a frantic people butcher on bare suspicion all those who do not think as they do, is to be responsible for all the murders that are perpetrated.

I do not attempt to palliate horrors which shake all my principles, but I endeavour to see things as they are; and I know that, if the people are ferocious, despots are no less so. Reckon the number of persons who, in Poland, have been the victims of a single woman.[1] Only reflect that this one woman, without provocation, without any

---

[1] Catherine II. of Russia.

s'attribuer à elle seule la mort de deux millions d'hommes. Pensez à Louis XIV., et vous conviendrez peut-être qu'on peut désirer encore le succès des armes Françoises, la destruction des Prussiens et des Autrichiens, sans offenser l'humanité. Si les François sont battus, je me résignerai à l'événement plus aisément que je n'aurois fait sans les horreurs commises. Mais je ne puis m'empêcher de frémir contre cette ligue qui ne sauroit être justifiée dans son principe, puisque les crimes les plus noirs du peuple François sont postérieurs à cette ligue, et principalement occasionnés par elle.

Nous vous attendons avec impatience. Adieu.

ET. D.

LETTER XCIII.

FROM LORD LANSDOWNE.

Dear Mr. Romilly, Bowood Park, Oct. 8. 1792.

I only wish you to like Bowood half as well as Bowood likes you.

---

cause whatever, may lay claim to the deaths of two millions of human beings. Think of Louis XIV., and you will perhaps admit that one may still wish for the success of the French arms, and for the destruction of the Prussians and Austrians, without offence to humanity. If the French should be beaten, I shall make up my mind to the event more easily than I should have done if these horrible scenes had never been acted. But I cannot help shuddering at this league, the principle of which it is impossible to justify, inasmuch as the blackest of the crimes of the French people were subsequent to it, and for the most part occasioned by it.

We expect you impatiently. Adieu.

ET. D.

As to the Warwickshire country gentleman, I am only afraid that he is the same with those of every other county in England. I thank God, the King has nobody about him cunning and wicked enough to advise him to meet the desire of reform, and compose a parliament of qualified men. I mean in the solid legal sense, for I verily believe a more corrupt, ignorant, and tyrannical assembly, would not be to be found upon the face of the earth, especially with a little scattering of a certain profession, which I will not presume to name, but which the King has found too useful, to consent to any reform which went to exclude them.

I pity the French very sincerely, particularly the clergy; but, after all, those who have any elevation of mind cannot be considered in such a desperate situation. I have always doubted whether an ambitious man, whose object is fame, gained most by being persecuted or favoured through life. So far as kings are concerned, I am sure they gain most by being persecuted; and people resemble kings so much, that I believe it makes no great difference, except that the people are sure to open their eyes sooner or later, and where they have been guilty of injustice, to repay with ample interest either the dead or the living. The clergy have no families; the harshness under which they suffer gives a dignity to their deportment, if they know how to assume it, and certainly no small degree of interest. I am sure there is not a priest of them all who will be half so miserable as the Duke of Brunswick, if he continues to have the worst of the campaign; but the clock

strikes six, and I am not dressed, and you know the government under which I live, so that I hope you will excuse my bidding you adieu so very abruptly.

Ever yours,
LANSDOWNE.

LETTER XCIV.

FROM MADAME G——.

Passy, 9 Décembre, 1792.

Il y a bien longtemps, Monsieur, que nous sommes privés de vos lettres; c'est bien notre faute, mais j'espère que vous n'aurez pas un seul instant accusé notre amitié, et plutôt les circonstances qui ont été si extraordinaires qu'elles laissoient peu de présence d'esprit.

Nous sommes bien sûrs que vous avez suivi, avec un intérêt souvent mêlé d'horreur, tous les évènemens qui se sont accumulés dans cette mémorable époque. Nous sommes toujours dans un chaos effrayant, et il ne reste pas le plus léger

---

LETTER XCIV.

Passy, December 9. 1792.

We have been for a long time, Sir, without letters from you; the fault is certainly our own, but I trust that you will not for one moment have attributed our silence to want of friendship, but rather to circumstances which have been so extraordinary as to leave but little time for thought.

We feel sure that you have followed up, with interest often mixed with horror, all the events which have crowded one upon another during this memorable epoch. We are still in a state of disorder the

rayon d'espoir de voir bientôt renaître un ordre de choses calme et paisible: tous les élémens révolutionnaires sont si bien réunis, et répandus avec tant de profusion dans toute l'étendue de la République; nous sommes si savans et si habiles en conjuration, qu'il est peu probable que des semblables talens ne cherchent pas à faire naître et durer toutes les circonstances qui leur seront favorables pour briller. Nous sommes donc destinés aux agitations de tout genre pour un temps illimité, et nous regrettons d'avoir une disposition d'esprit qui est entièrement contraire à cette manière d'être. Nous touchons dans ce moment à une catastrophe[1] horrible, qui laissera sur le nom François une tache indélébile, et qui aura des suites plus funestes qu'on ne peut le prévoir. On apporte dans ce procès une partialité, une injustice, qui ajoute encore à l'atrocité du forfait, et qui produit une indignation sourde, mais que la peur empêche de laisser percer;

---

most fearful; and not the slightest ray of hope remains of seeing any speedy return to a state of peace and tranquillity. All the elements of revolution are so well combined, and spread with such profusion over the whole surface of the Republic, we are so learned and skilful in conspiracies, that it is little probable that such talents as these should cease to encourage and keep alive every thing which may favour their display. We are, therefore, doomed for an unlimited time to agitation of every kind; and it is become matter of regret that the character of our minds should be wholly opposed to this kind of life. We are now on the eve of a horrible catastrophe[1], which will leave an indelible stain on the French name, and which will have more fatal consequences than it is possible to foresee. This trial is being conducted with a degree of partiality, of injustice, which, if possible, adds to the atrocity of the crime, and produces a silent indignation, which fear prevents from breaking out; for

---

[1] The trial of Louis XVI.

car il y a parmi les soi-disant honnêtes gens de la convention une lâcheté, qui égale la férocité barbare de l'autre parti. Ces circonstances affectent profondément, quelque effort qu'on fasse pour s'en distraire ou s'en désintéresser.

Nous sommes aussi très-affectés des nouvelles qu'on exagère, sans doute, de ce qui se passe en Angleterre. C'étoit là que nous allions nous réfugier en imagination, quand nous voulions trouver une liberté sage, et accompagnée du respect pour les lois. Nous nous flattons cependant que notre exemple vous sera utile, que vous saurez arrêter l'incendie à temps, et en modérer les effets. Nos vœux pour le bonheur de ce beau pays sont bien sincères, et votre opinion sur ce qui s'y passe nous seroit très-précieuse. Tout en gémissant sur les malheurs de l'humanité, nous jouissons cependant de tout le bonheur particulier qui nous est laissé. Comme il y a plusieurs sortes d'inconvéniens à passer l'hiver à Paris, nous sommes tous

---

there is amongst the self-called *honest* members of the convention, a degree of cowardice which equals the savage ferocity of the other side. One cannot but be deeply affected at all this, however much one may strive to divert one's thoughts from the subject, or to divest one's self of all personal interest in it.

The accounts, too, of what is passing in England, although no doubt exaggerated, give us great pain. It was the land of refuge for our imagination when we sought for an example of well-regulated liberty, combined with respect for the law. We trust, at least, that our example will not be thrown away upon you, and that you will know before it be too late how to arrest and moderate the flame of popular enthusiasm. Our wishes for the welfare of your noble country are very sincere, and your opinion of what is passing there would be highly valued by us. While mourning over the sufferings of human nature, we yet enjoy that domestic happiness which still remains to us. As a winter at Paris would be attended with many inconveniences, we are all united

en famille réunis à ce Passy où nous avons eu le plaisir de vous voir, et nous y savourons tous les genres de jouissances domestiques.

Nous trouvons qu'en général le commerce des hommes ne donne que des chagrins et du dégoût pour la pauvre humanité, et nous voudrions beaucoup nous en détacher, pour le remplacer par des études et des occupations qui ne laissent après elles aucun genre d'amertume. Vous comprendrez, j'espère, Monsieur, que ce qui cause notre misantropie nous rend encore plus chers et précieux les liens de l'amitié ; les sentimens que nous avons pour vous sont du nombre de ceux qui consolent de voir les hommes se dégrader par tous les excès que dictent les passions, parcequ'on sent qu'il y a des compensations. Nous vous prions de ne pas oublier que tout ce qui vous touche nous intéresse particulièrement, et nous vous demandons de nous prouver que vous en êtes persuadé, en entrant avec nous dans quelque détail sur ce qui vous concerne.

---

in our family circle at that Passy where we had the pleasure of seeing you, and here we taste with the same relish as ever all the various pleasures of domestic life.

We find that the intercourse of the world produces for the most part only sorrow and disgust for wretched humanity; and we would willingly keep aloof from it, and replace it by studies and occupations which leave no bitterness behind them. You will, I trust, understand that what makes us misanthropical, renders still dearer and more precious to us the ties of friendship ; the sentiments we entertain towards you are among those which console us when we see men degrading themselves by the commission of every excess which is prompted by their passions, because we feel that there are compensations. Pray do not forget that there is nothing which affects you, in which we do not take a lively interest; and we beg you to prove to us that you do not doubt it, by giving us a particular account of whatever concerns you.

Je suis obligée de fermer précipitamment cette lettre. Agréez toutes les assurances de notre amitié.

Letter XCV.

FROM MADAME G——.

Paris, 13 Mars, 1793.

Nous ne pouvons pas, Monsieur, laisser partir M. Dumont sans lui remettre quelques lignes, qui vous donnent de nouvelles assurances de notre amitié et de notre souvenir.

Quoique les sensations individuelles soient bien secondaires auprès des grands intérêts, qui agitent dans ces temps-ci, nous n'avons pu voir sans chagrin l'interruption, ou plutôt les difficultés de communication que la guerre apportera entre vous et nous. Cette rupture[1] nous a profondément affligés par les maux inévitables qu'elle doit causer

---

I am obliged to conclude my letter in haste. Believe ever in our friendship.

Letter XCV.

Paris, March 13. 1793.

We cannot allow Mr. Dumont to set off without making him the bearer of a few lines, to assure you that we have the same friendship for you, and that you are as often in our thoughts, as ever. Although all private feelings are of secondary importance, compared with the mighty interests which now agitate men's minds, it has been impossible for us to observe without pain the interruption, or rather the difficulty of communication between us which this war will occasion. We are deeply grieved to think of the inevitable evils which this rupture[1] will

---

[1] The National Convention declared war against Great Britain on the 1st of February, 1793.

aux deux pays. Combien l'humanité a lieu de gémir, quelques soient les suites de ce bouleversement général; lors même que la fin seroit parfaitement heureuse et glorieuse, il est impossible que tous les cœurs sensibles ne souffrent pas cruellement des moyens. Au milieu des calamités publiques nous conservons le même bonheur domestique; nous pourrions dire même que le nôtre en est augmenté: les liens de l'intimité se resserrent encore, dans les momens où le cœur froissé sent le besoin de ses consolations. D'ailleurs ce qu'on appeloit autrefois devoirs de société, les visites, les repas, les assemblées, n'étant plus de mise dans les circonstances actuelles, l'on se trouve plus habituellement auprès de ses vrais amis, et l'on les en aime davantage; l'on jouit de la douceur de gémir avec eux, mais vous savez que ce ne peut être que bien *bas*. Paris est violemment agité depuis quelques jours; on voudroit faire partir tout le monde pour l'armée, et il y a bien quelques op-

---

bring upon both countries. How much humanity has reason to lament, whatever may be the consequences of the general confusion; even though the end should prove glorious and happy, no feeling heart can fail to be cruelly affected by the means.

In the midst of public calamity, the happiness of our family circle is the same as ever. We might almost say that it is increased; for the ties of intimacy are drawn closer when the bruised heart feels the want of consolation. Besides, what were formerly called the duties of society, visits, dinners, and parties being no longer suited to existing circumstances, one is thrown more habitually amongst one's real friends, to whom, on that account, one becomes the more attached. One finds a pleasure in uniting one's lamentations to theirs, although you are aware that it must be only in a whisper.

Paris has been for some days in a state of violent agitation; every one is required to set off to join the army, and this meets with some

positions. Cependant il partira beaucoup d'hommes, et les sacrifices d'argent pour les bien payer et les bien habiller sont considérables. C'est bien le moment de vaincre ou de mourir, car quelle espèce de miséricorde pourrions-nous attendre de nos ennemis ? Nous vous comptons avec bien du regret dans le nombre, et nous tournons nos regards avec amertume vers le temps où nous vous faisions des sollicitations pour nous venir voir.

Mon mari se joint à moi pour vous assurer de notre inviolable amitié, et pour vous prier de penser à nous.

D. G.

Letter XCVI.

TO M. DUMONT.

Dear Dumont, September 14. 1793.

I have just received your second letter, and must with shame confess that no letter of mine to you has miscarried, for I have never yet written to you. You will, I am sure, do me the justice to believe that I have not been able to find half an hour's leisure since I left London, or you would

---

opposition. However, a great number of men will go, and great sacrifices are made to pay them well and clothe them well. This is indeed the moment to conquer or die, for what mercy could we expect from our enemies ? It is with pain we reckon you amongst the number, and we call to mind with bitter regret the time when we entreated you to come and visit us. My husband joins me in assuring you of our unalterable friendship, and in begging that you will sometimes think of us.

Yours, &c. &c.

D. G.

certainly have heard from me. At Edinburgh, which is the only place where I have been at all stationary, the business I came about occupied, on an average, five or six hours of every day. I had then to see the curiosities of the place, and the charming country about it, and I had every day dinner and supper parties in a very excellent society. You will easily believe that all this left me few moments of leisure, so few that I have hardly been able to read a newspaper, and that I know little more of what is passing on the Continent than what I have heard in conversation.

The society I have been living in has consisted principally of lawyers and men of letters. Among the last of these, the person whom I most saw and lived with at Edinburgh, was our friend Mr. Dugald Stewart, whom the more I know the more I esteem for the qualities of his heart, and the more I admire and respect for his knowledge and his talents.

He is at this moment printing two works; one, An Account of Adam Smith and his Writings, to be published in the *Transactions of the Edinburgh Society*; and the other, the heads of his Lectures on Moral Philosophy, a part of which only he has already published in the book which you are well acquainted with. This last work is only intended for the use of the students who attend his lectures, but he has promised me a copy. He has shown me part of his account of Adam Smith, which is very interesting. It contains a history of his different works; but Mr. Stewart has unfortunately resolved to be much shorter in what he says of the *Wealth of Nations* than he had once intended.

Smith's life, as you may suppose, does not abound with extraordinary events. There is one, however, which happened to him in his infancy, which is worth mentioning: he was stolen by some gipsies, and they had carried him to the distance of some miles before they were overtaken. A little more expedition on their part, or a little more delay on the part of their pursuers, and that acuteness and invention, which has produced a work that will benefit the latest posterity, would have been wholly exercised in finding out irregular expedients to preserve a precarious existence. I have seen many of Adam Smith's friends here, and he seems to have been loved and revered by every body who knew him.

Nothing is wanting to Edinburgh but a fine climate to make it the place in which I should prefer, before any that I have seen, to pass my life, if I were obliged to pass it in any town. Nothing can surpass the beauty of the country around it, which is rich, highly cultivated, well wooded, well peopled, and bounded on the different sides with the sea or with mountains. I have been pleased with every thing I have seen in Edinburgh and about it, except the persons of the women; I mean those of the lower ranks of life, who are certainly very plain; and the administration of justice, which I think detestable. I am not surprised that you have been shocked at the account you have read of Muir's trial; you would have been much more shocked if you had been present at it as I was. I remained there both days, and think I collected, in the course of them, some interesting materials.

You may judge, however, from the account I gave you of the manner of my spending my time, that I have not been able to collect any materials on any subject in a more faithful repository than my memory; and as that was never very good, is pretty much used, and is stuffed tolerably full, I am afraid I shall lose a good deal of what I have been collecting.

I write this letter, as you may guess from the different coloured inks, in different inns, just as I have five or ten minutes' leisure, and am at this moment at Luss, a little village on the side of Loch Lomond, in a most romantic country, by the side of an immense lake (Loch Lomond), which is enclosed with mountains and enriched with islands. My course from Edinburgh has been to Linlithgow, from thence to Falkirk and the iron-works at Carron, and so on to Stirling, which, as well as Linlithgow, was formerly the residence of the kings of Scotland. I am not much given to copy the inscriptions which I meet with on my travels; but I was very much struck with one I saw at Stirling. It was indeed so modern, having been only put up the last year, that no learned traveller would have deigned to look at it. It is upon some alms-houses, which were founded by a tailor. He had, in the exercise of his trade, earned a considerable fortune, which he chose to employ in this foundation, and in establishing a fund for repairing bridges. The inscription commemorates this fact, and then concludes with these words: "Forget not, reader, that the shears of this man do more honour to human nature than the swords of conquerors."

I have been perfectly astonished at the richness and high cultivation of all the tract of this calumniated country through which I have passed, and which extends above sixty miles, quite from Edinburgh to the mountains where I now am. It is true, however, that almost every thing which one sees to admire in the way of cultivation is due to modern improvements; and, now and then, one observes a few acres of brown moss, contrasting admirably with the corn-fields to which they are contiguous, and affording one a specimen of the dreariness and desolation which, half a century ago, overspread a country now cultivated and scattered over with comfortable habitations, and become a most copious source of human happiness. I complained to you formerly of the climate, and I never had more reason to be out of humour with it than at this moment, when the rain is pouring down, and spreading a veil between me and one of the most beautiful views that I have ever seen.

I take up my pen to conclude this long letter. While I was complaining of the rain it began to cease, and I soon afterwards set out for an island, on an eminence of which I had a beautiful view of the lake, its islands, and the surrounding country. I was accompanied by the minister of the parish, a Mr. Stuart, to whom Mr. Dugald Stewart gave me a letter. I afterwards dined with him, and found in him the hospitality and *naïveté* of a mountaineer, and the learning and cultivated mind of one who had divided his whole time between study and the society of a metropolis. I was quite delighted to make acquaintance with him. In the morning he preaches at his church in English, and in the afternoon in Erse; and he is now translating the Bible into Erse, a considerable part of which has been already printed. After dinner I proceeded to this place (Dumbarton), in my way to Glasgow, which I shall reach to-morrow morning. From thence I shall return to London, though not by the most direct road.

S. R.

Letter XCVII.

TO THE SAME.

Dear Dumont, Lincoln's Inn, Oct. 2. 1793.

I am so sensible of my fault in not having written to you oftener while I was in Scotland, that I have sat down with a firm resolution of writing you a very long letter now that I am returned, and nothing less than the interruption of a client shall prevent my keeping my resolution. Since my return I have been overloaded with business, and I have found accumulated for the few days I have to be here all the business which would have been thinly scattered through the last two months, if I had been in town. Of the little time I have had to spare, a part has been taken up with Mr. Guyot, whom I found here on my return from Scotland, and who is now set off for that country himself. I was very glad to see him, both on his own account, (for, with all the faults which you impute to him, he has many very estimable and amiable qualities,) and because he brought me some news of the D——'s. They are still well, and at Passy; and what may be deemed extraordinary good fortune, notwithstanding their riches, they have not yet been any of them fixed on as objects of persecution. The second son, however, has been compelled to take arms, but by special favour he has been permitted to enter into the corps of engineers, and has been allowed a little time to qualify himself for that situation, so that he has a short respite before he will be compelled to risk his life in defence of the oppressors of his country. The eldest son is still at Hamburg. G.'s brother, who was in the National Guard, has been murdered in a riot at Lyons. Guyot was at Paris in August and September of last year, and I have learned many more curious particulars of the events of that time, in a few hours' conversation with him, than are to be found in all the five or six hundred pages of Dr. Moore. He left Paris immediately after the massacres of September; and, although he was a foreigner, it was with great difficulty that he obtained a passport. Finding all other resources fail him, he resolved to try what influence he might have on Manuel, with whom he had once been intimate, and whom he had introduced to the D—— family. Accordingly he went to the Hôtel de Ville, and was there conducted into a room where a number of persons were assembled, all waiting to have an audience of Manuel. A profound silence prevailed among them, and the deepest melancholy and dejection was painted on every countenance. Guyot could not conjecture who they were; but he soon found that they were the relations and friends of persons, who had been confined in different prisons, come to inquire what had been their fate. The mode adopted to answer their inquiries, and to remove their anxious uncertainty, was this; they were taken one by one into a room, where were strewed about a number of fragments of clothes, torn, stained with dirt, or soaked in blood; and if, upon minutely examining these vestiges of massacre, they could discover nothing which they recollected, there was some faint hope that the son or the husband they were trembling for had escaped. While this tragedy was acting in the rooms of the Hôtel de Ville, a most disgusting farce was performed in the court below. Volunteers, who were setting out for the frontiers, came in crowds to take the oath to the new government before their departure, and as they came out of the Town House, each in his turn walked up deliberately to the prostrate statue of Louis XIV., which had been cast down with the other monuments of royalty, and p—— upon it in the midst of the shouts and laughter of a circle of women and children, delighted with this obscene ceremony, which lasted without interruption, during the two hours that Guyot was there, waiting for his passport.

I am sorry to find that you are wavering in your determination about going to Bowood, for I know how that sort of wavering generally ends in a person of your indolent disposition. I wish you would determine to go with me. It is pretty evident from your last letter that, if you have not quite laid aside Bentham's work, it occupies very little of your time; and as to K., it seems completely effaced from your memory. There may undoubtedly be some kind of enjoyment in sauntering away the whole morning with D., and hearing, during the whole afternoon, T.'s panegyrics on that loss of time which he professes to adore, and thus approaching so near to the quiescent state of death; but I really cannot persuade myself that it is an enjoyment fit for one of your talents, natural dispositions, and prospects of happiness. Indeed I am quite vexed, not only with you, but with myself, when I see such means of being useful to mankind as you possess, so lost as they seem likely to be. I reproach myself as being in some degree an accomplice, by not endeavouring to rouse you from so fatal a lethargy. Indeed, Dumont, you must come to a resolution of doing something that will be useful to posterity. Surely the hope of being able to prevent some of those calamities from falling on future ages, which we now see so dreadfully visiting the present, might be as strong a motive to excite your energy, as any that has ever hitherto called it forth.[1] I have a great deal more to say to you on this subject; but, not to fatigue you too much at present, I conclude.

Yours most affectionately,

SAML. ROMILLY.

[1] M. Dumont became subsequently the coadjutor of Bentham, and published eight volumes 8vo. of his works on subjects connected with Legislation.

Letter XCVIII.

TO THE SAME.

Dear Dumont, Oct. 4. 1793.

I was very much rejoiced to find that you were capable of reading my long letter quite to the end, and even of answering it in the same day: after so great an exertion, your case is certainly not quite to be despaired of.

You cannot think that I meant very seriously to censure you for sending my letter open to the Chauvets. They have said nothing to me about K.[1], nor I to them. However, my attack upon your indolence, loss of time, &c. was most serious, and I really think that it can be to nothing but your habitual want of exertion, that can be ascribed your using such curious arguments as you do in your defence. Your theory is this. Every man does all the good that he can. If a particular individual does no good, it is a proof that he is incapable of doing it. That you don't write, proves that you can't, and your want of inclination demonstrates your want of talents. What an admirable system! and what beneficial effects would it be attended with, if it were but universally received!

Indeed, I cannot condescend to refute a theory which I am sure it is impossible you can have seriously adopted. One would suppose by your letter that you thought the true criterion of a fine writer was, that he was fond of writing; but the

[1] Kïrkerbergher. See Vol. I. p. 415.

contrary is so true, that I doubt whether there ever was a great writer who took great pleasure in writing, and who had not, generally, when he began to write, a sort of repugnance to surmount. It must naturally be so. He must be difficult in the choice of expressions; he finds more pain from what is ill expressed, than pleasure from what is merely as it ought to be. He is sensible of the defects of his own style, and he feels more pain from them, than from defects in the style of others; and whatever pleasure his own performances may give him, when they are corrected to his mind, they afford him but little in their intermediate state. You recollect the labour which Rousseau had in writing, and the fatigue which he says it gave him; many other examples of the same kind might be mentioned.

S. R.

Letter XCIX.

FROM M. DUMONT.

13 Novembre, 1793.

J'avois compté, mon cher Romilly, de retourner incessamment à Wycombe, mais j'apprends que Madame de —— va s'établir à Londres, et en conséquence je resterai à Bowood, ce qui me privera du plaisir de vous voir, jusques vers la fin de l'année,

---

Letter XCIX.

November 13. 1793.

I had reckoned, my dear Romilly, upon returning forthwith to Wycombe, but I learn that Made. de —— is going to settle in London, and I shall therefore remain at Bowood, which will, in all probability, deprive me of the pleasure of seeing you till towards the

selon toute apparence. Ce long séjour n'est pas precisément ce que j'aurois choisi, surtout parceque, n'ayant point fait mon plan pour cela, je n'ai pas apporté les matériaux de mon travail. Cependant, pour ne pas mériter tout-à-fait vos reproches, je remplis ma tête d'histoire, avec un projet suivi, et j'amasse des pierres et du sable pour faire un jour un édifice, si mes forces peuvent seconder mes désirs.

Mais que font les livres ? Qui est-ce qui ne seroit pas dégouté d'écrire et même de penser, quand on voit la barbarie se reproduire dans le pays le plus éclairé de l'Europe ? Les hurlemens des sauvages sont moins affreux que les harangues des députés de la nation la plus polie et réputée la plus douce du Continent. On est presque réduit à souhaiter que les François eussent les vices de la lâcheté, comme ils ont ceux de la barbarie. Le courage du peuple est devenu l'instrument de la férocité de ses chefs.

Quoique j'aie condamné autant que vous la fac-

---

end of the year. This long stay is not exactly what I should have chosen, especially as, not having foreseen it when I made my arrangements, I have not brought with me the materials of my work. Nevertheless, that I may not altogether deserve your reproaches, I am cramming my head with history, and am endeavouring to lay down a connected plan; I am collecting stones and sand, which, if my powers do but second my wishes, may one day become an edifice.

But of what use are books ? Who can write or even think without disgust, when he sees the most enlightened country in Europe returning to a state of barbarism ? The howlings of savages are less frightful than the harangues of the representatives of a nation esteemed the gentlest and the most polished of the Continent. One is almost reduced to wish that the French added the vices of cowardice to those of barbarity. The courage of the people has become the instrument of the ferocity of their leaders.

Although I condemned, as strongly as you did, the faction of the

tion de la Gironde, pendant qu'elle attaquoit et renversoit la constitution, je vous avoue que l'horrible vengeance de la faction dominante m'a causé une profonde douleur. Je n'ai jamais aimé Brissot sous ses rapports politiques; la passion l'avoit énivré plus que personne; mais cela ne m'empêche pas de rendre justice à ses vertus, à son caractère privé, à son désintéressement, à ses qualités sociales comme époux, comme père, comme ami, comme défenseur intrépide de la cause des malheureux noirs. Je ne pense pas sans effroi qu'il avoit puisé une partie des principes qui l'ont égaré dans les écrits même de Rousseau, et qu'un cœur naturellement humain et honnête ne l'a pas défendu des illusions de l'esprit de parti. La vanité d'être regardé comme un chef a sans doute contribué à ses fautes; la légèreté de son jugement l'a précipité dans de fausses mesures, et la violence du peuple a fait le reste. Il étoit de ceux qui croyoient de bonne foi que tout étoit sanctifié par ce qu'on appeloit la volonté du peuple, et il a fait de

---

Gironde whilst it was attacking and pulling down the constitution, I confess to you that the dreadful vengeance taken on them by the dominant party gave me the deepest pain. I never liked Brissot as a politician; no one was ever more intoxicated by passion; but that does not prevent me from doing justice to his virtues, to his private character, to his disinterestedness, to his social qualities as a husband, a father, and a friend, and as the intrepid advocate of the wretched negroes. I cannot reflect, without a shudder, that he imbibed some of the principles which led him astray from the very writings of Rousseau; and that a disposition naturally kind and good did not preserve him from the delusions of party-spirit. The vanity of being looked upon as a leader no doubt contributed to his faults, the weakness of his judgment hurried him into false measures, and the violence of the people did the rest. He was one of those who sincerely believed that what is called the will of the people was a justification of every thing, and he

grands maux par l'enthousiasme de la liberté, comme tant d'autres en ont fait par l'enthousiasme de la religion. Le pouvoir d'*absoudre*, que s'étoit attribué l'Eglise Romaine, a précisément la même énergie sur les consciences que l'enthousiasme politique sur l'esprit. Je ne m'étois pas proposé de vous parler si longtemps d'un homme que vous n'avez jamais pu souffrir; mais je l'avois connu sous d'autres points de vue que ceux qui le rendoient justement blâmable à vos yeux, et la triste fin de cet homme[1], qui eut été excellent s'il fut né dans les Etats-Unis, m'inspire un sentiment de compassion qui ne me laisse voir dans ses fautes que l'effet de la contagion générale.

Mais que penser de l'abominable légèreté de ce peuple qui a compté, l'une après l'autre, les têtes de ces vingt victimes, à mesure qu'elles tomboient sous l'instrument fatal, sans paroître conserver le

---

has done as much mischief by the enthusiasm of liberty, as many others have done by the enthusiasm of religion. The power of *absolution* assumed by the Romish Church, has precisely the same hold on the consciences of men, as political enthusiasm has on their understandings. I had not intended to talk to you so long about a man you never could endure, but I had seen him in points of view different from those which made him justly blameable in your eyes; and the sad end of this man [1], who would have been excellent had he been born in the United States, inspires me with a feeling of compassion which prevents my seeing in his faults any thing more than the effect of the general contagion of the time.

But what are we to think of the abominable fickleness of that people who could count, one after the other, the heads of those twenty victims, as they each dropped under the fatal instrument of death, without seeming to retain the slightest recollection of the

---

[1] Brissot was executed at Paris on the 30th October, 1793, together with twenty other members of the Gironde party.

moindre souvenir des applaudissemens qu'il avoit donné, pendant plus d'une année, à des hommes qu'il regardoit comme les défenseurs de sa liberté? Cette réflexion ne devroit-elle pas effrayer ceux qui ont dirigé ces exécutions prétendues juridiques? J'espère que les scélérats qui dominent aujourd'hui ont signé leur arrêt de mort. Mais verrons-nous ce peuple férocisé revenir à l'humanité et à la raison? je n'en sais rien. La folie des Croisades a duré deux cents ans; la démence actuelle peut engloutir plus d'une génération.

Vous êtes plongé dans vos occupations judicielles. C'est presque un bonheur pour vous de n'avoir pas le tems de réfléchir, car toutes les réflexions aujourd'hui sont amères. J'espère que vous avez fait une provision de santé dans vos excursions. On parle ici de vous comme ayant donné plus de plaisir que vous ne pouviez en recevoir, et l'on se flatte d'un plus long séjour une autre année.

Adieu! Je vous écrirai bientôt une lettre moins lamentable. ET. D.

---

applauses which, for more than a year, they had bestowed upon them, as men whom they then looked upon as the defenders of their liberty? Ought not this reflection to alarm those who have directed these pretended legal executions? I trust that the ruffians who rule to-day have signed their own death-warrant. But shall we ever see this brutalised people return to humanity and reason? I know not. The madness of the Crusades lasted two hundred years; the present frenzy may swallow up more than one generation.

You are engrossed by your legal pursuits. It is almost a blessing for you that you have no time for thought, for all thoughts are bitter now. I hope that, in your excursions, you have laid in a good stock of health. You are spoken of here as having given more pleasure than you could have received, and a longer visit is looked forward to another year. Farewell! I will write you soon a less melancholy letter. ET. D.

Letter C.

TO M. DUMONT.

Dear Dumont, Lincoln's Inn, Nov. 22. 1793.

You would perhaps set some value on this letter, if you knew how many things I have to do at the moment I write it, and what excuses I must make to-morrow to some stupid attorney for having devoted to you the time which I ought to employ upon a bill in Chancery. You must have formed a very inaccurate idea of the insipid and uninteresting occupations to which I am every day enslaved, when you conjecture that I am so deeply absorbed in them as to pay little attention to what is passing in France. I have almost always present to my mind the state of that deplorable country. I cannot say that I felt no compassion even for Brissot and his party, but it is a compassion which reason cannot justify. They who have been teaching such bloody lessons, have no right to complain that they fall by the hands of the disciples whom they have themselves instructed. How fortunate it is that the torture was an aristocratical, or a monarchical invention; it is certainly that circumstance alone, and no degree of humanity, which prevents its being exercised on all the victims who are daily offered up to the populace of Paris. The Queen's[1] trial furnishes one among many instances, that the wretches who at present rule in France

[1] Marie Antoinette had been executed on the 16th October.

have been able to invent tortures for the mind, more cruel than any that had ever before been heard of. The French are plunging into a degree of barbarism, which, for such a nation, and in so short a period, surpasses all imagination. All religion is already abolished; and the next proceeding will undoubtedly be, a persecution as severe and as unremitting as any that has taken place in the darkest ages; for it is only in order to arrive at the persecution that religion is abolished. We may soon expect to see all books exterminated; history, because it relates to kings; poetry, because it speaks the language of flattery; political economy, because it favours monopolizers and freedom of trade; and so on through all other sciences, till the French preserve nothing of civilized life but its vices, which they will have engrafted on a state of the most savage barbarism.

Are you not astonished to see Sieyes in all this standing up in the midst of his fellow-murderers, and claiming applause for his having so long ago thought like a philosopher? Ill as I have long thought of him, I did not imagine him capable of such degradation.

I have been lately endeavouring to relieve my mind from the reflections which these hideous scenes suggest, by an account which has been lately published of the new colony of Kentucky, in America. It is no small consolation to one to think that there is at least one quarter of the globe in which mankind is daily increasing in happiness. The book is very interesting, though it is written, like almost all the other American compositions I have seen, in a style which has every possible defect, and not one merit; and though the author has the American mania of pretending to philosophize upon every thing, and to treat all nations but his own with contempt.

Yours ever,

SAML. ROMILLY.

LETTER CI.

TO MADAME G——.

London, July 29. 1794.

I can hardly express to you, Madam, the pleasure which I felt on opening M. G——'s letter, and reading the first four lines of it; by which I learnt that you were both, with your children, well in health, and out of France. My joy, indeed, was greatly damped by the rest of the letter, which gives me an account of the situation of M. D——; and yet, as I had heard a vague report of his having been arrested, unaccompanied with any particular circumstances, my anxiety for you had so much exaggerated the evil, and had so heightened your distress, that your letter brought me very great relief. I most earnestly pray that your endeavours may be successful, and that the time is not far off when you will again enjoy undisturbed that domestic happiness which you so well deserve. May I beg of you, when you write to your excellent mother, to mention my name to her, and to say how much I feel, and how anxiously

I interest myself for her? Would to God that you were wholly separated from the wretched country which you have quitted, and could have the full enjoyment of being once more in a land of peace and tranquillity! I have never read any of the accounts of those unexampled enormities which have been committed at Paris, without feeling, amidst the emotions of horror and pity which they excited in my mind, the strongest sympathy for you, who were doomed to be near the spot where all those atrocious crimes were perpetrated, and to have your imaginations alarmed, and your sensibility tortured, by a detail of a thousand circumstances of horror which we at this distance have escaped. I do not, however, wish to bring them back to your recollection, and should be happy if I could efface them from it for ever.

I have no news to send you, for happily this country produces no events worth relating. A great deal, indeed, has been said, both here and abroad, of the dangerous designs which are entertained and cherished by many persons in this country; but there has not hitherto been the smallest indication by any open acts of any such designs existing; and whatever interruptions of tranquillity have happened, have been by the too zealous friends of quiet and good order riotously demonstrating their loyalty and attachment to the constitution.

It is impossible not to be curious to hear particulars of the unhappy country you have left, and of which the public accounts here, where we never see a single French newspaper, are very imperfect; and yet I hardly know how to require them from you; "infandum renovare dolorem." But at any rate write to me. I can scarcely say how much I rejoice at the renewal of our correspondence. It seems as if we had met together after a long journey, and the lapse of many years. And what tragedies have filled up the interval! Our correspondence will, I hope, never again be interrupted, and I trust we shall, before many years have passed, meet in reality either in this country or in Switzerland.

I remain, &c.

S. Romilly.

Letter CII.

TO MR. DUGALD STEWART.

August 26. 1794.

I reproach myself very much for having so long delayed returning you thanks for the great pleasure which your account of Adam Smith afforded me. Some very pressing engagements made it very inconvenient to me to write to you for some time after I received it; and having once postponed writing, I have, ever since, gone on increasing my fault by being ashamed to own it. All my acquaintance who have seen the account of Adam Smith, think it extremely interesting. The only complaint I have heard respecting it is, that it is too short; and that you have withheld from the public the observations, which an analysis of the *Wealth of Nations* would have suggested to you.

I received, a few weeks ago, a letter from my friend G——, who married Mlle. D——. It was dated from Berne, and brought me the good news of his being safe there with his wife and his children. But M. and Mad^e. D—— are still in France, and he is in confinement; accused, however, of nothing but vaguely of being attached to aristocracy; and really guilty, I believe, of no crime but that of being rich. He is in a house in the neighbourhood of Paris, in a good air, with the use of a large garden, and in a very numerous and very good society of his fellow-prisoners. All these indulgences, however, are paid for at a very high rate; and I have heard it said (though G—— does not mention it), that this species of imprisonment of the rich is a source of corruption to those who are, or lately were, in power at Paris. Enormous sums are exacted, nominally for the board of the prisoners, but, in truth, to enrich some of the members of the governing committees. The lives of the persons so imprisoned are not supposed to be in much danger, because their deaths would put an end to a source of wealth to the persons to whose protection they are committed: but, for the same reason, their imprisonment is likely to be of long duration. The object of M. G——'s journey into Switzerland is to procure the Council of Berne to interpose in behalf of M. D——, who is still considered as a Swiss; and he seems to entertain great hopes of the success of that expedient. You told me, I recollect, that you had some thoughts of making a visit to London in the course of this year. I hope you have not given up all intention of that kind, and that I shall have the pleasure of seeing you here, where I shall probably pass the greatest part of my vacation.

I remain, yours,

S. R.

Letter CIII.

TO MADAME G——.

October 14. 1794.

Your excellent letter gave me inexpressible joy. I know that it is unnecessary to tell you so, but yet I feel pleasure in doing it. At the moment I received it, I was under great uneasiness on your account. I had, indeed, considered the overthrow of Robespierre's system[1] as the forerunner of M. D——'s liberty, and I had even sat down to congratulate you on that event, when I read in one of our newspapers that he was removed to the *Conciergerie*. I immediately destroyed my letter, lest my congratulations, reaching you at a moment when you were in the most tormenting uncertainty, should have only given you additional pain. I have ever since been waiting with great anxiety to hear from you. Judge then of the joy which your letter afforded me. May you long — long enjoy the society of the parents who are restored to you! I felt the most lively pleasure in learning that your excellent and admirable mother, whose virtues have been put to so severe a trial, and whose sensibility has been so tortured, was

[1] On the 27th July, 1794 (9th Thermidor, An. 11).

not indifferent to the interest which I take in every thing that concerns her. I please myself with thinking, that, before this letter reaches you, she will have joined you, and that when you read this, it will be by the side of that excellent parent, and that you will read it with a heart perfectly at ease, and in that calm and tranquillity which can enable you to enjoy the charming country which you now inhabit. I have at this moment before my eyes the very prospect which you are perhaps admiring. I once passed six weeks in the neighbourhood of Lausanne, and I every day beheld the sublime scene of the Lake of Geneva spread out at the feet of the rude mountains with fresh astonishment and delight. I think it never will be effaced from my memory. Unfortunately, I don't recollect the village of Cour, though I must several times have passed through it in going to Ouchy; but I lived above the town, in a house which then went by the name of the "Pavement." It has probably changed its name by this time, for it is now thirteen years ago: — it was just before I first visited Paris, and when I had the good fortune to be introduced to your family.

You are kind enough to reproach me for not talking about myself in my letters. It is, I assure you, because it is a subject upon which there is nothing to be told. If any events had happened in my life, which could afford either pain or pleasure to those who take any interest about me, I should not have failed to relate them to you, on whose friendship I so firmly rely. But mine is a life which passes without events. I am, I believe, exactly what I was when you last saw me, with the addition of five years to my age, with some alteration in my opinions produced by the terrible experience of public events, but with none, that I am aware of, in my dispositions. I am still unmarried, and, I think, likely to remain so. My success in my profession has been much greater than I could have had any reason to expect. My business has of late years greatly increased, and seems likely to increase much more. I devote myself indeed entirely to it, and it has been without much struggle with myself that I have twice refused a seat in Parliament.[1] My reasons for it I think you would approve of, were I to trouble you with them; but I have been long enough talking about myself, and if I have been too long, remember that the fault is yours.

Notwithstanding our total failure of success, the

[1] The following passage occurs, at the date of January, 1792, in a diary of events in the handwriting of Mr. Romilly: — "Lord Lansdowne offered me a seat in Parliament for Calne, in the room of Mr. Morris, who was about to resign. I refused it."

There is no account in these papers of the second offer here mentioned; but at a date subsequent to that of the letter in the text, the following correspondence passed between Lord Lansdowne and Mr. Romilly on the same subject: —

Extract from a letter of Lord Lansdowne, dated 27th June, 1795. —

"As you mention the possibility of its [a dissolution of Parliament] taking place in a few days, I send this by the coach to save time, for I cannot think of making any arrangement as to a new Parliament, without knowing your final determination in regard to yourself. I am persuaded it is unnecessary for me to say any thing on my part, as I have already explained myself so fully and repeatedly to you."

From a rough draft, in the handwriting of Mr. Romilly, dated 28th June, 1795. — "I return your Lordship my warmest thanks for your very obliging letter. Nothing which has happened since I had last the honour of conversing with you on the subject has in the least altered my sentiments with respect to Parliament; it is, therefore, with the truest sense of the obligation which I have to your Lordship, and with a great degree of reluctance, that I think myself obliged to decline profiting of your Lordship's kind intentions in my favour."

war seems, I think, as popular here as ever, at least in the part of the country where I have been, for I am but just returned to town. In London, I believe, and in other great trading towns, people begin to reflect, that no advantage can be gained by prosecuting a war, which has hitherto had no effect but to strengthen the system it was intended to overturn. As to the internal tranquillity of the country, there is no reason to fear its being interrupted, at least not for a considerable time. There are indeed many persons here who wish a total overthrow of our constitution, and many more who desire great changes in it; but the great majority of the nation, and particularly the armed part of it, (which is at present a very large portion, for volunteer regiments have been raised in every county,) are most ardent zealots for maintaining our constitution as it is, and disposed to think the reform of the most palpable abuse, which has been of long continuance, as a species of sacrilege. I am,

Yours, &c.

S. R.

1795—1802.

Letter CIV.

TO MR. DUGALD STEWART.

1795.

I know you do not very rigidly exact punctuality in your correspondents, but yet I am afraid you will think I have abused your indulgence by delaying so long to write to you. Very soon after I received your last letter, I delivered your book[1] to Lord Lansdowne; he desired me to return you many thanks for it, and to say, that as soon as he is sufficiently recovered from a fit of the gout, which he has had for a considerable time, to be able to hold a pen, he will write himself to thank you for it.

Since I had the pleasure of writing to you, I have received some account of M. D——'s family. I told you, I believe, that he was a long time in confinement for having, as was alleged, in his possession papers of a counter-revolutionary tendency. Soon after Robespierre's death, he was tried and acquitted; and he immediately removed with his family to Lausanne, in Switzerland. M. G—— and his wife have, however, since returned to Paris, and I believe they are

[1] Account of Adam Smith.

there at present. The eldest son, who went to America, and was at the head of a commercial establishment which his father had formed, died there after an illness of a very few days.

I understand the Ministers entertain very sanguine expectations from the expedition of the emigrants into Britany, though it seems hardly likely to produce any great effect at Paris; or, if it does, the most probable effect of it will be to restore the credit of the Jacobin party, whose vigorous measures may be thought the only resource in times of danger. The state of Paris seems very singular. There are no disturbances there but in favour of *moderantism*, and the only murders at present to be dreaded are likely to be perpetrated, as in the South of France, by those who are actuated by horror of the assassinations committed by Robespierre and his adherents.

Many persons who have been proscribed in France ever since the establishment of the Republic now appear with security, and even challenge the public attention by political publications. Among these, some of the most remarkable are Vaublanc, Dupont de Nemours, and Bergasse; but the most singular publications that have appeared at Paris are the different memoirs of the Girondistes, and which seem by the French papers to be very numerous. A few of them have been reprinted here; among others, that of Mad^e^. Roland, composed during her confinement in different prisons at Paris. It is written with uncommon eloquence, contains a great many curious facts, and gives some very well-drawn characters of the leading men in the different factions which have prevailed during and since the time of her husband's administration. But the most extraordinary character it paints is her own. Her enthusiasm, her party zeal, her masculine courage, and unalterable serenity under the most imminent dangers, are exactly calculated, in the present state of France, to excite the most enthusiastic veneration for her memory. Her eloquence, however, is much superior to her judgment; and the warmth of her zeal more remarkable than the purity of her morals. She expatiates on the extraordinary talents and virtues of Brissot, Buzot, Pétion, and, indeed, almost all of her own party: she applauds the famous letters of her husband to the King, which certainly, more than any thing else, contributed to the revolution of the 10th of August, and the consequent destruction of that unfortunate prince. She bestows high encomiums on the patriotism of Grangeneuve, who had laid a plan to have himself murdered, in order that the popular leaders who survived him might falsely accuse the King of the murder, and, by that means, inflame the indignation of the people against him. Another singular book, but much inferior in point of merit, is Louvet's account of his dangers and hair-breadth escapes, during his journey from Paris to seek an asylum in the Gironde, and back again from the Gironde to find a place of concealment at Paris.[1] The facts which it contains render it very interesting, though it is

[1] Le Récit de mes Périls depuis le 31 Mai, 1793.

written very much in the manner of a novel, and though nothing can exceed the extravagant absurdity of the author's political opinions. He is fully convinced, for example, that Robespierre was bribed by Pitt, and that the English army suffered itself to be beaten in order to gain the Jacobin party credit in France.

I am, &c.

S. Romilly.

Letter CV.

FROM M. DUMONT.

Bowood, Oct. 26. 1795.

J'ai été fort bien reçu ici, mon cher Romilly, mais je l'aurois été beaucoup mieux si je vous avois amené; il a fallu expliquer qu'il n'y avoit pas de ma faute, et rejeter sur la nécessité des affaires.

Si vous n'avez pas lu l'apologie de Garat [1], n'oubliez pas de vous la procurer. Il y a quelques détails extrêmement curieux, non pas sur lui-même,

---

Letter CV.

Bowood, October 26. 1795.

I have been very well received here, my dear Romilly; but I should have been much better received if I had brought you with me. I was obliged to explain that the fault was in no respect mine, and to lay it on pressing business.

If you have not read Garat's apology [1], do not forget to procure it. It contains some extremely curious details; not on himself, for, in

---

[1] Entitled *Mémoires sur la Révolution, ou Exposé de ma Conduite dans les Affaires et dans les Fonctions Publiques.* Paris, 1794.

car malgré tous ses efforts il ne peut jamais se donner qu'un rôle bien médiocre. Le morceau le plus soigné est un portrait de Danton, vers la fin de l'ouvrage ; mais, en le comparant avec Mad^e^. Roland, on voit combien tous les efforts d'un bel esprit sont impuissans pour arriver à ce style énergique et simple qu'elle a trouvé naturellement dans la trempe de son caractère. Au reste, il a dit aux Girondins une bonne vérité, c'est que par les lois les plus absurdes et les plus atroces, ils avoient armé eux-mêmes la commune de Paris de tous les moyens qu'on a ensuite tourné contre eux. Ils ont été détruits par les instruments qu'ils avoient préparé pour détruire les Royalistes.

Il me paroît bien difficile que la Convention puisse rester avec sûreté ou avec confiance dans Paris, après l'avoir couvert de victimes. Si elle transporte ses séances à Versailles, en abandonnant la capitale, ils perdent l'influence quelle exerçoit sur les provinces. Il me semble que le mécontente-

---

spite of all his efforts, he can nowhere make it appear that he played more than a very secondary part. The most laboured passage in it is a portrait of Danton, towards the end of the work; but in comparing him with Madame Roland one sees how powerless are all the attempts of a wit to acquire that simple and energetic style which she derived from the peculiar temper of her own mind. However, he has told the Girondists one home truth, namely, that it was by their own absurd and atrocious laws that they supplied the *commune* of Paris with all the powers which were afterwards employed against themselves. They have been destroyed by the weapons which they had prepared for the destruction of the Royalists.

It seems to me that it will be very difficult for the Convention to remain with safety or confidence in Paris, after having strewed it with victims; and, on the other hand, if they transfer their sittings to Versailles, they will, by quitting the capital, lose the influence which it

ment de Paris doit être une nouvelle source de révolution.

Vous verrez dans Garat qu'il a sauvé la vie à Mr. Vaughan ; que l'on alloit traîner devant le tribunal révolutionnaire comme espion de Pitt. Il ne le nomme pas, mais il le désigne pour ceux qui le connoissent, en parlant d'une lettre qu'il en a reçu de Basle.

Adieu, mon cher Romilly. Quand vous serez de loisir, envoyez-moi en deux lignes le bulletin de votre santé. Je voudrois bien vous transporter ici subitement. Je ne suis pas le seul à qui cela feroit plaisir. *Vale, et me ama.* En finissant comme notre ami Mirabeau, je me rappelle encore un trait de Garat qui a eu la lâcheté de l'insulter dans sa tombe, quoiqu'il aimât beaucoup sa compagnie et ses diners.

ET. D.

---

exercised over the provinces. It appears to me that the discontent of Paris must become a new source of revolution.

You will see in Garat, that he saved the life of Mr. Vaughan, who was about to be dragged before the revolutionary tribunal, as a spy of Pitt's. He does not mention him by name, but he points him out to those who know him, by speaking of a letter which he received from him from Basle.

Farewell, my dear Romilly. When you have leisure, send me in two lines the bulletin of your health. I wish I could suddenly transport you hither. I am not the only one to whom it would give pleasure. *Vale, et me ama.* In ending my letter like our friend Mirabeau, I am reminded of another trait of Garat's, who has had the meanness to insult him in his grave, although he was very fond of his company and his dinners.

ET. D.

Letter CVI.

TO M. DUMONT.

Dear Dumont, Lincoln's Inn, Oct. 27. 1795.

I have received your long-expected letter, and, as a gentle reproach, I answer it immediately. It would have given me great pleasure to have been with you at Bowood. I should certainly have passed my time much more agreeably than I have done here in the midst of Chancery pleadings; but I should have had so great an arrear of business as would have kept me hurried and fatigued throughout the whole winter. I do not much envy you any of your company at Bowood, except those who always reside there, and Robert Smith, whom I should be glad to know better than I do.

I have read Garat, and found many parts of it curious; but the most extraordinary thing in it is the spirit in which it is written. Surely none but a Frenchman could, after having acted such a part as he has done, speak of himself with pride and self-applause, and, in the midst of the ignominy in which he is involved, challenge the honours due to the most unexampled courage and patriotism. But such is the national character; no Frenchman is satisfied with a mere justification of himself; he must have a panegyric, and not to have done wrong is a praise which such heroes despise. Vilate, one of Robespierre's jurymen, who, as a matter of great merit, says that he never condemned any *fournées* (that is, he only murdered his victims one by one), has published a pamphlet[1] to blazon forth his own virtues, and above all his sensibility. But the vanity of no Frenchman surely is superior to that of Isnard. I have just been reading his memorial, which he has entitled *Proscription d'Isnard*, in which, in one modest tirade, he puts himself at least on a level with Curtius, Mutius Scævola, and Cato of Utica. He boasts that he never acted in concert with any man, "pas même pour faire le bien." "J'avois la manie," he says, "de former un comité à moi tout seul."

I have probably been reading many more French pamphlets than you, for a friend of mine has lent me a large cargo just imported from Paris. Among others are the papers found in the possession of Robespierre. Nothing can exceed the adulation of many of his correspondents. Louis XIV. was never exalted higher by the poets who cringed about his court, than Robespierre by his pretended republicans. He appears to have had spies, like those of the police under the old system. There are reports made by some of them to this mighty despot, in which they give an account where Tallien, and Thuriot, and others, went on such a day, and with whom they were seen, and much more of the same kind. The lists of the persons confined and transported, with the crimes imputed to them, which are also published, are much more curious than the Registers of the Bastile, which once excited so much indignation. Another curious pamphlet is *L'Almanac des Prisons*, and *Le Tableau des Prisons*, which consists of relations of what

[1] Entitled *Causes Secrètes de la Révolution du 9 Thermidor*.

passed in the different prisons, given by several persons who were confined there. There is, too, a history of Terrorism in the department of Vienne, by Thibaudeau, a deputy; but it is less interesting than one would expect. It contains an account of some of the enormities of Piorry and Ingrand, the two commissioners to whom that department was delivered up; but the author seems to think no persecutions so interesting to the public as those to which he and his own family were exposed, and to those he has accordingly mostly confined his narrative. There are likewise two volumes of other pieces relating to it. Among these is Tronsson de Coudray's defence of the Revolutionary Committee of Nantes, which contains such a picture of France, under the government of Robespierre and his proconsuls, as surpasses in horror the most hideous scenes that history, or even poetry, ever before presented. Perhaps you have seen all these publications; and yet I think you would have mentioned some of them if you had.

Bentham has been locking himself up at Hendon, and working, as he tells me, for you at his Civil Code. He has, too, a refutation of the French Declaration of Rights, which I encourage him to publish.

Yours ever,

SAML. ROMILLY.

Letter CVII.

TO M. DUMONT.

Dear Dumont, August 26. 1796.

Your description of Worthing is not very alluring, but yet there are some circumstances in it which are not to be despised, and I am by no means clear that I shall not make it a little visit. If I do, it will not be till after your ladies have left you. I wish, therefore, you would, some time in the course of the next week, give me some account of the plan of life which you have laid down for the season of adversity, that is, when they shall have left you. I take for granted we can dine together, in any lodging we may have, *tête-à-tête*; that is a circumstance upon which so much comfort depends, that, if I understood I must dine either with boarders in a house, or even in the public room of a coffee-house, it would be quite decisive with me not to set my foot in Worthing. You may recollect how poor a compensation I thought the goodness of the dinner for the badness of the company, when we were at Liverpool. I shall depend on your writing to me again, but you must not depend on seeing me. I may probably go for a week to the neighbourhood of Richmond: and, after all, the heat, the dust, the smoke, the closeness, and the stenches of London, at this season of the year, are not so oppressive to me as to those whom nature or fashion has moulded of a more delicate texture. The truth indeed is, that, though I reside in London, I spend most of my evenings in its environs; sometimes at my brother's, sometimes on the banks of the Thames, and now and then at Kensington; and for my mornings, I pass them in the enjoyment of my newly acquired liberty. Instead of law-books and chancery pleadings, I read and write just what I please. I am still devouring Mitford with unabated pleasure, and, that it may last the longer, I often consult his authorities, and am led away from him, for hours together, by the narrative of Pausanias and the charming simplicity of Herodotus. I have been writing, too, a good deal[1], and I cannot discover that want of exercise has had that sensible effect upon my style which you prophesied that it would: but, perhaps, together with the faculty of writing, I have lost that of judging; or, which is more probable, perhaps I never possessed those merits which you were apprehensive I should lose. But when I see you, you shall decide; and yet, what I have been writing is hardly likely to afford you much pleasure, since even in myself, with all an author's partiality, it has produced very mixed sensations. Have you ever read any of Charlotte Smith's novels? If not, get them at your circulating library. No doubt they have them; for, as she is either a native, or at least has been long resident in Sussex, her reputation there is even higher than in other parts of the kingdom. They will give you great pleasure, and are just suited to your present medicinal course of study. I forget

[1] Probably the first part of the Narrative of his own Life, which is dated 16th August, 1796.

the names of all of them but the *Old Manor House*, and *Ethelinda*, which are two of the best.

What do you think of Drouet's escape, and of the letters which he has written to the Five Hundred and to the public? If such facts as have appeared in the course of the French Revolution were to be found in Herodotus, they would be set to the account only of his credulity and his love of the marvellous.

Cura ut valeas, et ut ad nos firmus ac valens quam primum venias.

Saml. Romilly.

Letter CVIII.

FROM M. DUMONT.

Worthing, 29 Août, 1796.

Je suis plus content de Worthing, mon cher Romilly, que je ne l'étois dans les premiers jours. Je m'étois exagéré le bruit et la foule, parceque je m'attendois à une espèce de retraite ignorée. Il y a des environs fort agréables, et on peut varier ses promenades dans quatre ou cinq milles, de manière à déjeûner ou diner tous les jours de la semaine

---

Letter CVIII.

Worthing, ugust A29. 1796.

I like Worthing better, my dear Romilly, than I did at first. I had fancied the noise and the crowd greater than they really are, because I had expected to find a kind of secluded retreat. The neighbourhood is very agreeable, and one may vary one's excursions for four or five miles round, so as to breakfast or dine every day of the week in

dans quelque endroit différent. Je resterai seul dès Samedi matin ; si vous êtes tenté de venir, en supposant le temps beau, et nul sacrifice de votre part de quelque société aimable, marquez-moi le jour, et vous me trouverez à Steining, à huit milles d'ici, où l'on quitte la diligence, et où l'on prend une chaise de poste. Sans doute, il ne faut pas vivre dans la chambre publique d'un café, ni dîner à une table-d'hôte ; quoique j'aime assez de temps en temps cette variété, ce n'est pas lorsque je peux être tête-à-tête avec vous. Notre chaumière, un village voisin, un bateau, peut-être une excursion plus lointaine jusqu'à Arundel, ou telle autre place sur les bords de la mer, nous offrent plus de diversité qu'il n'en faut pour un temps si court.

Apportez-moi donc, je vous prie, quelque rayon de votre miel. Je vous dirai bien franchement mon avis sur sa saveur et le goût du terroir. Vous n'êtes pas dans l'âge des pertes ; mais quand je pense que Rousseau et Buffon, après plusieurs volumes admirés, sentoient encore eux-mêmes

---

a different spot. I shall be alone after Saturday morning, and if you should be tempted to come, assuming the weather to be fine, and no pleasant party to give up, let me know the day, and you will find me at Steyning, eight miles from hence, where you leave the coach and take a chaise. Of course, we must not live in the coffee-room, nor dine at a public table; although I like this well enough for a change now and then, it is not when I can be alone with you. Our cottage, a neighbouring village, a boat, and now and then a more distant excursion to Arundel, or some other such place by the sea side, will afford us more variety than we shall want for so short a time.

Bring me then, I beg of you, a sample of your honey. I will tell you frankly my opinion of its flavour, and of the garden in which it is produced. You are not in the age of decline; but when I think that Rousseau and Buffon, after several popular volumes, were conscious

leur progrès, je suis jaloux pour vous de tout ce qui vous retarde dans une carrière où vous pouvez aller si loin.

> " Quotque in flore novo pomis se fertilis arbos
> Induerat, totidem autumno matura tenebat."

Quoique mon écriture soit si mauvaise, ne l'attribuez pas à une main foible et tremblante ; je n'ai pour pupitre qu'un livre appuyé sur le dossier d'une chaise. Je me trouve mieux à tous égards, bon sommeil, bon appétit, et surtout bonne digestion, à tel point que, si nous avions encore deux mois de chaleur, je suis persuadé que je serois tout-à-fait rétabli. Adieu, mon cher Romilly. Je ne me suis pas encore livré à l'espérance de vous voir ici, et je ne le voudrois pas au dépens de vos plus légères convenances.

Tout à vous,

Et. D.

---

that they were still gaining ground, I am jealous of all that keeps you back in a career in which you may rise so high.

> " Quotque in flore novo pomis se fertilis arbos
> Induerat, totidem autumno matura tenebat."

Although my writing is so bad, do not suppose that my hand is weak and trembling : my only desk is a book supported on the back of a chair. I am better in all respects; good nights, good appetite, and above all good digestion ; so much so, that, if we have two more months of warm weather, I am persuaded I shall be quite well again. Farewell, my dear Romilly. I have not yet given way to the hope of seeing you here, and I would not wish it if it were in the least inconvenient to you.

Yours, &c.

Et. D.

Letter CIX.

TO M. DUMONT.

Dear Dumont, September 5. 1796.

But for your letter, I should have been, soon after the time when you receive this, at Worthing; your unexpected visiter, of course, immediately put an end to my plan. I have, however, little regret at it, for I had before given up the idea of passing a week or a fortnight with you in the friendly *tête-à-tête* which I had once promised myself, and my principal intention in visiting Worthing was to prevail on you to quit it.

I shall very much enjoy the party you propose. With respect to going to Bowood, I have not yet come to an absolute determination.[1] I intended to go, but the meeting of Parliament, which is certainly to be on the 27th of this month, quite deranges my plan. Lord Lansdowne will probably be in town; and indeed I intend to be, myself, in town at that time, and to be as constant an attendant in the gallery as I used to be before I was induced to sacrifice my love of politics and eloquence to my love of money.

Yours ever,

S. R.

[1] See *infrà*, Political Diary, Sept. 8. 1817.

LETTER CX.

TO MR. ROGET.[1]

My dear Peter, Hastings, Sept. 12. 1797.

I have for some time intended to write to you, but I have been so much occupied by business during these last two months, that till very lately I have never had half an hour which I could dispose of quite as I pleased. It would give me very great pleasure to entertain a regular correspondence with you; though, as your mother knows, mine is a correspondence in which I give but little, and require a great deal. The time, however, is, I hope, now not very distant when there will be a better intercourse between us than can be kept up by letters; when we shall see one another very often, and be connected, not merely by mere relationship and by warm affection, but by a most intimate and familiar friendship. I have heard lately from several persons of your application, and of the success of your studies; and it has given me great pleasure, but a pleasure not wholly unmixed with anxiety. I am afraid of your prosecuting your studies with more ardour and perseverance than your strength will allow of. I need not, certainly, impress on your mind the value of life and health, not on your own account alone, but for the sake of those who are most dear to you. But you really should consider, that it is with respect to knowledge as with many other things; by attempting to

[1] Now Dr. Roget, his nephew, who was then studying medicine at Edinburgh.

get too much we often lose instead of gaining, and a fortnight of too close occupation may make all study impossible for many weeks and months that may follow it. I have experienced this myself, when I was nearly of your age, and have been obliged to expiate, by several tedious months of languor and constrained idleness, the imprudent exertions which had exceeded my strength. You ought to reflect that relaxation is to the full as necessary as study to your success; and that the time which appears to be thrown away is really, even with respect to the advancement of your studies, time most profitably employed. I am at this moment putting in practice the doctrine I inculcate, for my only occupation here is to ride about the country, to enjoy the sea air, and to read books of amusement. I regret that your mother, in her rambles about England, never found out this spot. I think it would have exactly suited her. The town itself indeed has nothing to recommend it, nor yet much that can be objected to it: but the country about it is one of the richest, and one that affords the greatest variety of beautiful views, of any that I have seen in England; and it possesses in a very eminent degree, that which is unfortunately almost peculiar to England, a general appearance of prosperity, comfort, and content. I have been here about a fortnight, and am going from hence, with M. Dumont, along the coast as far as Chichester, and from thence to Bowood.

Remember me very affectionately to my sister, and to Nannette, and believe me to be,

Most affectionately yours,

SAML. ROMILLY.

LETTER CXI.

FROM M. DUMONT.

Kensington, 6 Jan. 1798.

Je n'essaye pas, mon cher Romilly, de vous dire tout ce que j'éprouve dans le sentiment de votre bonheur[1]: ce que je puis vous prédire d'après la connoissance de votre cœur, c'est qu'il augmentera encore, quoique peut-être aujourd'hui vous ne croyez pas cette augmentation possible. Vous êtes dans un tumulte de sentimens qui, en se calmant par dégrés, vous laissera plus propre à connoître, à goûter tous les charmes de votre nouvelle existence. Je vous attends à deux ans d'ici pour faire honneur à la justesse de mon discernement.

Nos amis, avec lesquels j'avois anticipé votre confidence, et vos raisons pour ne pas la faire vous-même, quoique ce fut déjà il y a quinze jours le

---

LETTER CXI.

Kensington, January 6. 1798.

I will not attempt, my dear Romilly, to tell you all I feel, when I think of your happiness[1]; but I may venture to predict, knowing your heart as I do, that you have still greater happiness in store, although you may now perhaps think this impossible. When the first tumult of emotion has gradually subsided, you will be better able to know and feel all the charms of your new life. I give you two years to do justice to the accuracy of my discernment.

Our friends, to whom I had already confided your secret, as well as your reasons for not having communicated it to them yourself,

---

[1] His marriage with Anne, eldest daughter of Francis Garbett, Esq., and Elizabeth Walsham, of Knill Court, Herefordshire, which took place on the 3d of January, 1798.

secret de tout le monde, m'avoient fait toutes les questions que l'amitié peut suggérer en pareille occurrence.

Si vous aviez prévu les questions auxquelles j'ai à répondre, vous auriez sans doute ajouté deux ou trois lignes à votre lettre sur le temps de votre retour, sur vos arrangemens, si vous prenez maison cet hiver, si . . . si . . . : tout cela veut dire au fond qu'on est très-impatient et très-curieux de voir la personne qui vous a fait passer sous le joug, parcequ'on sait bien, avec les sentiments qu'on a pour vous, que cela n'a pas pu se faire avec un mérite commun.

A présent, mon cher Romilly, je me recommande à vous auprès de M. Garbett et de sa famille; il faut qu'il me revienne quelque chose de leur amitié; réglez bien pour mes intérêts tous ces préliminaires.

Tout à vous,

Et. Dumont.

(although, for a fortnight, it had been no secret to any one,) beset me with every question which friendship can suggest on such an occasion. If you had foreseen all the inquiries I have to satisfy, you would no doubt have added two or three lines to your letter, respecting the time of your return, your plans, whether you take a house this winter, whether ——, whether ——; all which means, that there is great impatience and great curiosity to see the person who has made you pass under the yoke, because, from what we know of you, we are well aware that it is no common merit which could have brought about such an event.

And now, my dear Romilly, I commend myself, through you, to Mr. Garbett and his family; I trust to you to secure for me some portion of their friendship. Settle all these preliminaries to my advantage.

Yours, &c.

Et. Dumont.

LETTER CXII.

FROM MR. MANNERS SUTTON.[1]

Dear Romilly, Apethorpe, Jan. 8. 1798.

I have just read the paragraph of your marriage, and I do most sincerely and heartily congratulate you on that event. I am extremely glad on every account that you have taken this step; amongst many other reasons, I am sure it will contribute most essentially to your own happiness, and I think it must create a new interest in your mind in the situation of public affairs, and in some way or other give the country the advantage of an understanding, which I never thought much inferior to that of the ablest man in it.

I beg you will give my respects to Mrs. Romilly, and believe me, with great regard,

Yours very sincerely,
THOMAS MANNERS SUTTON.

LETTER CXIII.

TO MADAME G——.

Lincoln's Inn, Feb. 19. 1798.

You have sometimes reproached me for not speaking more of myself than I usually do in my letters; my excuse has been that in a life of so

[1] Afterwards Lord Manners.

even a tenor as mine, no event ever occurred worth communicating to you. I have not that excuse however at present; for, since I last wrote to you, an event no less important has taken place than that of my marriage. I remember telling you some time ago that I was unmarried, and likely to remain so; but I did not at that time know that such a woman, as I have now the supreme happiness of having for my wife, existed. You will naturally wish to have some account of her, but really I am unfit to give you that account. Were I to speak of her only as she appears to me, you would imagine I was exercising my talents in drawing the model of female perfection rather than describing a person who really exists. How happy should I be if uncontrollable circumstances had not placed us at so great a distance from each other; and if I could make intimately acquainted persons who are so formed to enjoy each other's society as you and my dear Anne!

S. R.

Letter CXIV.

TO THE SAME.

August 21. 1798.

Can you really have supposed that a natural effect of happiness was to make one forget one's best friends? Indeed the effect of it has been very different on me. Since I have been blessed with my dear Anne, I have thought of you even more frequently than I did before. I have often talked with her about you, your affectionate husband, and your excellent mother; and we have together frequently lamented that we are separated from you by so great a distance, and by other obstacles far more insurmountable than distance.

My time has, during the last winter and spring, been more engrossed by my business than ever; and, in addition to my usual occupations, two of my hours in every morning have been occupied with military exercises, which are now with us become the business of everybody. Fortunately, I have now at last a little leisure; and we are enjoying it by the sea side, in a most delightful country, and with the finest weather imaginable.

I return you thanks for M. Corancez's book.[1] I cannot however but say, that I was disappointed to find from a person who had frequently conversed with Rousseau for so many of the last years of his life, little more than anecdotes of his frenzy. When one recollects the two or three traits of Rousseau which M. de St. Pierre has related, one cannot but wish that he had seen him oftener instead of M. Corancez. It makes one's heart bleed to think what Rousseau must have suffered in the latter part of his life; and yet those sufferings were mild compared with what he must have experienced if he could have foreseen the events which have since happened, the horrors which have been committed by his pretended disciples, and the calamities which have befallen the countries which of all others were dearest to him.

[1] Corancez was one of the Editors of the *Journal de Paris*, from 1777 to 1790; and the work here alluded to was principally extracted from that Journal.

I wish our literature had produced any thing worth sending you, or worth giving an account of; but for a long time nothing has appeared of any considerable merit. Coxe's *Memoirs of Sir Robert Walpole* have been published; but they seem to have disappointed every body, although the expectations which they had raised were not very great.

You will be kind enough, I hope, not to lose any opportunity of letting me hear news of you; and that you will not with very scrupulous exactness wait for a letter from me, before you let me hear from you. My dear Anne joins in the wishes that I form, for the health and happiness of yourself and your family.

I am, yours,

S. R.

Letter CXV.

FROM M. DUMONT.

Hastings, 4 Août 1799.

Vous avez donc vu M. et Mad^{e}. G——. Je prends part à toutes vos joies mutuelles; grande impatience de toutes parts, grande curiosité à satisfaire. Je serois bien trompé si l'amitié des deux dames n'égaloit bientôt celle des deux amis. Dites-moi là, en confessional, si vous n'avez pas

---

Letter CXV.

Hastings, Aug. 4. 1799.

So you have seen Mr. and Mrs. G——. I take part in your mutual joy. Great impatience on both sides; great curiosity to satisfy! I am much mistaken if the friendship of the two ladies does not soon equal that of the two friends. Now, confess to me, in confidence: had you not a feeling of pride, after every other? In truth, you must have

eu un mouvement d'orgueil, après tous les autres. . . . . Il faudroit certes, comme disoit Mirabeau, que vous fussiez plus ou moins qu'un homme pour ne pas l'éprouver; mais on ne démêle pas cela dans l'agréable confusion de sentimens qu'occasionne une telle entrevue.

Je serai curieux de voir le mari et la femme après leur séjour dans le centre de cette révolution. Ils ont dû vous communiquer bien des anecdotes intéressantes; mais est-il possible de vivre si longtemps au milieu de tant de passions déchaînées sans en prendre soi-même? Il me semble qu'on ne peut pas venir de Paris avec une âme calme et modérée. Ce ne seroit pas même un fort bon signe, que de voir avec modération les actes et les acteurs de ce théâtre.

Un petit mot à l'oreille de Mad[e]. Romilly pour William; c'est d'éducation que nous parlons ensemble, et nous anticipons un peu. Je viens de lire, ou plutôt de relire, ce *Sandford et Merton*, dans lequel j'ai trouvé beaucoup d'esprit, de talent, de l'art de développer les idées, de les préparer, de les

---

been more or less than man, as Mirabeau used to say, if you had not; but it is not easy to distinguish it in the agreeable confusion of feelings occasioned by such an interview.

I shall be curious to see the husband and wife after their abode in the centre of the revolution. They must have told you many interesting anecdotes. But is it possible to have lived so long in the midst of so many unbridled passions and to have escaped the contagion? I can scarcely conceive any one coming from Paris with a calm and sober mind: indeed it would not be a very good sign to view with moderation the acts and actors on that theatre.

One word in Mrs. Romilly's ear about William. The subject is education, and a little premature. I have just been reading, for the second time, *Sandford and Merton*, in which I find a good deal of cleverness, of talent, of the art of developing ideas, of preparing them, and of intro-

faire entrer dans une jeune tête; mais ne trouvez-vous pas à cet ouvrage le défaut d'être une satire, et de jeter une espèce d'odieux sur les rangs plus élevés de la société, de donner constamment le beau rôle au petit fermier, et le mauvais au petit *gentleman?* et ce contraste continuel entre les deux est-il sans danger? On conviendra qu'il ne seroit pas trop bon entre les mains des petits fermiers; je conviendrai qu'il seroit moins mauvais entre les mains des petits *gentlemen* exclusivement, mais je crois encore que cette satire, cette sauce piquante, est de trop dans l'instruction, et j'opine pour que William ne le lise pas avant l'âge de quinze ans.

Tout à vous,

Et. Dumont.

Letter CXVI.

TO MADAME G——.

Knill Court, Sept. 4. 1799.

The letter, Madam, which my dear Anne wrote to you last Saturday, and mine to Mr. G——, were directed to Arundel Street, and may therefore

---

ducing them into the minds of children. But does not this work appear to you to have the fault of being a satire, and of throwing a sort of odium upon the higher ranks of society, by always making the little farmer play the good part, and the little gentleman the bad one? and is this perpetual contrast between the two without danger? Every one will admit that it would not be a very good book for little farmers; I allow that it would do less harm in the hands of little gentlemen, but I still think that this satire, this high seasoning, education would be better without, and my advice is, that William should not read it till he is fifteen years old.

Yours, &c. &c.

possibly have miscarried. I send this therefore to your new residence, for it would be great injustice to ourselves, as well as to you, to suffer you to entertain the idea that this beautiful country, even with all its charms, can so soon have made us forget the pleasure which your company afforded us. As you say nothing of your sweet children, I conclude that they are both in good health. Our little William improves every day. He walks about, laughs, and is as happy as his little means of happiness will allow him to be. Every body that sees him is surprised that so healthy and strong a child should have been nursed in London.

Your La Harpe affords me great entertainment; though I have not yet got to that which I guess to be the most entertaining part of his works—his criticisms on modern authors. He has certainly a great deal of taste, his observations are generally just, his illustrations are new, and he is always amusing. It is remarkable, however, how much afraid he seems of ever going alone. He is continually a critic upon other critics; and he seldom judges of one author but through the medium of another. He gives his own opinion on dramatic poetry, on the sublime, and on oratory, in the form of a review of Aristotle's *Poetics*, Longinus's *Treatise*, Quinctilian's *Institutions*, and Cicero's *Dialogue*. To praise Homer, he finds it necessary to refute Lamotte. To defend Sophocles he attacks Voltaire; and to explain his own opinion of Horace and Juvenal, he undertakes to show how much Duraulx had mistaken the characters of both those satirists. He seems to me like a man who had long followed the business of a reviewer of new publications, and who could not sufficiently divest himself of the habits of his past life, when he set about a great work, which required to be treated upon general principles, and with method. The disposition of his work appears to me to be made in defiance of all order. He begins with dramatic poetry; then proceeds to the sublime; next to a comparison of the French and ancient languages; then to epic poetry; then again to dramatic. The division of the work between the ancients and moderns appears to me to be most injudicious, since he must necessarily, in both parts of it, have to compare the moderns and ancients together. I will not, however, tire you with my observations; I should rather say, I will not tire you any longer with them; but will thank you again for the great pleasure which the book has afforded me. Indeed you can hardly think what pleasure, after the drudgery of the last winter and spring, I have in passing a few days just as I like; in reading what I please; in walking when I please; in strolling about, or taking a ride with my dear Anne; in carrying about my little William; and in laughing only because he shakes his little sides with laughter.

Yours, &c.

S. R.

Letter CXVII.

TO THE SAME.

Cowes, September 29. 1800.

I am afraid you will both carry away a much less favourable opinion of this country than you brought into it, but I think you have seen it under disadvantages; and though I believe that many things are altered among us for the worse since the French revolution, which has had a most important effect on the whole nation, yet I really do not believe that our national character is so much changed as Mr. G. seems to think it. I must own, however, that what is now going forward in almost every part of the kingdom is not calculated to give a favourable opinion of the wisdom of my countrymen. Never, to be sure, were there such temptations held out to riot and insurrection as the resolutions which, in consequence of the late riots, have been entered into in different parts of the country respecting the price of provisions. London is almost the only place in which the rioters have not been triumphant; every where else, although the riots have been stopped by an armed force, yet the price of provisions has for a moment been lowered; the rioters have consequently carried their point; and the success of one commotion has constantly produced others in other places. Nothing can be more foolish than the expedients which have been adopted for lowering the price of provisions: they are such, indeed, as will probably produce that effect for a short time (I believe a very short one), but as must of necessity greatly increase them hereafter. The effect thus produced, while it lasts, will be naturally attributed by the rioters to their exertions; they will feel the necessity of interposing their authority again, and will consider a fresh violation of the law as an act of patriotism and a public duty. I have so little doubt of this effect being produced, and of fresh riots breaking out, that I should really think the state of the country most alarming, if the number of armed volunteers that are spread throughout it did not make it impossible that any commotions, in which only the lowest part of the community takes part, should be carried to any formidable length. The poor misguided wretches who engage in these riots are greatly to be pitied. They feel the scarcity and the high price of the necessaries of life most severely; great pains have been taken by persons in high authority to persuade them that what they suffer is not to be ascribed to those natural causes which were obvious to their senses, but to the frauds and rapaciousness of the dealers in provisions. They are told that there are severe laws in force against these crimes, and yet that the crimes are every where committed: it is clear, therefore, that no justice is done for the people till they do it for themselves. Then indeed resolutions are entered into, which the persons who make them admit to have been necessary, but which they never thought of entering into while they only saw their poor neighbours starving around them, and till the moment arrived when their own barns were about to be burnt, and their houses to be pulled down over their heads. Certainly a poor man, who, actuated by such considerations, has the courage to expose himself and his family to ruin for the public good, acts most meritoriously, though the men who have contributed most to mislead him will be the first to send him without pity to the gallows. To this very moment

I cannot find that the least attempt has been any where made to undeceive the people; but, on the contrary, an opinion the most repugnant to common sense, that is, that provisions of all kinds bear a higher price than the persons who deal in them can well afford to sell them at, is, without the least enquiry upon the subject, every where acted upon as an established truth.

Yours, &c.

S. R.

Letter CXVIII.

TO M. DUMONT.

Dear Dumont, Saturday, Jan. 9. 1802.

A thousand thanks for your letters; next to the pleasure of being at Paris, and comparing with one's own eyes the Paris of to-day with that which existed before the Revolution, is that of receiving such interesting details.

I am extremely rejoiced to hear that you and Bentham are about to make your appearance in public so soon. It is very entertaining to hear Bentham speak of it. He says that he is very impatient to see the book[1], because he has a great curiosity to know what his own opinions are upon the subjects you treat of. The truth I believe is, that he has a great curiosity to read these opinions in print; for when you gave them to him

[1] *Traités de Législation Civile et Pénale*, which was shortly afterwards published at Paris.

in manuscript, he had so little curiosity that I believe he read very little of them. He says that he thought what he read very insipid, principally because there was nothing new or striking in the expressions. This, however, was not said to me, and was so confidential that he would exclaim against a double treachery if he knew that I told you of it.

Have you yet seen Dugald Stewart's *Life of Robertson?* It is well done, but inferior to the *Life of Adam Smith.* The most interesting part of it consists of the Letters, particularly those of Hume. The sincerity and cordiality with which he interests himself about the writings, and rejoices in the success, of a contemporary and rival historian, do him the greatest honour. If Dugald Stewart's book be a good criterion by which to judge of the spirit which at present prevails at Edinburgh, it must be more intolerant than ever. Our friend thinks it necessary, upon most of the subjects which he incidentally mentions, to say that he would not be understood to adopt the opinions which he relates; and he has carried his caution so far as to suppress some letters, which were extremely characteristic of the writers of them, because he thought they might scandalize his pious and loyal countrymen. Amongst others, one that I have seen, in which Hume, after reproaching Robertson for speaking without disapprobation of some enormities which were committed by the Scotch Reformers, concludes with saying, " But I see you are a good Christian and a Whig, and I am therefore your very humble servant, David Hume."

I have read with very great pleasure the papers you left with me; they are extremely interesting, and seem to me new, though I believe that there is very little in them that I had not heard from you in conversation.

Ever and most sincerely yours,

SAML. ROMILLY.

DIARY

OF

A JOURNEY TO PARIS IN 1802.

Aug. 30. 1802. Left London on a journey to Paris.

Sept. 3. We passed through Abbeville, where we found most of the large houses shut up, and the streets full of beggars. The cause, we were told, was, that the woollen manufactures, which had once flourished so much at this place, were totally ruined.

Sept. 4. Slept at Chantilly. The magnificent castle at Chantilly is a heap of ruins, and its beautiful garden has been laid waste. The stables, the private apartments in which the Prince de Condé lived, and a range of buildings erected for the Prince's servants, is all that remains of the splendid piles of building which once constituted and adorned this palace.

Sept. 5. Arrived at Paris. The rooms which had been taken for us were in the Hôtel de Courlande, Place de la Concorde, the place once known by the name of Place de Louis XV., and afterwards Place de la Révolution. This was the spot upon which the unfortunate Louis XVI., and afterwards the Queen, and Mad[e]. Elizabeth, suffered death; and where, under the reign of Robespierre, daily executions of a number of victims took place before a gigantic statue of the Goddess of Liberty which was then placed there, and as a sacrifice to whom so many victims were offered up. In the last six days, before the tenth Thermidor, the Revolutionary Tribunal condemned two hundred and thirty persons to death.

During our journey, which was entirely through a corn country, we found the land every where cultivated; no waste land to be seen; but we saw no pasture, and no turnips. A number of small new farm-houses have been built, and the condition of the middle and lower ranks of the people seems to have been much improved. In general, they plough with only two horses, which are yoked a-breast; and one person alone can, by a long rein, drive the horses and plough at the same time. We once saw a woman alone ploughing and guiding the horses.

Sept. 6. We went to Passy with Mad[e]. Gautier.

Sept. 7. Mad[e]. Gautier procured for me the reading of the original MS. of Dr. Franklin's Life. There are only two copies—this, and one which Dr. F. took with a machine for copying letters, and which is in the possession of his grandson. Franklin gave the MS. to M. Viellard, of Passy, who was guillotined during the revolution. Upon his death, it came into the hands of his daughter or granddaughter, Mad[e]. Viellard, who is the present possessor of it. It appears evidently to be the first draft written by Franklin; for, in a great many places, the word originally written is erased with a pen, and a word nearly synonymous substituted in its place, not over the other, but farther on, so as manifestly to show that the correction was made at the time of the original composition. The MS. contains a great many additions made upon a very wide margin; but I did not find that a single passage was any where struck out. Part of the work, but not quite half of it, has been translated into French, and from the French re-translated into English. The Life comes down no lower than to the year 1757.

Sept. 8. Called on Talleyrand, who received me with great politeness. I afterwards called on Le Chevalier, Talleyrand's secretary; in a short conversation I had with him, he told me that in his opinion nothing could restore good morals and order in the country, but, as he expressed it, "la roue et la religion de nos ancêtres." He knew, he said, that the English did not think so, but we knew nothing of the people; even Fox, with whom he had just had a conversation, knew nothing of them, for he had said the same thing to him, and Fox had been shocked at the idea of restoring the wheel as a punishment in France.

We went to the Musée Central des Arts, where all the fine statues and pictures brought from Italy, from the Netherlands, and from different parts of France, are collected together: the Apollo Belvidere, the Laocoon, the Dying Gladiator, the Torso, &c.

We dined at Mad^e^. G——'s at Passy with Mad^e^. Lavoisier, the widow of the famous chemist.

Sept. 9. Mad^e^. Lavoisier took us to see a celebrated picture of M. Girodet. The subject is, Victory introducing the shades of Desaix, Dampierre, Marceau, Joubert, and the other officers who have died in the war, to the heroes of Ossian. The execution is, if possible, more ridiculous than the subject. All the figures, except Victory, and an eagle which is soaring in the sky, are painted as if seen through a mist to represent shades. The nymphs who attend Ossian are hospitably regaling the subordinate heroes, the private soldiers and drummers, with the nectar of Ossian's time, good beer, in shells; and some of these *manes* of drummers and soldiers are represented as smoking their pipes, and are such burlesque figures, that they might well have a place in Hogarth's *March to Finchley*. M. Girodet's reason for putting one of these figures in his picture I thought a curious one. He told us that he had placed him there (a little ugly fellow beating a drum and smoking a pipe) to serve as a foil to one of his heroes (I think Dampierre), who was not much favoured in his person by nature.

Sept. 10. Gallois breakfasted with us, and afterwards accompanied me to the Palais. At the Tribunal Criminel I heard part of the trial of a woman accused of having stolen some jewels and money belonging to her mistress, upon her mistress's death; and of the brother of the servant, who was accused of being an accomplice and a receiver. The only part of the trial that we heard was the speech of the counsel of the prisoners, and the summing up of the judge. The summing up was very masterly; the judge recapitulated, and observed upon the evidence with great ability, and without the assistance of any notes; all his observations were against the prisoners. It seems that it has been found that juries very often acquit the prisoners whom they ought to convict; which may account for the judge's summing up strongly against the prisoner. It is said that the frequent acquittals prevent witnesses from giving their testimony. They foresee that, notwithstanding whatever they may depose, the accused will be acquitted, and that by their evidence they will only have provoked the vengeance of a desperate villain who is shortly to be turned loose upon the public.

The juries are required to decide, not upon the single question, guilty or not guilty, but upon a series of questions unnecessarily numerous.

In the court in which the criminal tribunal is held are the busts of Brutus and of J. J. Rousseau. There are also two unoccupied stands for busts, on which were formerly placed those of Marat and Le Peletier St. Fargeau.

I afterwards went to the *Tribunal de Cassation*, the *Tribunal de Première Instance*, and the *Tribunal de Police Correctionelle*. Dined at Mad^e^. G.'s with Camille Jourdan, Portalis, (the son of the minister, and who is to go as secretary to General Andréossi in his embassy to England,) and Girodet.

Sept. 11. Attended again at the *Tribunal Criminel;* six men were tried together for forgery. There was no jury. The trial by jury for the *Crimen falsi*, and likewise for the crimes of setting fire to barns of corn, &c., was taken away by a law made last May, or *Floréal*. Till then, crimes of this description were tried by what was called a special jury, consisting partly of persons who by their profession were most likely to understand the subject (a sort of *experts*). The reasons given for superseding juries, as to these crimes, were, that the crimes had become very common, were extremely dangerous to society, and ought to be suppressed without delay. But, in truth, all crimes ought to be suppressed as speedily as possible, and if the trial by jury does not tend to the due execution of justice, and consequently to the prevention of crimes, the trial by jury ought to be abolished universally. The men I saw tried were, according to the last law, tried by six judges; their judgment must be unanimous to condemn.

After every witness was examined, an examination took place of the prisoners by the judges. This would have much shocked most Englishmen, who have very superstitious notions of the rights and privileges of the persons accused of crimes. It should seem, however, if the great object of all trials be to discover the truth, to punish the guilty, and to afford security to the innocent, that the examination of the accused is the most important, and an indispensable part of every trial. I observed one objection to it, however; which is, that the judges often endeavour to show their ability and to gain the admiration of the audience by their mode of cross-examining the prisoners. This necessarily makes them, as it were, parties, and gives them an interest to convict. They become advocates against the prisoners; a prisoner who should foil the judge by his mode of answering his questions, particularly if by that means he should raise a laugh from the audience, would have little chance of obtaining a judgment from him in his favour.

Having heard a sentence of a man who was to be executed at the *Place de Grève* cried about the streets, I walked thither. The scaffold was erected, and the guillotine ready; a great crowd of persons were assembled, principally women. The ideas which the guillotine must awaken in every body's mind, naturally render it an object of horror; but, independently of those ideas, the large slanting axe, the hole through which the neck of the sufferer is placed, smeared round of a different colour, and seeming to be yet stained with the blood of former malefactors, the basket placed to receive the head, and the large wicker chest in which the body is afterwards thrown, render it altogether a most hideous instrument of death. It seems to answer very well the idea of Montaigne, who I think somewhere recommends as the most proper public punishments, those which make the strongest impression on the spectators, but inflict the least pain upon the malefactor. From the Place de Grève I walked back towards the Palais; and I there saw the prisoner brought out to be led to the place of execution. A small party of dragoons attended him: he was placed in a cart, his body naked, with a red cloak (or, according to the terms of the law, *une chemise rouge*,) tied round his neck and hanging loose over his shoulders. He had been convicted of a murder and robbery.

On all the public buildings at Paris are inscribed

the words, *Unité, Indivisibilité de la République, Liberté, Egalité, Fraternité:* the words "*ou la mort*" followed in all these inscriptions, but are now effaced; and in some places the words *Justice, Humanité*, are substituted in their place. Under one of the windows of the Louvre an inscription was placed during the reign of Robespierre to commemorate that it was from that window that Charles IX. fired upon the people. This inscription too is now effaced. Upon the Château of the Tuileries, next the Place de Carousel, are the marks of the cannon-balls fired on the famous 10th of August, and over each of those marks is an inscription still remaining, 10 *Août*, 1792.

We went this morning to the Petits Augustins, where are collected the monuments out of most of the churches of France, the remains of the *vandalisme* (as it is called) which prevailed during the most extravagant times of the republic. The inscription upon the monument of *Le Brun*, the famous painter, may give some idea of the folly and extravagance of those supposed republicans. The words *in italics* have been struck out with a chisel, and the rest of the inscription was suffered to remain. "A la Mémoire de Charles Le Brun, Ecuyer, Sieur de Thionville, premier Peintre *du Roi*, Directeur des Manufactures *Royales* des Gobelins, Directeur *Chancelier de l'Académie Royale* de Peinture et de Sculpture. Son génie vaste et supérieur le mit en peu de temps au-dessus de tous les peintres de son siècle. Ce fut lui qui forma la célèbre Académie de Peinture et de Sculpture que *Louis le Grand* a depuis honorée de sa *Royale* protection, &c. &c. pour marque éternelle de son mérite. *Louis le Grand* le fit son premier peintre, lui donna des lettres authentiques *de noblesse*, et la combla de ses bienfaits, &c. &c."

We dined at home, went afterwards to the *Théâtre de la Rue Feydeau*, and then to Mad^{e}. Lavoisier. We met there a party of about a dozen persons; amongst others, the Abbé Morellet, MM. Suard, Barbé Marbois, one of the ministers (ministre du Trésor National), Dupont, Gallois, Girodet the painter, M. and Mad^{e}. de Souza (formerly Mad^{e}. de Flahault). The conversation was very pleasant, and principally literary; not a word of politics: this, however, seemed to proceed rather from indifference than from caution.

Sept. 13. I called with Gallois upon the Abbé Morellet, Suard, and Baert. We went to the Panorama of Lyons, and Mad^{e}. Delhi's manufactory of china, formerly called the Angoulême manufactory, and afterwards to the Prison of the Temple.

Went to the Opera Buffa. "Il Barbiere di Seviglia."

Sept. 14. Dined at home. Erskine and his son dined with us.

Went after dinner to the Opera, to the first representation of "Tamerlan." We saw there General Moreau, Cambacères, Mad^{e}. Tallien, Mad^{e}. Recamier, &c. &c. We were going the next day into the country, and, to give our horses some rest, we had a hackney coach brought to take us home from the Opera. The consequence of this was, that though we quitted our box before the last dance was over, we were obliged to wait till almost every body else was gone before we could get away. Every gentleman's carriage (no matter in what order they stood) had precedence over our contemptible hackney coach; and we waited three quarters of an hour while the numerous carriages of the politer part of the audience drove up and carried off their company. I could not but think this a singular order of police, enforced as it is by dragoons and foot-soldiers, in a city where it is impossible to stir a step without seeing the word "Equality" displayed upon some public building, or at the corner of a street, in conspicuous characters.

Sept. 17. On my return from the country, I found an invitation from Talleyrand to dine with him to-day at his house at Neuilly. I went there, of course, without Mrs. Romilly. A large company was assembled; we waited a long time for Talleyrand; soon afterwards dinner was announced. We sat down about thirty. Among the men were Count Cobenzl (the Austrian ambassador), the Danish ambassador, General Andréossi, Admiral Brieux, Rœderer, Portal (a physician), and about ten or twelve Englishmen, particularly Charles Fox, General Fitzpatrick, Lord Holland, St. John, and Adair. After dinner the company very much increased, and amongst those latter visiters were General Bournonville and Cardinal Caprara. Talleyrand received me coldly enough, with the air and manner of a great minister, and not of a man with whom I once was intimate. The dinner, and the assemblage after dinner, were so grave and solemn, that one might have conceived one's self rather at the court of some little German prince than in the house of a man of good society in Paris. The dinner was one of the most stately and melancholy banquets I ever was present at. I had the good fortune to sit next to Charles Fox, and to have a good deal of conversation with him. But for this circumstance, I should have found this dinner a very irksome and unpleasant task which I had imposed on myself. After dinner, in the room in which we took coffee, two young women, dressed *à l'Angloise*, and, as it is said, English women, walked in, and burned incense; after staying some time in one part of the room, they walked to another corner, still burning incense, till the whole room was perfumed.

Sept. 18. We went by water to St. Cloud, in the hope of being able to see the inside of the castle. Nobody is admitted, even into the outer court of this place, since it has been determined that it is to be the habitation of the first Consul, without producing a ticket; and, after getting into the first court, the visiter is stopped by every sentinel in his way, and ordered to produce his ticket, till he gets into the palace. Into this palace, so difficult of access, have been transported some of the finest pictures of which the gallery of the Louvre has been despoiled, — pictures which had long been exhibited there, which the public of Paris have been accustomed to admire and to feast their eyes and their vanity upon, as part of the spoil won from the nations with which France has been at war. This public property is thus appropriated to adorn the private residence of the first Consul, into which the unhallowed feet of the Parisian mob are not suffered to penetrate. This, more than any thing I have met with, proves to me in what scorn Bonaparte holds the opinions of the people. He seems to despise their favour; and, if he supplies them with frequent festivals, it is less to gain popularity than to occupy and amuse them.

One can hardly pass through a street in Paris without seeing a lottery office, or meeting fellows offering lottery tickets for sale. The Constituent Assembly abolished all lotteries, as being destructive of the morals of the people. Under the Directory they were restored, and they now are encouraged and flourish to such a degree, that this most mischievous temptation to the most ruinous kind of gaming is held out unremittingly, and almost in every village, to the lowest class of society. Under the old government there was only one lottery, which was drawn at Paris; but now there is a lottery by authority of government, not only at Paris, but at Lyons, Strasbourg, Bordeaux, and Brussels.

Sept. 20. Went to the Exhibition of the Productions of the Arts at the Louvre; afterwards to the Palais, where a man and two women were tried for forgery; then to Nôtre-Dame, and lastly to the Cabinet of Mineralogy at the Hôtel de la Monnoye. At Nôtre-Dame all the crucifixes and statues were removed, while public worship was prohibited, and the church was called the Temple of Reason. In the great choir is a Mosaic pavement, with the arms of France, the *fleurs-de-lis*, and a crown over them. This was not removed, but the following inscription is engraven upon it: — "Sous le règne des lois, la liberté, après avoir écarté tous les objets qui pouvoient blesser les yeux républicains, a conservé ce pavé par respect pour les arts." Dined at home. Gallois and Bentham dined with us. In the evening at the Théâtre François, Tartuffe, &c.

Sept. 21. Went to the Jardin des Plantes with Mad[e]. Gautier, Erskine, and his son. Saw the Cabinet d'Histoire Naturelle, the Gardens, the Ménagerie, and the Cabinet of Anatomy of Cuvier, which Cuvier himself showed us. Called on the Duchess de la Rochefoucauld. Went in the evening to the Théâtre François — Phédre. Mlle. Duchesnois, a new actress, who has very considerable merit, appeared in the character of Phédre: the rest very bad.

Sept. 22. Went again to the Louvre to the Exhibition of the Productions of the Arts, in the hope of seeing Bonaparte. He was there; and we had an opportunity of seeing him very well, he being close to us during a pretty long conversation he had with Mongolfier, who explained to him a machine he had exhibited. None of the prints of him are very like. He has a mildness, a serenity in his countenance which is very prepossessing; and none of that sternness which is to be found in his pictures. His painters seem rather to have wished to make the picture of a very extraordinary man, than to paint a portrait very like him. Went with Bentham to see the hall of the legislative body, which is built on what was formerly the Palais Bourbon. The hall is very beautiful, and admirably adapted to a country where the nominal legislature is a mere ornament, a toy to amuse the nation with. Went in the evening to a meeting of the National Institute—the Class of the Sciences: Monge, president; La Grange, La Place, Bertholet, Cuvier, Guyton de Morveaux, Prony, &c. A paper read of Aldani, a nephew of Galvani, on experiments of Galvanism; some, on the heads and bodies of two men immediately after they had been guillotined.

Sept. 23. 1 *Vendémiaire.* Anniversary of the republic. Talleyrand sent me word, by Charles Fox, that I might be presented to-day to the first Consul, together with Erskine, at his levee at the Tuileries. I had been disgusted at the eagerness with which the English crowded to do homage at the new court of a usurper and a tyrant, and I made an excuse.

The illuminations and fireworks. The illuminations at the Place de la Concorde and the Tuileries were very fine. The illuminations of private houses were miserable. In England, the finest part of a public illumination consists of the lights in the windows of private houses; in France, it is only in the illumination of public buildings and gardens that one finds any thing to admire. It is a trifling circumstance, but it characterizes the two nations. In France, almost all great works are undertaken by the public; in England, they are carried on by private projectors.

Sept. 24. Dined at Talleyrand's at Neuilly;—a solemn dinner, like the former, and still more numerous.

Sept. 26. Dined at Passy with M. Garnier, (the translator of Adam Smith, and the present prefect of the department of the Seine and Oise,) Bentham, Dumont, Lord Henry Petty, &c.

Sept. 27. Saw the Hotel of the Invalides with M. Treipzac, the architect, who lost a leg and was wounded in many places by the explosion of the infernal machine, 3d Nivose. *A-propos* of the conspiracy of the 3d Nivose, every body here is firmly persuaded that it was suggested and paid for in England. Windham is universally considered as the principal machinator. Bonaparte spoke of it to Charles Fox, and was astonished at Charles Fox assuring him that he was fully convinced that there was not the least ground for the imputation.

At the Invalides, in the inscriptions under all the pictures, the word "Roi" is every where effaced, and nothing substituted in its place. "Maestricht pris par le ——." "Entrée du —— dans la ville," &c. &c.

Sept. 28. Went to the gallery of the Museum; met West there, who showed us the pictures which are not public. The Transfiguration of Raphael; the demoniac and his father, and a figure immediately behind him, were left unfinished by Raphael, and were painted by Julio Romano. The portrait of Cardinal Bentivoglio, by Vandyke, the finest of his portraits. West told us the pictures were most judiciously repaired, and that no injury whatever was done to them by repairing them. There is not a single picture of Salvator Rosa or of Gaspard Poussin in the Gallery.

Sept. 29. Dined at Madame Lavoisier's, with

Dupont, Baert, Dumont, and Lord Henry Petty. Went afterwards with Dumont and Lord H. Petty to Neuilly to Talleyrand's. Saw Saint Foix there.

Oct. 1. Went to Versailles; breakfasted at Little Trianon; saw the castle. A miserable collection of pictures, all of the French school.

Oct. 2. Dined at home. Went to the Théâtre François—The Cid, Lafont, in Rodrigue, received great applause, but appeared to me to be one of the worst actors I ever saw.

Oct. 3. Went to see the houses of Lucien Bonaparte, General Murat near Neuilly, and Madame Bonaparte, the mother. We could not help contrasting the fresh splendour and magnificence of the habitations of the present reigning family, with the tarnished grandeur and neglected appearance of Versailles; the palace of the Bourbons in the days of their prosperity, and the ruinous cottages and temples of the Little Trianon, which the last queen had made the principal abode of her pleasures.

Oct. 10. Went to the castle of Meudon and to Bellevue; returned to Passy. The road to St. Cloud at the bottom of the garden at Passy was crowded for many hours with the carriages of persons going to and returning from the levee of the first Consul, or rather of Madame Bonaparte, at St. Cloud. We dined at Passy, and in the evening Matthieu de Montmorency, the ex-constituent, came in. He seems unaffected, unassuming, possessed of good sense, and of an excellent disposition.

Oct. 12. Went to the Hospice of the Enfans Trouvés in the Faubourg St. Jacques, formerly the Port Royal, and a prison during the reign of terror.

Oct. 13. Went to the National Library. The Professor Millin showed us the antiquities, and M. Dacier the manuscripts. Among the most curious were, the famous Virgil from the Vatican Library; the Terence, which is supposed to be of the ninth century, with a commentary interlined. A Latin translation of Josephus on the Egyptian Papyrus, and written in the running hand of the Romans, and said to be of the fourth century, but supposed by the best critics to be of a later date by two or three centuries. The letters of Henry IV. to his mistress. A most beautiful MS. of Petrarch, with illuminations, and a part of Dante in the same MS. Another MS. of Dante, with very curious illuminations. The "Heures" of Anne of Brittany, with a great variety of plants and insects, beautifully drawn. The "Heures" of Louis XIV. The campaign of Louis XIV. The original MS. of Telemachus, in the handwriting of Fénélon, with many interlineations and corrections, &c.

Went in the evening to M. Suard's; met there the Abbé Morellet, Lally Tolendal, Camille Jourdan, &c.

Oct. 14. Left Paris.

Oct. 19. Got home to Gower Street.

There is at present in France the greatest abundance of specie. All payments, except of large sums, are made in gold and silver. Gold is scarce, as compared with silver; but not in a greater degree than it was before the revolution. If a banker pays a sum in Louis-d'or, he deducts three or two sous upon every Louis, although there has not been, since the beginning of the revolution, any coinage of gold. The principal part, too, of the silver that is current, consists of crowns of six livres of the old monarchy. Soon after the first acts of violence which attended the commencement of the revolution, gold and silver coin became extremely scarce; there was a general cry, and almost a universal belief, that the coin had been carried into foreign countries, and very strict, but very futile, regulations were made to prevent what was thought so great an evil. To men of reflection, it was very obvious that the only possible cause of a scarcity which was so sensible, must be the general alarm which had spread throughout the country, and which must have induced most persons who were possessed of money to bury or conceal it, as the only resource they could have when their other property was gone. The creation of assignats operated in the same way, but to such a degree as to make all coin disappear. It was obvious to every body that a time would come when assignats would be of no value; every body therefore who was inclined to save any thing saved in coin and paid in assignats. If assignats had not been created, coin, however scarce, must have continued in circulation. A man possessed of coin must have parted with some of it, or must have refused himself the necessaries of life; and no future evil which he was disposed to provide against could be greater than that of starving. As soon as the assignats were put an end to, gold and silver coin again immediately appeared in the very same Louis-d'or and crowns which it was supposed had been exported into foreign countries and melted.

The facility with which the currency of assignats was stopped, and the perfect tranquillity which attended that operation, is one of the most extraordinary political phenomena of the revolution.

Bank notes of the *Caisse d'Escompte* are current, but only for large sums; the smallest I have seen are for 500 francs.

The only silver coin there has been during the revolution is of pieces of five francs, which are not very common; there is coinage of silver and copper mixed, consisting of pieces of 30 sols and 15 sols; and a copper coinage of pennies, all of which are very common. Money is lent here at an enormous interest, as high, I have been told, as 12 per cent. upon good security. Mortgages of real estates of the old possessors of them produce an interest of 10 per cent.; and Government borrows money at 10 or 11 per cent., to be repaid in a few months by the receipt from the taxes. As long as this lasts, none of their great commercial enterprizes which the French seem in general to expect, can possibly take place. What must be the trade in which a man can afford to pay 12 per cent. for the money he uses in it? and who that can sit quietly at home, dine with his friends, go to the Opera every evening, and then to Frescati, and with all this receive 12 per cent. for his money, will devote his time, undertake the trouble, and incur the risk of any trade?

It is very curious to consider what France is, to recollect what it has been during the last fourteen years, and to speculate upon what it is likely to be. A more absolute despotism than that which now exists here France never experienced: Louis XIV. was never so independent of public opinion as Bonaparte is: the police was never so vigilant or so well organised. There is no freedom of discussion; the press was never so restrained, as at present, under Louis XIV. and XV.; the vigilance of the police in this respect was eluded, and books, published in other countries, containing very free opinions, were circulated at Paris: but that is not the case now. Among other restraints, all English newspapers are prohibited; and it is said that even the foreign Ministers are not permitted to receive them by the post. An opinion is entertained, whether with or without foundation I do not know, that persons of character, and who mix in good society, are spies employed by the police, and consequently that a man is hardly safe any where in uttering his sentiments on public affairs. It should seem, however, that few persons have any desire to utter them. I have been in several societies in which there was certainly the most perfect security, and where politics seemed the last subject that any body wished to talk upon. It may seem at first very wonderful by what means Bonaparte can maintain so absolute a power. It is not by the army; for if he is popular with the soldiers, it is only with those he has commanded: he does not seem, however, to have been ever very popular even with them. His character is of that kind which inspires fear much more than it conciliates affection. He is not loved by any of the persons who are about him, not even by the officers who served with him; while Moreau is universally beloved by all who have served with him. It is impossible to say that it is by the force of public opinion that Bonaparte reigns: there is certainly an opinion very universally entertained, highly favourable to his talents both as a general and as a politician: but he is not popular; the public have no attachment to him; they do not enjoy his greatness. Bonaparte seems, indeed, to despise popularity; he takes no pains to gain the affections of the people. All the public works which he sets on foot are calculated to give a high opinion of himself, and to immortalize his name, but not to increase the happiness of the people, or to alleviate the sufferings of any particular description of them. To increase the beauty and magnificence of the city, to build new bridges, to bring water by a canal to Paris, to collect the finest statues and pictures of which conquered nations have been despoiled, to encourage and improve the fine arts, are the great objects of Bonaparte's ambition in time of peace. That he meditates the gaining fresh laurels in war can hardly be doubted, if the accounts which one hears of his restless and impatient disposition be true. His literary taste may serve to give some insight into his character: Ossian is his favourite author.

When the Bastille was stormed by the mob of Paris, there were not found in it I think more than five or six prisoners; and to those the Bastille served as an hospital rather than a prison; for they were advanced in age and without friends. — I am assured that there are, or at least very lately were, more than seventy prisoners confined in the Temple, the bastille of the present day; persons of the most adverse principles and opinions, some of them violent Jacobins, others emigrants and aristocrats.

As persons of the most opposite opinions are subject to persecution, so are they, as indiscriminately, objects of favour. Fouché, who till a few days ago was minister of police, and was supposed to have the confidence of Bonaparte, was at Nantes one of the most violent revolutionists, in the very spirit, it is said, of Carrier. It is reported of him, that he used at one time to wear in his hat the ear of an aristocrat, in the manner of a national cockade.

What strikes a foreigner as most extraordinary at Paris, is that the despotism which prevails there, and the vexatious and trifling regulations of the police, are all carried on in the name of liberty and equality. It was to establish liberty and equality on their true basis, according to Bonaparte's own declaration in the legislative assembly at St. Cloud on the 18th *Brumaire*, that he commanded his grenadiers to charge the assembly with fixed bayonets, and obliged most of the members to seek their safety by escaping through the windows. Liberty and equality are still sounded as high, and displayed in as conspicuous characters as ever. In the front of the Tuileries, one of the most magnificent palaces of Europe, the most sumptuously furnished, filled with the finest pictures, continually surrounded with guards, and inaccessible but to those who are connected with the first Consul, who makes it his place of residence, is displayed the word *Egalité* in large letters. You attempt to pass through an open passage, and you are rudely stopped by a sentinel, who, with the voice of authority, halloos out, "On ne passe pas par ici." You turn your head, and for your consolation behold inscribed in characters which seem indelible, *Liberté*.

And has it been only for this, and in order that a number of contractors, of speculators, of persons who have abused the military or civil authority they have possessed, may enjoy securely their ill-gotten wealth, that rivers of blood have been shed, that numbers of individuals, who by their talents and acquisitions were the ornaments of one of the most enlightened nations in the world, have perished on the scaffold, that the most opulent families have been reduced to misery and languished out their wretched lives in exile! Such an exclamation is very natural. It is, however, to all these horrors of the revolution, that Bonaparte owes his power. If public opinion is not strongly expressed in his favour, it is strongly expressed against every thing in the revolution which has preceded his consulate. The quiet despotism, which leaves every body who does not wish to meddle with politics (and few at present have any such wish), in the full and secure enjoyment of their property and of their pleasures, is a sort of paradise, compared with the agitation, the perpetual alarms, the scenes of infamy and of bloodshed which accompanied the pretended liberties of France.

Bonaparte is said to entertain a very bad opinion of mankind, at least of the nation he governs. In consequence of that opinion he distrusts every body, and does every thing himself.

Almost all the French I have seen entertain a very high opinion of Mr. Pitt, and a proportionally mean opinion of the English opposition. They admit that Mr. Pitt did not carry on the war with great ability, but they think that his talents alone saved us from a revolution, such as they have themselves experienced.

It is astonishing how much the French are disposed to refine, to account for every thing that happens in an extraordinary way, and to find deep design and contrivance in the most simple transactions. There is hardly a Frenchman who is not satisfied that Pitt's conduct with respect to the slave trade was only a trap laid for France, and into which she unfortunately fell. I remember to have heard this very thing said in France in 1788, of the measures taken in England to procure the abolition of the slave trade. The expedition of Quiberon was, according to this refined way of thinking, undertaken with no object of succeeding in it, but merely to send to their graves all the best naval officers that France had to boast of, and who happened then to be emigrants and in England; and in this point of view it is considered as a great stroke of policy, and as one of the achievements which prove Pitt's great talents.

Letter CXIX.

TO MADAME G——.

November 2. 1802.

Anne's two letters from Dover and London will have informed you, my dear Mrs. G., of our safe arrival here, and of our having found our children perfectly well. The contrast between France and England is not greater than that between our present mode of existence, and that which we have lately enjoyed. From a life of gaiety, of seeing sights, and of going into company, Anne's is become perfectly domestic, and she sees scarcely any but the faces of relations; and for myself, from a life of complete idleness, I have passed into the midst of great business, and have the near prospect of much more. The time, indeed, is so fast approaching when I shall hardly have a moment which I can call my own, that I am fearful of suffering this season of comparative leisure to pass without thanking you for all your kindness to us. We are indeed indebted to you, and your most amiable family, for almost all the enjoyment we have had at Paris; but what we have most reason to thank you for is, for enabling us to know you so much better than we had done before. It was necessary to have lived with you, to have seen you in your own house, and with your own family; to have known all that you have gone through, and how you have gone through it, to appreciate justly all your merit. Our friendship and affection for you hardly could increase, but at least we have now many additional motives for them. I can hardly express how much I am obliged to you, for the memorial of my most excellent friend, your husband. I had read the book often, but I have read it again with new delight, because it was his; and I have been most sensibly affected by some passages which he had marked; and particularly that in which Lælius laments the loss of the best of friends, in Scipio, and exclaims, that although snatched away from him, yet, in his memory he still lived, and would live for ever; and that the virtues which he loved in him had not perished with that part of him which was mortal. It will often be a source to me of exquisite though melancholy pleasure.

I hope to God that a renewal of war is not at hand; but there does not seem much of a friendly disposition either in your or our governors. There is no describing to you the effect which Bonaparte's proclamation against the Swiss has produced in this country. The language of all the newspapers, of all parties, has been the same upon it, and they certainly only express the indignation which has been universally felt here. I hope, however, that our ministers are not weak enough to mistake this for a wish on the part of the nation to plunge into all the miseries of war; but I will not answer for it.

We have a work just published here by Paley, entitled *Natural Theology;* which, from an observation you made when we were seeing Cuvier's cabinet, I think would afford you great pleasure; and I will send it to you by the first opportunity I meet with. It is the only book worth noticing, which has been published during our absence.

I am yours, &c.,

S. R.

Letter CXX.

TO M. DUMONT.

Dear Dumont, May 31. 1803.

It is vain to wait for a moment of leisure; I may as well write to you, therefore, now that I have not an instant to spare, as at any other time. Anne told you, I believe, that there is no mention of you in the third number of the *Edinburgh Review*. I don't think you have any reason to be sorry, unless you think it would be of use to your book[1] to have it abused. The Editors seem to value themselves principally upon their severity, and they have reviewed some works, seemingly with no other object than to show what their powers in this particular line of criticism are. They begin their account of *Delphine*, with these words: — "This dismal trash has nearly dislocated the jaws of every critic among us with gaping." Of Fivée's *Letters*, they say, "It is some advantage to have this kind of standard of *pessimism*, to see the utmost extent to which ignorance and petulance can go;" and of Dugald Stewart's *Life of Dr. Ro-*

[1] *Traités de Législation Civile et Pénale.*

bertson, which, upon the whole, they treat with comparative indulgence, they say at the conclusion that a Life of Robertson is a work yet to be written. There are, however, many articles in the last number of great merit, and it is, I think, upon the whole, very much superior to the second number.

Nothing has been published here since you left us, except a pamphlet, by Lord King, on the Restriction on Payments in Specie by the Bank, which has great merit. He has rendered clear and familiar a very obscure and difficult subject. I suspect that our friend Whishaw has contributed something to the merit of the work.

I suppose you see our newspapers, and that you have consequently read the papers which our ministers have published as their justification for proceeding to hostilities against France. The first day's debate which took place on the subject of them has not been published, for, owing to a new regulation which was made respecting the admission of strangers into the gallery, none of the newswriters were able to get in. Pitt's speech is universally allowed to be one of the finest, if not the very finest, he ever made. His influence and authority in the House of Commons, shown upon the debate I have just mentioned, and still more on the day when Fox moved that the House should recommend the Crown to accept the mediation of the Emperor of Russia, exceeds all belief. The ministry seem, in the House of Commons, in comparison with him, to be persons of no account. An administration whose talents were generally thought so meanly of, or I may say who were so universally despised, was never before at the head of a great country. There does not seem likely, however, to be any great change. It is said that Tierney is immediately to be in office, and it seems probable enough; but the King is supposed to object more firmly than ever to Pitt's return into administration.

You will have heard, to be sure, before this that Bonaparte, under pretence that to make captures at sea before a formal declaration of war is contrary to the law of nations, has made prisoners of all the English between the ages of eighteen and sixty within the French territory. Mr. Liston, our ambassador at the Hague, Lord Elgin, who was at Paris on his way to London, and Mr. Talbot, the secretary of Lord Whitworth, are said to be of the number of persons who are not permitted to return to England. All the other Englishmen are made actual prisoners; the men being sent to the Temple, or the Conciergerie, and the women to Fontainebleau. If it had been Bonaparte's object to give strength to the British ministry, and to make the war universally popular in England, he could not have devised a better expedient.

I have not seen Bentham for a long time; but I understand the ministry intend to propose, among other measures of finance, a tax on Successions, resembling that which he sometime ago suggested. This will, no doubt, be not a little agreeable to him, and will probably, for a time, divert him from his present occupation, which is, I conjecture, writing on that particular question of the Law of Evidence, which has lately been discussed in our Courts. Ever most sincerely and affectionately yours,

SAML. ROMILLY.

LETTER CXXI.

TO MADAME G——.

August 9. 1803.

The uncommonly warm weather we have had lately, has made me very much enjoy the cool and refreshing evening air at Kensington; and now and then a walk by moonlight, after passing sometimes nine or ten hours of the day in a crowded court of justice. You pity me for not passing more of my time in this retreat, and in the company of my dear Anne; and I am not so dull as not to perceive the gentle reproof which is concealed under your pity. You think that I am sacrificing real and certain happiness for an imaginary and uncertain good — that domestic comfort which I might now enjoy, for riches and honours which I may never live to attain. But in this you are very unjust to me. In the course of life which I am following, I think I am only discharging my duty; and that the only chance I have of rendering any important service to others, is, by just proceeding as I am now doing. If I am not mistaken in this, you will admit that I have an excuse, or rather that I do not stand in need of excuse, for being so many hours separated from one with whom it would be my greatest happiness to spend every moment of my existence. Just at the present moment I am less deserving of your compassion than at any other time. In a few days my labours will cease, and we hope to quit London till the end of October. We shall first pass ten days or a fortnight at Lord Lansdowne's at Bowood; a place which I now always visit with fresh pleasure, as it was there I first saw my dear Anne, and every spot of that delightful abode brings to my recollection scenes which were only an earnest of that unmixed happiness which I have ever since enjoyed. But I say too much, when I call it quite unmixed, for though I cannot consider the irksome and laborious duties of my profession as a real interruption of my happiness, yet it is in truth interrupted by the reflection, that in this life every thing is subject to change; and that our condition can hardly change but for the worse. From Bowood we shall go into Herefordshire, into a retreat which, I think, if you were to see it, you would say was worthy of Switzerland.

EVENTS IN 1805.

The Chancellorship of Durham having become vacant by the resignation of Mr. Baron Sutton, who did not think it compatible with his situation as a judge, although it had formerly been held by Mr. Justice Yates and Mr. Justice Willes, after their promotion to the Bench: the Bishop of Durham appointed me to the office. He came to me one day below the bar in the House of Lords, after the business I was attending on was concluded, and offered it to me with many compliments more flattering than the offer itself. Till then the Bishop had been almost a stranger to me. I had indeed been counsel in different causes in the Court of Chancery both for him and against him, but I had never met him in company, and had spoken to him only once before. The occasion of that conversation was this. The Bishop and his friend, Mr. Bernard, were great patrons of the society for bettering the condition of the poor, and were zealous promoters of a number of different plans for advancing the general good of mankind; all set on foot with the best intentions, but many of them, as it appeared to me, more remarkable for goodness of intention, than for enlarged views or sound policy. I happened to mention to Mr. Bernard one day, when the conversation had turned upon the subject of the sufferings which mute animals were wantonly made to endure, that I thought he and his friends might do a great deal of good by endeavouring to bring into general use a mode of slaughtering cattle, which would be attended with much less pain to the animal than that which is commonly practised, such as had been suggested by Mr. Bakewell of Leicestershire, and warmly recommended in some of the agricultural reports; and I observed, that perhaps this might be done, by offering rewards to butchers who should practise it, and whose vanity might be the more flattered by receiving a prize for their humanity, as it was a virtue of which they are generally supposed to be least susceptible. Mr. Bernard pressed me to put down something upon the subject in writing. I did so, and in the few lines I wrote, I insisted principally on the importance, in a moral and political point of view, of weaning men from the habit of contemplating with indifference the sufferings of any sensitive beings. The proper remedy for the evil would, perhaps, be a law prescribing the mode in which cattle should be put to death, and prohibiting any other. But such a statute, unless the mode which it pointed out was generally known, and was already by some persons practised, would probably, as it were by general consent, remain unexecuted. It was, therefore, of great importance to introduce the new practice without any legislative interposition, and this was my reason for suggesting the measure to Bernard. He showed my paper to the Bishop, who adopted the idea very cordially, and some time afterwards introduced himself to me in the House of Lords. After expressing his surprise that a lawyer, in so much business as I was, could find time to think of such matters, he told me that he had spoken to several persons who had taken up the idea with much zeal, amongst others, Lord Somerville, who was at the head of the Board of Agriculture, Mr. Mellish, the great contractor for victualling the Navy, and the First Lord of the Admiralty, who had all promised to do every thing in their power to promote and bring into general use Mr. Bakewell's plan, and that he had great hopes that it would, before long, be effected.

Whether this circumstance had given the Bishop a favourable opinion of me, or whether he was merely influenced by the consideration that, of the barristers who attended the Court of Chancery, I was in the most practice, I do not know; but I understood that some earnest and very powerful solicitations were made to him on behalf of other persons, when he appointed me, who had not solicited, and who did not wish for the office. Though I had not wished for it, I accepted it. The emolument attending it I knew to be very inconsiderable, not much more than the amount of the expense of going to Durham to discharge its duties. The honour is not generally considered, either in or out of the profession, as a very high one, and certainly had no charms for me: and it was impossible I could look to the office as the source of any pleasure. I yielded, therefore, in a great degree, in accepting it, to public opinion. Attorneys and Solicitors General had of late hardly thought themselves at liberty to refuse it; and I was partly afraid of incurring the reproach of being solely intent upon amassing a fortune by my labours. I was actuated, too, by another, though not a very powerful motive. I was desirous of trying the experiment how I should acquit myself, and how I should feel in a judicial office. The experience, however, which the office could afford me was very inconsiderable: there had not been, upon an average of many years back, more than four or five causes in the Court in a year, notwithstanding that, for a part of that time, some of the ablest equity lawyers in the profession, amongst others, Lord Eldon and Lord Redesdale, had presided in it. In truth, there are several concurrent causes which must ever prevent the business of the Court from being considerable. One of the principal is, the narrow extent of its jurisdiction. Out of the County Palatine, the decrees of the Court cannot be enforced — one of the first acts I had to do as Chancellor, was to issue a sequestration against a man who had been ordered to pay a sum of 900*l.* No sooner was the decree pronounced against him, than he quitted his old place of residence, and having taken up his abode only a few miles off, in the county of Northumberland, was disposed to set the Court and its decrees at defiance. Fortunately he had some land in Durham, which could be sequestrated; but it will not be thought surprising that there is not much business in a Court which can enforce its decrees only against those who happen to have real property in one small county.

But though a Chancellor of Durham has not the comfort of reflecting that his services are of much public utility, he may, if he be fond of such things, enjoy the grandeur and magnificence and homage which attend him. The castle of Durham, the episcopal palace, is, when the Chancellor arrives, given up to him by the Bishop. It is his house; the servants attend upon him as the lord of it; a costly dinner is given to the dignitaries of the church, to the counsel, the officers of the court, and the neighbouring gentlemen; and this, though at the Bishop's expense, is, by a kind of legal fiction, considered as the Chancellor's dinner. The invitations are sent in his name; he presides at the table; and when the Bishop is at Auckland, the Chancellor invites and receives him as his guest. Though I was, in some degree, prepared for this, I could not, upon my arrival at Durham, but feel very forcibly the ridicule of all this mimic grandeur. It was night when we got there, for my dear Anne, who had been accompanying me on a short and hasty tour to the Lakes of Cumberland, was with me. We found that we had been long expected; and as we drove through the gates into the spacious court, and the porter sounded the great bell, we saw the servants hurrying out with lights. In the midst of bows and compliments, and by numerous attendants, we were conducted through long lighted galleries into a drawing-room, where some of the officers of the court and their wives were waiting to receive us, and "My Lord" and "Your Honour" ushered in every phrase that was uttered. So sudden a transformation into a great man, and the lord of an old feudal palace, reminded one of Sancho's government of Barataria; and still more of Sly, the drunken cobbler of Shakspeare. But to me all this ceremonial was not more ridiculous than it was irksome. The necessity of making conversation with persons I had never seen before, and of presiding at table and doing the honours of a great dinner, were to me so disgusting and painful, that the experience of two tedious days passed at Durham would have been sufficient to cure me of all ambitious desires, if I could have imagined that the duties of a Chancellor of England bore any resemblance to those of a Chancellor of Durham. The decision of the few causes which came before me, in none of which did any question of difficulty arise, hardly deserves the serious name of a duty, when compared with the more arduous task of acting the part of Lord of a castle not my own, and of considering as my welcome guests the numerous strangers whom I met at table.

In the autumn of this year a very unexpected offer was made to me by the Prince of Wales, of a seat in Parliament. It was made through my friend Creevey, in a letter which I will transcribe.

"Dear Romilly, Brighton, Sept. 18. 1805.

"You will be surprised at receiving a letter from me, no doubt, and perhaps still more so at the subject of it; but I am desired to write to you by a person whose desires, in the courtly language of this place, are considered as *commands*. I will proceed, therefore, to state to you my case. In the course of the few weeks I have been here, I have had various conversations with the Prince of Wales, principally upon the subject of political parties, and respecting which he is very ardent and not a little communicative. On Monday last, the day after his return from Weymouth and London, in the course of a very long discussion upon these matters, he said he had done one excellent thing during his absence,—"he had got a seat in Parliament for Romilly." He then went at great length into your history and your merits; pronounced you to be the chief of your profession, and a certain future chancellor; and expressed the greatest desire for *himself* to be the means of your coming into Parliament. He said he had mentioned this in an interview with Fox, in town last week, who had likewise expressed the greatest delight at it. You would have been amused had you heard the familiarity with which he handled the possible objections to this measure: he said your parliamentary business was principally in the House of Lords, with which it would not interfere, and that you seldom or never attended election committees. You may readily imagine I was not so unskilful as to omit this opportunity of mentioning my acquaintance with a person whom I heard so highly panegyrised; but I hazarded no conjecture as to the conduct you would pursue upon such an offer, or as to any objects you might have in view, parliamentary or political; indeed, I wished the subject to end as it then stood, that I might have an opportunity of preparing you for some official communication upon this subject. Yesterday, however, he renewed the subject, and expressly desired me to write to you; and now I can only state to you what I have here written. I do not know the name of the place he means; the time when it would be vacated: nor do I know distinctly whether the seat was to be gratuitous; certainly the impression upon my mind was such, but unfortunately princes are very vague discoursers, and, still more unfortunately, one has no means of cross-examining them, or compelling them to put their sentiments down upon paper. You must, therefore, use your own discretion in the answer you send to this very blind information, and coming from such a quarter. You must see the necessity of my showing him your letter in answer to this when it comes, and of course will frame it accordingly; you may, at the same time, give me any private instructions, and I will take care to obey them. I am to dine with him to-day, and doubtless you will again be displayed; if I collect any more detail as to this matter I will send it, and in the mean time I think my ignorance of your present residence furnishes you with a sufficient apology for some delay in sending the *official* answer to this communication. It would be very presumptuous in me to give any opinion as to whether you should politically connect yourself with this same Prince; on the other hand, in the course of things, he is to be King, and a connexion with him now is a connexion with a most powerful party, and a party certainly the most respectable of parties in the country — to say nothing of the political opinions of him and his party being those which I presume you would think most advantageous for the country. At all events you must, I am sure, feel much gratified at this homage from him in conjunction with Fox, and I leave you to make such reply to it as you think fit.

"I beg you to present my respects to Mrs. Romilly, and believe me to be very truly yours,

"THOMAS CREEVEY."

When I received this letter, I had not had any intercourse whatever with the Prince, direct or indirect, except upon the subject of a cause in the Court of Chancery, in which he took a very great interest. It related to the guardianship of a daughter of Lord Hugh Seymour, who had remained, at the death of her parents while she was of very tender years, under the care of Mrs. Fitzherbert. With that lady she had been left by her family till she was between five and six years old, and they then required to have her returned to them. Being an orphan, and without a legal guardian, no person had a right to remove her, and the principal object of the suit was to have a guardian for her appointed. On the one side were proposed for this office Lord Euston and Lord Henry Seymour, who had been named by Lord Hugh in a will made before the birth of this little orphan, the guardians of all his children in a certain event, which did not happen; and on the other, Mrs. Fitzherbert, with whom the child had been placed by both her parents when they went from England, (Lady Horatia, the mother, on account of her health, and Lord Hugh as captain of the ship which he commanded,) who had from that time considered and cherished the child as her own, and who had in truth become a mother to it. The Master, to whom the matter was referred, approved of Lord Euston and Lord Henry Seymour as guardians; and from his decision Mrs.

Fitzherbert brought the matter, by an exception to the report, before the Lord Chancellor, who, after a long hearing, and with less than his usual deliberation, confirmed the Master's report. While the cause was depending, the Prince of Wales, who lived at Mrs. Fitzherbert's house, as his own, was extremely anxious about the event of it. He loved the child with paternal affection, and the idea of having her torn from him seemed to be as painful to him as it was to Mrs. Fitzherbert. It was upon the occasion of this cause that he desired once that I, who was one of the counsel for Mrs. Fitzherbert, would meet him at her house. I met him accordingly, and had a very long conversation with his Royal Highness; but it was confined entirely to the subject on which he had desired to see me.

I was very much surprised therefore to receive such an offer from the Prince. I had not a moment's hesitation as to refusing it, but the difficulty was to find a proper mode of giving that refusal. I could not say that I had determined never to go into Parliament, for it was my intention to obtain a seat in it. I could not give any good reason for wishing to delay it long, for if I ever thought of taking any part in politics, I had not much time to lose. To give my real reason, that I was determined to be independent, and not to enter the House of Commons as the agent of another person, even though that person were the heir-apparent of the Crown, would, I suspected, be extremely offensive to the Prince, and be thought by him the highest degree of insolence. But offensive though it was, I had no other resource; and I determined, therefore, with as much respect as I could, to assign that reason for my refusal. What increased my embarrassment was, that Creevey, to whom my letter was to be addressed, was himself brought into Parliament solely by Lord Petre. But there was no help for it, and I returned him this answer.

"Dear Creevey, Little Ealing, Sept. 23. 1805.

"I have but just received your letter, which by mistake was sent after me to Durham, and did not arrive there till after I had left it. It has, indeed, very much surprised me, and I am afraid my answer to it will occasion as much surprise in you. I cannot express to you how much flattered I am by the honour which the Prince of Wales does me. No event in the whole course of my life has been so gratifying to me, and I have only to fear, that it proceeds from much too high an opinion which his Royal Highness has formed from some partial and exaggerated account of me. I have formed no resolution to keep out of Parliament; on the contrary, it has very long been my intention, and is still my wish, to obtain a seat in the House of Commons, though not immediately. My politics you are already well acquainted with: if I had been a member from the beginning of the present Parliament, my vote would have been uniformly given in a way which I presume would have been agreeable to the Prince of Wales. Upon all great questions, and indeed it does not at this moment occur to me that I need make any exception, I think that upon all questions I should have voted with Mr. Fox; and yet with all this

I feel myself obliged to decline the offer which his Royal Highness has the great condescension to make me. This must seem very strange and paradoxical, and it certainly does require a good deal of explanation. I will endeavour to give it in the best way I can. When I was a young man, a seat in Parliament was offered me; it was offered in the handsomest manner imaginable. No condition whatever was annexed to it. I was told that I was to be quite independent, and was to vote and act just as I thought proper. I could not, however, relieve myself from the apprehension that, notwithstanding all these declarations which I believe were made with great sincerity, the person to whom I owed the seat would consider me, without perhaps being quite conscious of it himself, as *his* representative in Parliament; that he would be surprised, and perhaps chagrined, if his politics were not on all important occasions mine; and, in a word, that I should have some other than my own reason and conscience to account to for my public conduct: and even if these were not his sentiments, that they would be the sentiments of the public. In other respects, the offer was to me a most tempting one. I had then no professional business with which it could interfere. I took a much greater interest in political contests than I have ever done since, and as a young man I was vain and foolish enough to imagine that I might distinguish myself as a public speaker. I weighed the offer very maturely, and in the end I rejected it. I persuaded myself that (although that were not the case with others) it was impossible that the little talents which I possessed could ever be exerted with any advantage to the public, or any credit to myself, unless I came into parliament quite independent, and answerable for my conduct to God and to my country alone. I had felt the temptation so strongly, that in order to fortify myself against any others of the same kind, I formed to myself an unalterable resolution *never*, unless I held a public office, to come into Parliament but by a popular election, or by paying the common price for my seat. As to the first of these, I knew, of course, that I must never look for it; and as for the latter, I determined to wait till the labours of my profession should have enabled me to accomplish it without being guilty of any great extravagance.

"It is true, that when I formed that resolution, the possibility of a seat being offered me by the Prince of Wales had never entered into my thoughts; and that the rules which I have laid down to regulate my conduct ought perhaps to yield to such a circumstance as this. But yet I have so long acted upon this resolution, the principles on which I have formed it have become so much a part of the system of my life, and that life is now so far advanced, that I cannot convince myself, proud as I am of the distinction which his Royal Highness is willing to confer on me, that I ought to accept it. The answer that I should wish to give to his Royal Highness, is to express in the strongest terms my gratitude for the offer, but in the most respectful way possible to decline it; and at the same time to say, that if his Royal Highness thinks that my being in Parliament can be at all useful to the public, I shall be very glad to procure myself a seat the first opportunity that I can find. But the difficulty is to know how to give such an answer with propriety; I am fearful that it may be thought, in every way that it occurs to me to convey it, not sufficiently respectful to his Royal Highness, and from this embarrassment I know not how to relieve myself. My only resource is to trust that you will be able to do for me, what I cannot do for myself, and to convey my answer in a way which will express all the respect and gratitude I feel.

"You will undoubtedly not have understood me, when I said that it was not my wish to go into Parliament immediately, to mean that I was waiting till I might have gained sufficient to make the consideration to be paid for a seat a matter of little importance to me. I already consider it as a matter of very little importance, but I was desirous for a little longer to devote myself entirely to my profession. A close attendance in Parliament is not quite compatible with a close attendance at the Rolls, and you know very well that in the present state of the Court of Chancery, by very much the greater proportion of causes are heard there; this however is also a consideration of very inferior importance.

"This long letter will, I am afraid, have quite exhausted your patience, but I knew not how to explain myself more concisely.

"I remain, dear Creevey,

"Ever and most sincerely yours,

"SAML. ROMILLY."

At the same time I addressed a private letter to Creevey in these words: —

" Dear Creevey, Sept. 23. 1805.

" I send you enclosed the official answer you desire, though I am afraid you will think for an official answer it is in a very odd form. The truth is, that though I had no hesitation as to refusing the Prince's offer, I found myself much embarrassed to know what reasons to give for doing so; at last I thought, as is often the case in matters of difficulty, the simplest and most obvious course to take is the best, and that I had nothing to do but just to speak the plain truth upon the subject. If it gives offence to the Prince I shall be sorry; but my consolation will be that the evil was inevitable. You will smile, perhaps, at the solemnity of my letter, and at the long and important history of myself; but while you are disposed to think this ridiculous, pray do not forget how it is forced from me. I have been making a very hasty tour to the lakes of Cumberland, and have since been acting the part of a chancellor at Durham. The most important, and by much the most disagreeable, part of my duty has been to preside at a formal and very numerous dinner of persons, not one of whom except Losh I had ever seen before.

" I am sorry to be unintentionally the cause of so much trouble to you, but you will easily guess that I shall not be sorry to learn how my answer is received."

How my letter was received will appear from the following account which I received, about a week afterwards, from Creevey: —

"Dear Romilly, Chichester, October 1. 1805.

"I am afraid you will think me long in giving you any information upon the subject of your letter, and the way in which it was received. On Wednesday last I saw the Prince on horseback at a review, and he called me to him, and, amongst other things, asked if I had heard from you. I told him I had your answer to my letter in my pocket; and, after having shortly stated to him the substance of it in the way I thought most likely to give a favourable impression to him, I gave it to him. As he had not then an opportunity of reading it, he put it in his pocket and took it home with him; and on Thursday evening I saw him reading it over and over again. He then called me to him, and began a conversation about it: he *professed* himself to be perfectly satisfied with it, but he was evidently mortified. He repeated all his former sentiments respecting you, and said he hoped you certainly would come into Parliament upon your own terms. 'That if you would not permit him to *give* you a seat (which would have been his greatest delight), he would take care you should be sure of one, when you wanted it, in any way you chose to have it.' I pressed upon him repeatedly the superior advantage you could render to him, to his opinions, to his party, and to the country, by sitting in Parliament in the way you proposed, rather than by owing your seat immediately to him; to all of which he assented, but still conveying to me always the impression that he was hurt. This is so natural a consequence of your refusal, that of course you must have anticipated it. I took for granted you would do as you have done, and I am sure you have done right. It seems to me impossible that this conduct on your part can produce any injurious consequences, either to yourself or the public. You must feel every kind disposition to the Prince in return for an offer so handsomely made; and he is much too clever not to value you far more highly for this specimen of your independence. A connexion thus begun between you is, I think, of the most promising kind; the most likely to afford you ultimate influence over the Prince (if he is accessible to influence at all), and of course the most likely to be beneficial to the country. At the close of our conversation I asked him if he wished to keep your letter: but he said, as it contained political opinions of yours, he did not think himself justified in doing so; and he returned it, and it is now in my possession, to be disposed of as you shall direct. I delayed writing to you for some days, thinking the conversation might be renewed, but we have had nothing but the Duke of York, and generals, and reviews, since. I meant to have written from here last night, but was too late for the post. I am now just returning to Brighton, and if any thing more occurs upon this subject you shall learn it. I beg you to present my kind respects to Mrs. Romilly, and believe me to be, dear Romilly, very truly yours,

"Thos. Creevey."

I had spoken the truth in my letter, but I had not spoken the whole truth; nor was it fit I should. I was averse to being brought into Parliament by any man, but by the Prince almost above all others. To be under personal obligations of that kind to him, to be in a situation in which, as a lawyer and as a politician, he might repose a particular confidence in me, was what I, above all things, dreaded. I knew, from some conversations which Lord Lansdowne told me had taken place between him and Lord Moira some years before, that the Prince had expressed a wish to know some lawyer upon whose advice he could safely rely, and in whom he might place unbounded confidence; and that he was desirous of forming such a connexion before his accession to the throne. The subject of this desired confidence was also mentioned to me; and it was one upon which I imagined the best advice was likely to be the least acceptable. These circumstances occurred to me when I wrote my answer; and I thought it might perhaps prove a fortunate circumstance that I had thus early an opportunity of letting the Prince know what I was. If, such as he found me, he should be disposed to advance me to any high honour, I might, indeed, hope to be able to render some important services to the public; if, on the other hand, this specimen of my independence should prove an obstacle to my promotion, it would be clear that I could not obtain it but upon conditions understood, if not expressed, to which I never would submit.

I showed this correspondence soon after it had taken place to ——. When he had read it, he asked me if I was serious in saying that I meant to buy myself a seat, and whether that were a measure which I could easily reconcile to my conscience. I had so long considered this as almost the only mode by which Parliament was accessible with honour to one who had no family connexion, or local interest which could procure his return, that I was surprised at the observation even from a person who had lived so long secluded from the world, and had been so much accustomed to consider our constitution in its theory rather than in practice, as ——. Certainly it would be better that burgage-tenure boroughs should not exist, or that, existing, the owners of them should never make the high privilege of nominating representatives of the Commons of England in Parliament a subject of pecuniary traffic, but should, in the exercise of it, select only men of an independent spirit, whose talents and integrity pointed them out as most worthy of such a trust. But while things remain as we now unfortunately find them, as long as burgage-tenure representatives are only of two descriptions, they who buy their seats and they who discharge the most sacred of trusts at the pleasure, and almost as the servants of another, surely there can be no doubt in which class a man would choose to enrol himself; and one who should carry his notions of purity so far, that, thinking he possessed the means of rendering service to his country, he would yet rather seclude himself altogether from Parliament than get into it by such a violation of the theory of the constitution, must be under the dominion of a species of moral superstition which must wholly disqualify him for the discharge of any public duties.

If, however, I should be supposed by any one into whose hands this paper may chance to fall, to mean to convey a universal censure upon all persons who suffer themselves to be placed in Parliament by the proprietors of boroughs, he will as much have misunderstood me as if he supposed me ready to maintain that all persons who buy their seats are honest independent men, who go into parliament from no motive but to promote the public good. There are exceptions to all general rules. A man who has already established his public character may be brought into parliament by a private individual without the smallest reproach: it is his past and not his future conduct, what he has done, and not what is expected from him, to which he owes his seat.[1] And even where no prior services have given the individual any claims, there may be circumstances in the character of the giver and the acceptor of the seat, in their mutual confidence, and their mutual friendship, which may make such a connexion an honour to both of them. I could myself name several private individuals, from whom I should never have hesitated to accept a seat in Parliament; but they were men who had not and who never could have any

[1] See *Parliamentary Diary*, November 23. 1812. — Ed.

seats to dispose of. The recollection, therefore, of cases which might indeed be stated to be possible, but nothing more, could not prevent me from adopting as a general rule that which I have stated. It was a rule too laid down for myself alone, and founded upon circumstances peculiar to myself, upon my station in life, my family, my particular profession, upon my own peculiar character, upon my past life, and the future expectations of me which I knew my friends had formed, and which I had been accustomed to form myself.

In the November following the Prince sent to me to desire that I would go to him at Carlton House. I obeyed his summons (November 11.). He said a few words upon the subject of his offer, thanked me for having written so fully on the subject, and said that I must come into Parliament, but in my own way. He then entered into some conversation on the subject of Miss Seymour's cause. After despatching these subjects he proceeded to the matter which he said had been the cause of his desiring to see me. It was one, he said, of the most confidential nature and of the greatest importance. He then stated to me, very circumstantially and at great length, facts which had been communicated to him relative to the Princess of Wales, through the intervention of the Duke of Sussex, by Lady Douglas, the wife of one of the Duke's equerries. He told me that the account was to be put down in writing, and that it should be then sent to me, that I might consider with Lord Thurlow, to whom it was also to be sent, what steps it would be necessary to take.

Near a month elapsed before I heard anything more on the subject, but at the end of that time Colonel M'Mahon brought me, from the Prince, the narrative of Lady Douglas. After I had read it, by desire of the Prince I called (December 15.) on Lord Thurlow. Colonel M'Mahon accompanied me. Lord Thurlow had been very ill, which had been the cause of our interview being postponed for a week. He was still indisposed, and appeared to be extremely infirm; he was, however, in full possession of his faculties, and expressed himself, in the conversation we had together, with that coarse energy for which he has long been remarkable. He said that he had not been able to read all Lady Douglas's narrative, it was written in so bad a hand; but that he had gone rapidly over it, and collected the principal facts, (and, in truth, it appeared, from the observations he made, that no fact of any importance had escaped him;) that the first point to be considered was whether her account were true, and that, for himself, he did not believe it. He said that there was no *composition* in her narrative (that was the expression he used), no connexion in it, no dates: that some parts of it were grossly improbable. He then said, that when first he knew the Princess, he should have thought her incapable of writing or saying any such things as Lady Douglas imputed to her, but that she might be altered; that to be sure it was a strange thing to take a beggar's child, but a few days old, and adopt it as her own; but that, however, Princesses had sometimes strange whims which nobody could account for; that in some respects her situation was deserving of great compassion. Upon the whole, his opinion was, that the evidence the Prince was in possession of would not justify taking any step on his part, and that he had only to wait and see what facts might come to light in future. In the mean time, however, that it would be proper to employ a person to collect evidence respecting the conduct of the Princess; and he mentioned Lowten as a person very fit to be employed. At Colonel M'Mahon's desire, I wrote down for the information of the Prince what I collected to be Lord Thurlow's opinion. It having been manifest, from Lord Thurlow's manner, that he was not disposed to enter fully into the consideration of the subject, I understood from Colonel M'Mahon that the Prince would be governed by my advice. I wished, however, to decline being the single adviser of the Prince in a matter of such very great importance, and I suggested the propriety of Erskine being consulted. The papers were accordingly put into Erskine's hands, and we met upon them. I could not, however, easily engage him to consider what I thought the matters principally deserving of consideration; I therefore, by myself, put down in writing what appeared to me to be the principal difficulties to be decided on, and gave it to Colonel M'Mahon to be delivered to the Prince.

In the mean time Erskine and I agreed that, as Lord Thurlow had recommended, Lowten should be employed for the purpose. Erskine accordingly appointed Lowten to meet us both; but, on the night preceding the day fixed for our meeting,

Erskine's wife died: it was therefore impossible for him to attend the meeting, and I saw Lowten alone (Dec. 27.), put him in possession of the facts I was acquainted with, and delivered to him Lady Douglas's statement.

Dec. 30th. Lowten called on me, and informed me that he had seen Lord Moira and Colonel M'Mahon, and that from them he understood that it was the Prince's wish that I should see Lady Douglas.

Dec. 31st. I saw Lady Douglas with Sir John Douglas, Lord Moira, and Lowten, at Lowten's chambers. Lady Douglas answered all questions put to her with readiness, and gave her answers with great coolness and self-possession, and in a manner to impress one very much with the truth of them.

DIARY

OF

HIS PARLIAMENTARY LIFE,

FROM ITS COMMENCEMENT IN 1806 TO ITS TERMINATION IN 1818.

1806.

Feb. 8th. I this day received information from Mr. Fox, that I was appointed to the office of Solicitor-General.

This is the commencement of my public life. May I (though it is more than I dare expect or hardly hope for) be as happy in it as I have hitherto been in privacy and obscurity. I have determined to keep a journal of all those transactions of my life, which can be of any importance to the public or to myself. I may hereafter probably find it very useful to ascertain past events with more accuracy than a memory so defective as mine could enable me to do; and in recording every day the acts of my life, I shall be compelled to reflect on them, and on the motives by which I have been actuated, and, as it were, to pass a judgment on my conduct before it is too late for any self-confession to be of use.

My appointment has not only been unsolicited, but it has been made without connexion with either Lord Grenville or Mr. Fox, by whom the administration has been formed. I owe it principally, I believe, to the Prince of Wales. After the King had sent for Lord Grenville and had directed him to form a new administration, Colonel M'Mahon called on me, and informed me, that he had the Prince's commands to say to me, that he had told both Lord Grenville and Mr. Fox that it was his particular wish that I should hold some office in the administration that was to be formed. I have certainly never paid my court in any way to the Prince. His Royal Highness was kind enough, not many months ago, to offer me a seat in Parliament, which I very respectfully, but very decidedly declined.

Although the new administration has been formed in general of the public men of the greatest talents and highest character of any in the country, yet there are some few appointments which have been received by the public with much dissatisfaction, and none with more than that of Erskine to be Lord Chancellor. The truth undoubtedly is, that he is totally unfit for the situation. His practice has never led him into courts of equity; and the doctrines which prevail in them are to him almost like the law of a foreign country. It is true that he has a great deal of quickness, and is capable of much application; but, at his time of life, with the continual occupations which the duties of his office will give him, and the immense arrear of business left him by his tardy and doubting pre-

Erskine Lord Chancellor.

decessor [1], it is quite impossible that he should find the means of making himself master of that extensive and complicated system of law which he will have to administer. He acts, indeed, very ingenuously on the subject; he feels his unfitness for his office, and seems almost overcome with the idea of the difficulties which he foresees that he will have to encounter. He called on me a few days ago, and told me that he should stand in great need of my assistance, that I must tell him what to read, and how best to fit himself for his situation. "You must," these are the very words he used to me, "you must make me a Chancellor now, that I may afterwards make you one."*

10th. Piggott told me to-day, that Mr. Fox had desired him to say that the administration would bring us both into parliament without any expense on our parts. I cannot have any scruple about so coming into parliament. Not having the least hesitation at accepting the office of Solicitor-General under the present ministry, I cannot hesitate at accepting a seat in parliament from them. If I had come in as a private individual, I would not have accepted a seat from anybody. But, as long as I hold the office to which I have been appointed, I must support the administration. As soon as they appear to me unworthy to be supported, it will be my duty to resign.

* Before the Great Seal was given to Erskine, it had been offered to each of the two Chief Justices. Mansfield declined it on account of his age; and Lord Ellenborough because his office is almost as lucrative and is held for life, and perhaps because, being unaccustomed to courts of equity, he thought himself unfit for the office.

---

[1] Lord Eldon.—Ed.

Romilly sworn into the office of Solicitor-General.

12th. I was this day sworn in, together with Piggott, the new Attorney-General, and we attended the levee at the Queen's House, and kissed the King's hand on our appointment. His Majesty was pleased to knight us both, greatly against our inclination. Never was any city trader, who carried up a loyal address to his Majesty, more anxious to obtain, than we were to escape, this honour. We applied to Lord Dartmouth, the lord in waiting, to Lord Grenville, Lord Spencer, and everybody on whom we thought it might depend, to deprecate the ceremony which awaited us. But the King was inflexible. For the last twenty years of his reign, it has pleased his Majesty to knight all attorneys and solicitors general and judges on their appointment, though for the first five and twenty years he had never seen the necessity or propriety of it; and now, every man who arrives at these situations must submit to the humiliation of having inflicted on him that which is called, but is considered neither by himself nor any other person an honour. Perceval, the last Attorney-General, had been permitted to decline knighthood because he was an Earl's son.

Chief Justice of the King's Bench a member of the Cabinet.

March 1st, *Sat.* At Mr. Fox's desire, I attended a meeting at his house of several members of the House of Commons, to consider the question, expected to be brought on in the House on the Monday following, on the subject of Lord Ellenborough having a voice in the Cabinet. That there is nothing illegal or unconstitutional in this, seems clear. It is certainly very desirable that a judge should not take any part in politics; but this is not according to the theory of our Constitution, nor consistent with practice in the best times of our history. The chiefs of all the three courts are always Privy Councillors; and the Cabinet is only a committee of the Privy Council, and, as a Cabinet, is unknown to the Constitution. In the reign of Geo. II., and in the beginning of the present reign, when Regencies were established by Act of Parliament, in the event of the King's dying while his successor was in his minority, Councils were appointed to assist the Regents; and those Councils consisted, in each case, of the first officers of the State, such as are commonly Cabinet Ministers, with the addition in each case of the Archbishop of Canterbury, and the Chief Justice of the King's Bench; and in both cases it was the Chief Justice for the time being.* In Queen Anne's reign, Lord Justices were appointed, in whom the whole executive government was to remain, till the successor, if at the Queen's death he were out of the realm, should arrive in the kingdom; and the Chief Justice of the King's Bench was appointed one of the Lord Justices.† The first of these Acts met with great opposition from the Tories of that time; particular persons were objected to as Lord Justices, and a protest was entered in the House of Lords; but no objection whatever was made to the Chief Justice being of the number.

Romilly elected for Queenborough.

21st. I was elected to serve in Parliament for the borough of Queenborough. Mr. Geo. Peter Moore, who had been returned at the last general

* See the statutes, 24 Geo. 2. c. 24.; 5 Geo. 3. c. 27.

† See 4 Anne, c. 8.; and 6 Anne, c. 7.

election, accepted the Chiltern Hundreds at the request of Mr. Fox to make room for me. There was no opposition; but yet it was expected and considered indispensable that I should be present at the election. The borough is very much under the influence of the Ordnance; but, at the last election, Prinsep and Moore were chosen in opposition to the government, and in defiance of all the exertions of the corporation. Between 140 and 150 voters polled at the election. I found all parties very well disposed towards me; not only there was no opposition, but apparently I had the cordial support of all the electors. In less than four days after my election, I received applications from two of the electors to procure places for them; and of these, one, whose name is B——, had tired me, when I was at Queenborough, with long conversations to explain to me the politics of the borough, and to state the grievances of the freemen; in the course of which he told me twenty times that he was speaking for his brother freemen only, and did not at all consider himself.

Took his seat.

24th. I took my seat in the House of Commons, and was, on the same day, appointed one of the committee to manage Lord Melville's trial.

27th. Mr. Whitbread wrote me a letter to desire, on behalf of all the managers, that I would undertake to sum up the evidence on the trial of Lord Melville, which I suppose I cannot, with any propriety, decline.

Cruel punishment in the navy.

April 1st. *Tu.* Attended the Privy Council upon the examination of Mr. Stephens, a lieutenant in the navy, under the statute 33 Hen. 8. c. 23.

He was charged with the murder of three seamen at Bombay, in the year 1801. They had been flogged without any court-martial being held on them; and the punishment was inflicted with such horrible severity, that they all three died in less than twenty-four hours after it was over. Stephens had been present at the punishment, but he acted only in obedience to the orders of his superior officer, Lieutenant Rutherford, who, the Captain being absent, had the command, and who had ordered and presided himself at the execution. A warrant had been issued by the Council to apprehend Rutherford; but, upon the messenger's arriving at his ship, he threw himself overboard, and was supposed to have been drowned. All the witnesses who established the fact (for there had been several meetings of the Council before this, some of which I had attended) were seamen, who, acting under Rutherford's orders, had joined in inflicting the punishment; the men having been made to run the gauntlet. The witnesses were all in the same situation as Stephens. In strict law, they seem to have been all guilty of murder. Under all the circumstances, however, the Council thought it would not be advisable that a commission should issue to try Stephens; and they agreed (subject to what the Chancellor should think, who was unable this day to attend) to report to the King that measures should be taken to discover Rutherford, if he were living; and that Stephens, as well as the seamen, should be required to enter into recognisances to appear and give evidence against Rutherford, if he should be discovered.

In the course of these examinations it appeared, that it was not uncommon for officers, of their own authority, and without any court-martial, to inflict very severe punishments; and that they supposed this to be legal. I had some conversation with Mr. Grey[1] (First Lord of the Admiralty) on the subject; and he agreed that measures ought to be taken to prevent this in future. I will take an opportunity of speaking with him again upon it, and upon the enormous severity of punishments inflicted by courts-martial, which surely require to be restrained.

Slave trade.

Wilberforce came and sat by me to-day in the House of Commons, and renewed our acquaintance, which has been interrupted (but not by any fault of mine) for I think about nine or ten years. He said that he came with a petition to me; it was, that I would speak in support of the Bill he meant to bring in for the abolition of the slave trade; as he was sure that my speaking, as I was quite new in the House, would be of great use. I told him that I would do every thing in my power to ensure the success of the measure, and that, if I found that my speaking on it could be of any use, I would certainly do so.

Severity of military punishments.

3d. As I sat next to Mr. Grey to-day in the House of Commons, I renewed our conversation on the punishment in use in the navy. His idea is, that nothing more is necessary than that instructions should be given from the Admiralty prohibiting punishments, or at least severe punish-

[1] Now Earl Grey.—Ed.

ments, inflicted without the sentence of a court-martial; and, as they are already illegal, an Act of Parliament on the subject is certainly not necessary. But it is to be feared that the Admiralty instructions will in time fall into disuse, and that the practice of inflicting these unauthorised punishments will be revived. Mr. Grey thought that any measure which would draw the public attention to the subject was very objectionable. In this I cannot agree with him. In the short conversation we had together, I observed to him that something should be done to mitigate the punishments which were legal and regular, but which were most inhumanly severe. He seemed to agree with me in disapproving them, and the punishments in the army too, which he thought were still more severe; but he seemed to think it dangerous, or at least inexpedient to interfere with them.

Mr. Windham to-day introduced into the House his plan of military defence. His principal object is to improve the condition of the soldiers, by enlisting them for a stated period, and not for life, and by giving them an increase of pay, and other rewards for long service. But he did not propose any mitigation of the cruel punishments to which they are subject; and, indeed, he observed, that a very severe discipline was what he conceived to be necessary. For myself, I have no doubt that the savage and most inhuman punishments, to which soldiers and sailors alone of all British subjects are exposed, have a most fatal influence upon the discipline of the army, and upon the character of the nation.

6th. *Easter Day.* At Mrs. Fisher's, Ealing; stayed there till the 10th.

Lotteries. 12th. Lord Henry Petty[1], the Chancellor of the Exchequer, dined with me. I took occasion to observe to him, in the course of the day, how desirable it was that lotteries should be discontinued. He agreed with me, but said that, during the war, he thought it would be hardly possible to go on without them; that, however, they would not be extended, though a plan for that purpose had been in agitation, and had been much pressed on the Ministry. This plan was to put them on nearly the same footing as they are in France, where lotteries are drawn in the provincial towns, as well as at Paris; and, by means of those provincial lotteries, there is a lottery drawing almost without interruption throughout the year. Tierney, he said, was a great friend to this plan; but that it certainly would not be adopted. He observed too, that lotteries did much less mischief, now that all insurance upon tickets was abolished, than they did formerly. This may be; but they are still attended with most pernicious consequences.

Law of Evidence. 17th. I spoke for the first time in the House of Commons. It was in a committee of the House, upon the Bill to declare that a witness could not by law refuse to answer a question, on the ground that his answer might subject him to a civil suit. The Master of the Rolls, though he had declared himself an enemy to the Bill altogether, proposed a proviso, that it should still be open to a witness

[1] Now Marquis of Lansdowne.—Ed.

to object to answer any question, which, as a defendant to a bill in equity, he could not be compelled to answer; and that the judges should decide on that objection. I thought such a proviso, which proceeded on the supposition that the rules of evidence were to be governed, or which at least left it doubtful whether they might not be to be governed by the doctrines of courts of equity, extremely improper, and I therefore opposed it. The rules of evidence being part of the common law, it was impossible that they could depend on the doctrines of equity, which are all of very modern origin. The Bill had originated in the House of Lords; the Attorney-General had moved the first and second reading of it, and had carried it through the committee without proposing such a proviso. Now, however, that it was re-committed for the purpose of having this proviso moved, he supported the proviso with some earnestness, and at considerable length. Mr. Fox joined with me in opposing it, and it was rejected without a division.

Liberty of the press.

18th. In the House of Commons, Sergeant Best[1] moved for leave to bring in a Bill to prohibit under severe penalties the publication in the newspapers of proceedings before justices of the peace, or of applications to the King's Bench for leave to file informations. The ground stated for this measure was the prejudice which was often excited in the minds of the public against persons who were afterwards to be put on their trial; and which

[1] Now Lord Wynford.—Ed.

in many instances might influence the persons by whom the prisoners were to be tried.

This may be an evil, but it seems unavoidable, unless all such proceedings were to be had in secret. It is an evil which is far outweighed by the advantage of having the proceedings of justices of the peace under the control of public opinion. The proposed measure is at the best a very dangerous restraint upon the liberty of the press.

22d. Sergeant Best, upon conversing with Mr. Fox and the Attorney-General, and finding that his bill will be opposed, has, as I understand, abandoned it.

Law of Evidence.

23d. *First day of Term.* Upon the third reading of the Witness Bill, I spoke in support of it. My argument was, that the Bill had for its object to declare the law, as the majority of the judges had stated it to be, in their opinions lately delivered in the House of Lords, but delivered only in a legislative proceeding, and therefore not considered as of authority to govern future decisions. That if it were doubtful (though it did not appear to me that it was so), whether the Bill did not go beyond the opinions of the judges, yet, it had not been disputed by any one that the law, as so declared by the Bill, was the law upon the subject; and even if that could be matter of doubt, yet, if regard were had to the inconveniences arising from the law being such as the minority of the judges had declared it, there could be no doubt that the law ought to be such as the Bill declared it: and that there would be no evil in the Act, though intended to be merely declaratory, being to some extent enacting. In civil cases, ought a man to be permitted to suppress facts in his knowledge, necessary to establish the just demand of a plaintiff, or to defeat an unjust demand made on a defendant, because if those facts were disclosed, the witness too may be compelled to do justice to one from whom he withholds it? In criminal cases, shall offenders go with impunity, or an innocent man suffer the punishment of the guilty, rather than a witness be compelled to discover what will enable a third person to recover from him that which he unjustly withholds? But it is said to be very dangerous to expose witnesses to a temptation to commit perjury wantonly or unnecessarily. So to expose them is undoubtedly an evil; but, where their testimony is necessary to the due administration of justice, the exposing them to such a temptation must be regarded as an evil that is unavoidable.

The Bill was carried upon a division of 51 for it, to 18 against it.

Sheridan.

Mr. Sheridan, speaking upon quite a different subject[1], took occasion to say that he should oppose Sergeant Best's bill in every stage of it.

Lord Melville's trial.

29th. On this day the trial of Lord Melville, upon the impeachment of the Commons, commenced in Westminster Hall.

May 10th. As one of the managers of the Commons, I summed up the evidence which had been given in support of the impeachment; I spoke for three hours and twenty minutes; but more than

[1] The charges against Lord Wellesley.—Ed.

eight days had been occupied in receiving the evidence.*

Slave Trade.

16th. The Bill for abolishing the Slave Trade with any foreign colonies, which had passed the House of Commons, was, on this day, read a third time in the House of Lords, and passed. It was opposed, and the House divided upon it: the numbers for the bill were 53[1]; against it 18. Of this 18 one third were the King's sons; the Dukes of York, Clarence, Cumberland, Kent, Sussex, and Cambridge, having all voted against it. The Duke of Gloucester spoke and voted for the Bill.

Lord Melville's trial.

17th. The proceedings on Lord Melville's trial in Westminster Hall closed on this day, being the 15th day of the trial.

Princess of Wales.

18th. At the Prince's desire I called on Lord Thurlow, at his house at Dulwich, on the subject on which I had before seen him in December in the last year. I have preserved a memorandum of what passed on the former occasion. The evidence which has since been discovered is not very important. Lord Thurlow desired me to tell the Prince that the information he had received was

* The day before I summed up the evidence, I had some conversation on the subject with *Mr. Fox;* in the course of which, he told me that he was not acquainted with my manner of speaking, and therefore could not give me advice, except that he advised me not to be afraid of repeating observations which I thought very material; that it was much better that some of my audience should observe that I repeated, than that any of them should not understand me; that he had himself been reproached for repetitions, but he was not convinced that he was wrong.

---

[1] In Hansard, the numbers for the bill are stated to be 43.—Ed.

too important for it to remain in his possession, without some steps being taken upon it; that he ought to communicate it to Mr. Fox, and consider with him what was to be done upon it; and that the information had remained already too long in his Royal Highness's possession not proceeded on. In the course of the day I waited on the Prince, and communicated this message to him.

At Lord Thurlow's I met Mr. Forster, the solicitor, who had come at the Prince's request to speak with him respecting Miss Seymour's[1] cause, which is likely to come on soon in the House of Lords, and about which the Prince is extremely anxious.

Mr. Forster persuaded me to go round by his house at Sydenham on my way home, telling me it was only a mile about. I found it, however, between three and four miles about, which was very inconvenient to me; but I did not repent of having yielded to his persuasion, for, on our way, he told me of a plan which he had formed for shortening the duration, and diminishing the expense of proceedings in Chancery. It had been shown to Lord Redesdale, Mr. Madocks, and other persons in great practice at the bar, and had had the benefit of their corrections. Forster gave it to Lord Thurlow, when he was Chancellor; who, in his usual way, deferred taking any step upon it, and resigned the Great Seal, leaving the practice as he had found it. Forster has promised to send me a copy of it. As he is a very sensible man,

Practice of the Court of Chancery.

[1] See *suprà*, p. 117.—Ed.

and very well acquainted with the practice, I expect a great deal from it.

Planting Church Lands.

He told me too of another project of his, to encourage the lessees of church lands to plant and improve them. Lord Eldon adopted it, and last session brought a bill into the House of Lords to carry it into execution, but afterwards abandoned it. He pressed me very much to bring a bill for the purpose into the House of Commons.

Princess of Wales.

23d. I saw Lord Grenville on the subject of the Princess of Wales's conduct, and his Lordship desired me to state the most material facts, from the written declarations which have been put into my possession, in order to their being laid before the King. Lord Grenville seemed to think that the birth of the child[1] would render it impossible to avoid making the matter public, and the subject of a Parliamentary proceeding.

24th. I went to Ingram's at Twickenham, and stayed there for the Whitsun holydays till the 28th. I drew up the paper Lord Grenville desired, and sent it to him on Monday the 26th.

The Lord Chancellor read the paper to the King; and his Majesty authorized the Lord Chancellor, Lord Spencer, Lord Grenville, and Lord Ellenborough to inquire into the subject, and to report to him the result of the examinations they should take.

31st. I met the Lord Chancellor, Lord Spencer, Lord Grenville, and Lord Ellenborough, at Lord Grenville's; and it was settled that they would proceed the next day upon the examination.

[1] See *infrà*, p. 150. — Ed.

June 1st. *Su.* We met accordingly; no person being present but the four noblemen mentioned above and myself. Lady Douglas underwent a very long examination. Sir John Douglas was also examined; and the anonymous letters were produced, and were put into my possession.

2d. In the House of Commons, I spoke in support of Mr. Windham's plan for enlisting men for the army for a period of seven years only, and a further term of three years if the first seven shall expire during war, instead of enlisting them for an indefinite period of time, that is, for life. The ground upon which I principally supported it was, that it was repugnant to the principles of our Constitution, that there should exist in it an army composed of an order of men quite distinct from the rest of the community, and who have given up those liberties, which are incompatible with military discipline, never to resume them; that men who enlist for a limited period of time continue citizens, and have before them the prospect of once again enjoying that personal liberty and those privileges; that this not only renders the army less formidable to the liberties of the country, but much more formidable to the enemy to which it is to be opposed. I cited Blackstone, vol. i. pp. 408. 414. I wished to have said something upon the severity of military punishments; but as the other doctrines I had to maintain were, I knew, very unpalatable to many of the persons who heard me, I was afraid of doing harm rather than good.[1]

Army enlisting for limited time.

[1] On a division, the question was carried by a majority of 206 to

Princess of Wales.

6th. In the evening I attended at Lord Grenville's house, when Cole and Bidgood, two of the Princess's pages, attended and were examined.

7th. I attended at Lord Grenville's from between one and two o'clock in the day till half-past eleven at night. The whole of our time, with a short interval for dinner, was occupied in examining witnesses. The four Lords of the Council had granted an order to bring before them six of the Princess's most confidential servants* from her house at Blackheath, to be examined. The order was executed without any previous intimation being given to the Princess, or to any of her servants. The Duke of Kent attended, and stated to the Princess that reports very injurious to her reputation had been in circulation; and that his Majesty had therefore ordered an inquiry to be instituted on the subject. The Princess said that they were welcome to examine all her servants, if they thought proper. In addition to the servants, Sophia Austin was examined. The result of the examination was such as left a perfect conviction on my mind, and I believe on the minds of the four Lords, that the boy in question is the son of Sophia Austin; that he was born in Brownlow-Street Hospital on the 11th of July, 1802; and was taken by the Princess into her house on the 15th of November in the same year, and has ever since been under her protection. The evidence of all the servants as to the general

* Charlotte Sander, Sicard, Stikeman, Roberts, Frances Lloyd, and Mary Wilson.

105; and the Bill was ultimately passed in the House of Commons on the 6th of June.—Ed.

conduct of the Princess was very favourable to her Royal Highness; and Lady Douglas's account was contradicted in many very important particulars.

10th. The hearing of the appeal from Lord Eldon's order, appointing Lord Euston and Lord Henry Seymour guardians of the infant, youngest daughter of Lord Hugh Seymour, in opposition to the proposal of Mrs. Fitzherbert to be appointed her guardian, came on to-day in the House of Lords, and I was heard for the appellant.

Slave Trade.

In the evening of the same day, I had the satisfaction of expressing in the House of Commons my abhorrence of the slave trade. It was on the motion of Mr. Fox that the House should resolve, that it would with all practicable expedition take the most effectual measures for the abolition of the slave trade, at such time and in such manner as should be found most expedient, or to that effect. I did not attempt to argue the question, whether the slave trade ought to be abolished. This I considered as long ago decided; and that the trade could now be defended only by already refuted arguments, and disproved assertions. I spoke principally to impress on the House a sense of the reproachful situation in which the country stood with respect to this subject; since it had, now above fifteen years ago, had the courage to inquire minutely into the subject, and had ascertained, by a great body of evidence which stood recorded against the nation, that the trade was carried on by robbery, rapine, and murder; and had yet, with the full conviction of this, persisted in the trade for so long a period of years; and had, since it had ascertained and made public all these facts, dragged from the coasts of Africa by this trade not less than 360,000 human beings. The words "robbery, rapine, and murder," gave great offence to some gentlemen, particularly to General Gascoyne (one of the members for Liverpool), Sir William Young, and George Rose. But, as I should think it criminal to speak of such a trade otherwise than as it really is, I shall probably use the same expressions again, when I have next occasion to speak of it. The resolution of the Commons was agreed to by the Lords, on the 24th of June.[1]

Lord Melville acquitted.

12th. The peers gave their judgment in the case of Lord Melville; and acquitted him by a great majority.

Guardianship of Miss Seymour.

14th. I replied in the House of Lords in the appeal respecting the guardianship of Miss Seymour. The order of the Lord Chancellor was reversed; and Lord and Lady Hertford were by the House appointed the guardians. Several peers voted against this, but there was no division.* I counted between eighty and ninety peers who

* This decision was attended, some years afterwards, with consequences of considerable importance. It occasioned a great intimacy between the Prince and Lady Hertford, which ended with her entirely supplanting Mrs. Fitzherbert in the Prince's favour; and it produced that hostility towards the Catholics, which the Prince manifested when he became Regent, and his determination to place his confidence in those Tory ministers, whom he had always before considered as his personal enemies.

1 The resolution was carried in the House of Commons by a majority of 99; the numbers being for it 114, against it 15. In the House of Lords the numbers were for concurring in the resolution of the Commons 41, against it 20.—Ed.

were present: the Prince, who was as anxious that Mrs. Fitzherbert should continue to have the care of the child as he could have been if the child had been his own, and who knew that Lord and Lady Hertford would not remove her, had earnestly entreated all his friends to attend. I had, on the Prince's account, done every thing that depended on me to prevent this; and which was only to represent to Colonel M'Mahon what I thought of such a proceeding. The question was certainly one which involved no legal consideration whatever, and which every peer was as competent to decide as a lawyer could be; but yet to canvass votes for a judicial decision is that which cannot be too strongly reprobated.

Mr. Justice Fox.

19th. *Th.* The House of Lords this day put an end to all the proceedings[1] against Mr. Justice Fox, by adjourning them for two months, when it was known that Parliament would not be sitting. There is no doubt that the mode in which this matter has hitherto been proceeded in is extremely oppressive to the party accused, and to all the witnesses, who have been brought from Ireland during three successive Sessions of Parliament without any thing being decided, or the prospect (if it is to be proceeded on in the same way) of any thing being decided for many years to come. Not one charge is yet gone through;

[1] By a majority of 25 to 16. These proceedings originated in several petitions presented to Parliament in May and June, 1804, complaining of the arbitrary and violent conduct of Mr. Justice Fox, in the discharge of his judicial duties at the Summer Assizes for the counties of Donegal and Fermanagh, during the preceding year, 1803.—Ed.

and when all should be gone through in the House of Lords, the matter would be to be brought before the Commons, that they might concur in an address to the Crown for the judge's removal. But though this proceeding be not proper, some other should be resorted to. It will be most disgraceful to Government, if, after what has been stated at the Bar of the House of Mr. Justice Fox's conduct, he is suffered to remain a judge. He ought unquestionably to be impeached.

Princess of Wales.

The proceedings which have taken place respecting the Princess of Wales have, it seems, become public. Her Royal Highness has thought proper to make them so; and will, no doubt, in her own justification, endeavour to excite all the public odium she can against the Prince. His conduct towards the Princess on former occasions may have been extremely unjustifiable. Upon this occasion he could not have acted otherwise than he has done; and if he is to blame, it is for having used too much caution, and delayed too long laying before the Ministers the important facts which had come to his knowledge.

23d. Attended again at Lord Grenville's with the Chancellor, Lord Spencer, and Lord Ellenborough; and examined two witnesses respecting the conduct of the Princess.

25th. The same to-day.

The King's power to legislate for conquered colonies.

26th. The cases which are laid before the Attorney-General and myself by the Secretaries of State and the Privy Council are so numerous, and the questions upon them generally so unimportant, that they are not worth noticing here; but the subject upon which we gave our opinion to-day is so important, and may be attended with such serious consequences, that it may be right to make a memorandum of it. The question was referred to us by Mr. Windham, and was this: — Whether the King could, by order in Council, and without the intervention of Parliament, prohibit the importation of slaves into the island of Trinidad, which was conquered by the British arms in the last war, and ceded to Great Britain at the peace? The Attorney-General was of opinion that the importation could be prohibited only by Act of Parliament; I thought differently; and we wrote separate and contrary opinions. My opinion was founded upon the doctrines laid down in the celebrated case of Campbell *v.* Hall, in Cowper. The King has, as I conceive, authority by proclamation to alter the laws of a conquered country in all cases where the Parliament has not interposed. He cannot, indeed, give to the country such laws as are repugnant to the principles of the British constitution, or as would be a violation of the law with respect to his other subjects. He cannot, for example, dispense with the Navigation Act, or the Laws of Trade, in favour of his subjects inhabiting Trinidad; because that would be a violation of the law as to the rest of his subjects; but he may make laws for the internal government of the island; and it appears to me, that to prohibit the increase of the number of slaves in the island by importation is clearly matter only of internal legislation.

This is a question of very great importance; because, after the measures which have already been adopted respecting the Slave Trade, there is, as I understand, great repugnance in Ministers to bring any further Bill on the subject into Parliament during the present Session, and some doubt entertained whether they could carry such a Bill through. In the mean time, the number of slaves which are imported annually into Trinidad, the horrible mortality that prevails amongst them, and the certainty that (with the prospect which there now is that the Slave Trade will, before long, be entirely abolished) the importation for the next year, if it is not prohibited, will greatly exceed what it ever has been, render it most important that the prohibition should very speedily be adopted. I was not able to understand the Attorney-General's difficulty; but it seemed to arise out of the Laws of Trade, and the Act of 37 Geo. III. c. 77., making the port of San Josef in Trinidad a free port; and the Consolidating Act, 45 Geo. III. c. 57.

Amendment of Bankrupt Laws.

In the House of Commons I this day moved for leave to bring in a Bill to amend the Bankrupt Laws. The object of it is merely to prevent the evils which arise from the honest transactions of bankrupts being set aside by secret prior acts of bankruptcy, and from commissions being overturned by secret acts of bankruptcy prior to the petitioning creditor's debt. There are three ways of remedying the evil:—1st, By making the party bankrupt only from the time of the commission being taken out; and not, as he now is, by relation back from the time of the first act of bankruptcy committed. The objection to this is, that it would open a great door to fraud, by giving validity to all transfers of the bankrupt's property at a time when it was known that his circumstances were desperate. 2d, By declaring that no commission shall be taken out founded upon any act of bankruptcy which has taken place more than a limited time (six or three months) before the commission is sealed. This is a remedy which Mansfield, the present Chief Justice of the Common Pleas, and Lord Eldon lately thought of applying; and Lord Eldon has declared that he would bring in a Bill for the purpose. But the objection to it is, I think, unanswerable: if the time limited is short, a great many very proper commissions will be prevented; if it is long, the evil will not be remedied, but a great many honest transactions with bankrupts will be set aside. 3d, The only other remedy that occurs to me is that which I have adopted,—to declare that all conveyances, payments, contracts, and dealings with bankrupts shall be valid, notwithstanding prior acts of bankruptcy, if the parties dealing with the bankrupts had not notice of such acts.

It certainly is not from an abundance of leisure that I have undertaken this; for I am obliged every day to refuse to answer cases which are brought to me, because I have not time to answer them.

Princess o Wales.

27th. Attended at Lord Grenville's, at the examination of Mrs. Fitzgerald relative to the Princess.

July 1st. Again at Lord Grenville's on the same business. The Prince had put into my hands several original letters of the Princess to himself, and to the Princess Charlotte. I took them with me; and, upon a comparison of the hands, no one of the four Lords had any doubt that the anonymous letter, the inscriptions upon the obscene drawings, and the directions upon the envelopes in which the drawings were enclosed, were all of the Princess's own handwriting.

3d. There was a meeting again to-day at Lord Grenville's; but, through a neglect of giving me notice, I did not attend it.

Amendment of the Bankrupt Laws.

The notice which I gave of my intention to bring a Bill into Parliament to amend the Bankrupt Laws (a Bill which, by the bye, I have since brought in, and which has been read a second time), has drawn upon me a most voluminous and numerous correspondence. A day has not passed without my receiving five or six long letters; some signed, some anonymous, but all suggesting some evil in the Bankrupt Law, and proposing a supposed remedy, or leaving it to me to find one out. One man recommends me to abolish the whole system, and substitute a new one in its place; another would make the obtaining certificates more easy; a third would enlarge the description of persons who may be made bankrupts; a fourth would have permanent official assignees; a fifth suggests that my Bill will so much diminish the business and consequently the profits of the Commissioners, that I ought, in justice to them, to propose to increase their fees to twice their present amount. But most of my correspondents tell me very honestly that it is their own particular cases that they have in view. An attorney from Dublin writes to complain that attorneys cannot, as such, be made bankrupts; and from the King's Bench and the Fleet I have sent to me the complaints of bankrupts, stating the hardship of their cases, and the oppressions of their creditors, and requesting that a clause may be inserted in the Bill for their relief. Not one of these letters has suggested to me a single idea that can be of any use. Nor is it by letter only that my time is broken in upon. Persons call on me to state their notions of reform; and I never enter into the House of Commons without being importuned by one or other of the Members for the City, to provide a remedy for the case of acceptors of bills of exchange, who, at the time of the bankruptcy, have not paid their acceptances. I seem to have become a kind of public property; and, because I would reform evils which most immediately call for reform, to have come under some obligation to make the Bankrupt Laws perfect. And this, too, they would have done in a moment, by some hasty clause to be inserted in the Bill, without any consideration, just as they may crudely suggest. All this importunity satisfies me that a man cannot, even as to reforms which every body agrees are proper, do good with perfect impunity.

Lord Wellesley.

4th. I flatter myself that I contributed to-day, in a great degree, to prevent a measure which would in my opinion have brought the greatest disgrace upon the House of Commons. Lord Temple moved, pursuant to a notice given some time past, that the charge against Lord Wellesley upon the transactions in Oude should be immediately taken into consideration. Mr. Paul, who had preferred the charge, declared that he was not ready to go upon it; and that there had not yet been a production of all the papers which the House had ordered to be produced, and which appeared to him necessary to support the charge. Lord Wellesley's friends, however, (and there was a very numerous attendance of them,) with Lord Temple at their head, insisted that the charge should be immediately proceeded on; in order, no doubt, that it might be dismissed as unfounded, the accuser not being prepared to make it good. The only ostensible ground upon which this motion could be supported, and upon which it was supported, and by the Master of the Rolls among others, was the unreasonable delay of the accuser. The debate had been protracted till near 11 o'clock, and the House was very clamorous for the question when I rose. I endeavoured, by calling the attention of the House to the dates which had been stated by Paul, and which, not being contradicted, I supposed to have been stated accurately, to show (what was really quite palpable) that there was not the least foundation for imputing delay to him; on the contrary, that he had proceeded with great activity and diligence; and that it was not through any fault of his that he was not prepared at that moment to maintain his charge; and I endeavoured to impress the House with the reflection how deeply their own honour was concerned, and how important it was not to give countenance to any notion which might have gone abroad, that, where a man who had filled high public offices was accused, the same principles of justice, and the same rules of proceeding were not adhered to, as in the case of an obscure individual. When I concluded, there was no call for the question; little was said afterwards in the debate; and Lord Temple, after consulting with Sir Arthur Wellesley and Mr. Wellesley Pole, desired to withdraw his motion, but said that he should renew it on that day se'n-night.

Two or three days after this, Lord Wellesley's friends said in the House, that nothing could be farther from his wish than to have the discussion prematurely gone into, and that they should therefore acquiesce in its standing over till next Session.

Princess of Wales.

12th. Attended at Lord Grenville's, when his lordship read the draft of the report[1] of the four commissioners for inquiring into the conduct of the Princess of Wales which he proposes to make. Some few verbal alterations were made upon the suggestion of each of the Lords present, the Chancellor, Lord Spencer, and Lord Ellenborough, and one or two at my suggestion. It states the opinion of the commissioners, that there is no foundation for either of the assertions, that the Princess was delivered of a child in 1802, or that she was pregnant in that year; but that the conduct sworn to have been observed by the Princess towards Capt. Manby is of a kind that deserves the most serious consideration.

[1] This report is printed at p. 1117. of Vol. XXIV. of Hansard's Parliamentary Debates.—Ed.

Amendment of the Bankrupt Laws.

22d. Lord Redesdale had a very strong inclination to oppose, in the House of Lords, my Bill for the amendment of the Bankrupt Law. He stated his objections to me (not indeed till I had asked him for them), but I could not feel the force of any of them. He stated them to Lord Ellenborough, to the Chancellor, and to Lord Eldon; but he could not find any body disposed to oppose the Bill, or to agree with him in thinking that the measure ought to be postponed for further consideration. At last he contented himself with moving, as an amendment to the Bill, a proviso, that the sealing a commission, or striking a docket for a commission, should be deemed notice to all the world of an act of bankruptcy, if any prior act should have been committed. As far as relates to striking a docket, which is never matter of public notoriety, this appears to me to be objectionable; but I did not think it of sufficient importance to resist it, and I hope that little harm will be done by it.* With the exception of Lord Redesdale's moving this amendment, no word of objection or observation was made in either House, in the course of the Bill passing through Parliament. It received the royal assent to-day.†

Parliament prorogued.

23d. This day, Parliament was prorogued. Since I have had a seat in it, very little has passed that was either very instructive or very amusing. Some admirable speeches, indeed, of Fox's; but the great powers of his mind are not called forth by the

Mr. Fox.

* It was afterwards repealed, at my suggestion, by 49 Geo. 3. c. 121—6.

† Stat. 46 Geo. 3. c. 135.

puny antagonists he has now to contend with, as I once remember them; and for the last month, ill health has wholly prevented his attendance. The Opposition has objected to every thing which has been proposed by the Ministry, except the Property-tax, which was originally a measure of their own party; but, as they do not act upon any great public principles, they are obliged to take very narrow ground. They affect an extraordinary anxiety for the King's prerogative, which nobody has thought of invading; they scrutinize minutely all the details of the Bills brought into Parliament, to find some inconsistency or inaccuracy in their most unimportant provisions. They endeavour to render the Ministers unpopular, by exciting jealousy among the volunteers; they revive, for this purpose, expressions used by Windham three years ago; and they misconstrue or mis-state every thing that he says, or that he has said. Upon every measure, they talk of the opinions and the plans of Mr. Pitt; or, in their language, the great statesman whose death the nation finds every day more reason to deplore. There is nothing very formidable in all this; and it surely is not very encouraging to a party to have no leader but one who is dead, and to be driven to support their feeble pretensions to power upon the remains of that leader's reputation.

Conduct of the Opposition.

Aug. 23d. I set out for Durham, to hold the court there, as Chancellor of the County Palatine. As the Attorney-General intends staying all the autumn in London or its neighbourhood, and as one of us may very well be absent during the vacation, I think of going farther north; perhaps into Scotland, and even as far as the Highlands. To have a perfect relaxation from business, to breathe the pure air of the country, and to enjoy the society of my dear Anne quite undisturbed, are my only objects. Of course she accompanies me; and as my eldest son is now arrived at an age at which, though he can profit but little by travelling, he may suffer very materially by being left at home under the care and in the society of none but servants, he must be of our party.

Fees in the Court of Chancery of Durham.

28th. Held the court at Durham. The business very inconsiderable. The Deputy-Registrar and Examiner of the Court ascribe the small number of causes in it to the fees of the solicitors, (as they have been long established,) being much lower than those allowed in the Court of Chancery of England; so much lower, that it is far more profitable to a solicitor to institute a suit in London, and pay an agent there for doing the business of it, than to file the bill at Durham and transact all the business himself; and, as it depends on solicitors where the bills of their clients should be filed, almost all are filed in London. There is no reason why the fees should not be the same here as in the English Chancery, where they certainly are not too high.* In many cases, it would be extremely beneficial to the inhabitants of Durham to have their suits instituted and decided in their own city†,

* The expense of Chancery proceedings is most oppressive; but this is to be ascribed to stamp duties, and to other causes than the amount of the solicitors' fees. The fees were increased by Lord Erskine, soon after this was written.

† I speak of causes that may be considered almost as amicable. The jurisdiction is too confined for adverse suits.

instead of having them sent, at great expense, and with much delay, to London. I think, therefore, of raising the solicitors' fees to the same rate as in the English Chancery. This, however, will require a good deal of consideration.

31st. I arrived at Edinburgh, and remained there till the 8th of September, when I set out for Stirling in my way to the Highlands.

Reform of the Courts of Justice in Scotland.

During my stay at Edinburgh, Clerk, the Solicitor-General for Scotland, with whom I have been long acquainted, showed me the sketch which he has made of a Bill for carrying into execution the resolutions come to by the House of Lords in the last Session, respecting the administration of justice in Scotland; and we had a good deal of conversation on the subject. The objects of the plan, which relates only to Civil cases, are two:—1st, To take from the Judges of the Court of Session the decision of all questions of fact, and give it to juries, or rather *restore* it to juries; for in Scotland, before the fifteenth century, a jury decided all disputed facts in Civil causes as well as upon Criminal trials. And 2dly, to diminish the number of appeals to the House of Lords, by erecting an intermediate Court of Appeal, and not permitting an appeal to the Lords till after the final decision of the cause in the inferior court. These objects are extremely important, particularly the first of them; and, if it is accomplished in Scotland, it may lead to a very great improvement in English jurisprudence, by establishing the trial by jury for all disputed facts in our Ecclesiastical Courts.

The projected reform will, however, be attended

with considerable difficulties. The principal of these, as far as relates to the introduction of juries in Civil cases in Scotland, will be how to model the forms of the procedure, so as to ascertain with precision what are the disputed facts, and to reduce them to plain questions for juries to decide. I suggested to Clerk (and he seems, I think, inclined to adopt my suggestion) that, amongst other regulations which must be established to execute his plan, it would be very desirable to abolish altogether the oath of reference, which still exists in the Scotch law; and, in lieu of it, to give each litigant party power to examine his antagonist upon oath *vivâ voce*, just like any other witness before the jury. If this novelty should be successfully introduced into Scotland, it may lead to the adoption of it in England, and may enable us to substitute that more effectual mode of obtaining a discovery from an adverse party, in the place of our expensive and inefficacious equitable bills of discovery. With respect to the Court of Appeal, various plans, it seems, have been suggested. It is intended that the Court of Session, which consists of fifteen Judges, shall be divided into three chambers, each consisting of five Judges; and that every pursuer or plaintiff shall be at liberty to institute his suit in whichever chamber he pleases. Each chamber will in truth be a distinct court; but, instead of describing them as such, they are to be called Chambers or Sessions of the Court of Sessions, that there may not appear to be any violation of that article* of the Act of Union, which declared that the Court of Session

* Art. 19.

should remain in all time coming as it was constituted before the Union. From the decision of the chamber in which the action is brought an appeal is in all cases to lie to an intermediate court, before the dissatisfied party can be allowed to carry the cause to the House of Lords. How that intermediate Court of Appeal shall be constituted, is a question which has produced much difference of opinion. It is to consist, according to one project, of the ten Judges of the Court of Session who are not members of the chamber appealed from; and, according to another, of certain commissioners, the Presidents of the different chambers, the Chief Baron of the Exchequer, and some noblemen holding high offices in Scotland, and who would answer in some degree to the extraordinary Lords of Session of former times;—not lawyers, but men of high rank, whose presence would give dignity to the court, and who would keep the ordinary Judges in awe, and prevent that partiality to particular suitors which exists, or is supposed to exist, in the present members of the court, and from which, in a small society, it is probably very difficult for Judges to be wholly exempt. A third proposal is, that the Court of Appeal shall consist only of five persons, the Presidents of the two chambers not appealed from, the Justice Clerk, the Chief Baron, and the senior Lord of Session. To this there seems great objection, arising principally from the particular characters and connexions of the individuals who now fill those offices. The present President of the Court of Session, Justice Clerk, and the Chief Baron, are men so connected together, so swayed by general and local politics, so much disposed to concur in every thing and to support each other, that to place the whole administration of Civil Justice under their control and at their ultimate disposal (as it would necessarily be if they constituted the majority of a Court of Appeal), could not fail greatly to aggravate those very evils which have been found to result from the present judicial system, and which call so loudly for reform. The connexion between the Judge and the suitor has for many years, perhaps one might say for ages, been a subject of complaint in Scotland. Justice, we are told, was never better administered there than by the Englishmen whom Cromwell, during his usurpation, appointed to be Judges; and it is said that, when this remark was once made before an old Scotch Judge, he observed that there was no great merit in their deciding impartially, for they were a kinless pack. The best Court of Appeal seems, without all doubt, to be that of the ten Lords of Session not members of the chamber appealed from. I find, however, that thoughts are entertained of making some addition to it; which, however the parties concerned may disguise the matter from themselves, is not, I fear, suggested by the most disinterested motives. The Lord Chancellor of Scotland, when that office existed, was president of the Court of Session. It has been intimated that it might be expedient to revive that office, but not to give the Chancellor any other judicial function than that of presiding over the Court of Appeal, which should consist only of himself and the ten Lords of Session. The expense of this scheme, and the increase of ministerial patronage which would attend it, are alone considerable objections to it. But there is another, and, as it seems, a still more weighty objection to it. The business of the courts in Scotland is confined to so few persons, that, if Judges were chosen, not as we have seen them, but most conscientiously and with the most scrupulous regard to their fitness for the situation, it may well be doubted whether it would be possible to find at any one time fifteen men, qualified by their learning, talents, and experience, for the judicial office. Where the persons qualified are so few, and the offices so numerous, to institute a new magistracy, and to make it so pre-eminent in rank, dignity, and emolument, that it must necessarily be considered as the first reward of the profession; what is it, but greatly to increase the evil, and to make it matter of necessity that the most important judicial offices should be filled by men quite incapable of executing the duties of them? But, besides this, the services that a Lord Chancellor of Scotland could render the public, if, as is proposed, he were merely to preside in the Court of Appeal, must be inconsiderable. Appeals, in all probability, would not be frequent, and the revival of this high office would only afford the means of intercepting, in his way to the bench, a man who would be a very meritorious and valuable Judge, to make him almost a useless but a highly honoured and a well-rewarded Chancellor. It is obvious, however, that if there were now to be a Lord Chancellor for Scotland, Henry Erskine, the present Lord Advocate, would be appointed to that office; and he is, with reason, most listened to by Lord Grenville and the rest of the ministry, on the subject of the proposed reform.

Mr. Fox's death.

Sept. 21st. It was at Fort Augustus that I received the intelligence of Mr. Fox's death, which happened on the 13th. How unfortunate, that so soon after the country had recovered from its delusion respecting him, and was availing itself of his great talents, those talents should be extinguished!

Oct. 1st. I determined to return to London some weeks earlier than I had originally intended, that I might attend Mr. Fox's funeral.

9th. I arrived in London.

Mr. Fox's funeral.

10th. Mr. Fox's funeral. I attended it as one of the mourners. Nothing could be more solemn and affecting. It was very numerously attended; and most of the persons present seemed as if they had lost a most intimate, and a most affectionate friend.

Parliament dissolved.

24th. Parliament dissolved.

Election at Queenborough.

29th. I was re-elected for the borough of Queenborough; William Frankland, recently made a Lord of the Admiralty, was elected with me. There was not any opposition; Alderman Prinsep, who had sat for the borough in the last parliament, having now given up all his pretensions to it.

Letter of the Princess of Wales.

Nov. 27th. I received from Lord Grenville a copy of the letter which the Princess of Wales has addressed to the King, as an answer to the Report of the four Lords of the Privy Council, and a justification of her conduct. Instead of the dignified defence of an injured and calumniated

Princess, it is a long, elaborate, and artificial pleading of an advocate; and no person as much accustomed as I am to Plumer's manner can doubt that he is the author of it.* As a pleading, however, it is conducted with great art and ability. It is manifestly intended to be at some time or other published†; and is likely, when published, to make a strong impression in favour of the Princess. The most remarkable circumstance in it is, that the Princess, instead of demanding that a further investigation of her conduct should take place, and that she should have an opportunity of proving her innocence and confounding her enemies, earnestly deprecates any further inquiry. It is true, however, that she speaks of an inquiry by the same Lords, and conducted in the same manner as that which has been already prosecuted; and she leaves the matter as if it had never occurred to her Royal Highness or her advisers that there might be an inquiry before the Privy Council, to which she might be a party. Lord Grenville desired me to put down in writing the observations which occurred to me in reading this letter;

* I have been since informed, in a manner that leaves me no doubt, that, though Plumer has altered and corrected it, it is drawn up by Perceval.

† It has since come to my knowledge that this letter was printed under the superintendence of Perceval, with a view to its publication. The change of administration, however, rendered the publication unnecessary to the men whose object it was to make the transactions the means of bringing odium on their political opponents. The pamphlet was therefore suppressed. Some copies of it, however, surreptitiously got into the hands of different persons; and the editor of a Sunday newspaper having given notice, in very mysterious terms, that he should publish it, he was prevented only by an injunction of the Court of Chancery, granted on the 11th of March, 1808, upon a private hearing by Lord Eldon, in his room at Lincoln's Inn Hall. The name of the cause was the *Attorney-General* v. *Blagden*.

this I have done, and have transmitted them to him. Dec. 6.

Cause of a Purcell *v.* M'Namara in the Court of Chancery.

Dec. —. A proceeding which has recently taken place in the Court of Chancery so strongly characterizes the Chancellor, that it may be worth remembering. A bill was filed some time ago, by a lady of the name of Purcell, against John M'Namara, to set aside several deeds conveying to him a moiety, which she was entitled to, of a very valuable estate in the island of Tortola, as having been obtained from her by advantage taken of her ignorance, and an abuse of the confidence which she had reposed in him. The cause was heard by Lord Eldon when Chancellor, and he decreed that all the deeds should be delivered up by M'Namara to be cancelled, and that he should pay the costs of the suit. As soon as the present Chancellor succeeded to the great seal, M'Namara petitioned to have the cause reheard. It seems that he had in early life been an acquaintance of the Chancellor's; and he had the folly to boast that he should certainly obtain a reversal of the decree, and to invite his friends to come and witness his triumph. The Chancellor, not choosing to trust himself with the sole decision of the cause, or thinking that there might be considerable difficulty in the case, desired the Master of the Rolls to assist him upon the rehearing. During the first two or three days of the cause being reheard, the Chancellor, with great rashness, expressed a very strong opinion that the decree could not be supported. The Master of the Rolls, after his usual manner, remained perfectly silent. In truth, the Lord Chancellor did not, at the time he so discovered his opinion, at all understand the cause; nor had he then heard of some of the most important facts in it; for M'Namara's counsel began, and, as might be supposed, did not open a very strong case against their own client.

When he had heard the counsel for Miss Purcell, and had talked with the Master of the Rolls upon the case, he became sensible that it was impossible to reverse, or even to alter, the decree. In truth it was a very gross case, in which M'Namara, under pretence of rendering service to the plaintiff, her brother, and her sister, had obtained from them a conveyance of every thing they were possessed of; and had reduced them to subsist upon small annuities received from himself, and for which he compelled the plaintiff to sign receipts acknowledging that she had no right to her annuity, but owed it to his generosity and charity. The decree was affirmed. The day after this judgment was pronounced, M'Namara caused to be inserted, in two of the daily newspapers, a long article which professed to be an account of the cause, but which was in reality a misrepresentation of the facts, the arguments of counsel, and the judgment of the court, calculated throughout to disguise the case from the public, to exculpate M'Namara, and to represent Miss Purcell in the most odious light. The most important circumstances were entirely suppressed; and with respect to one very important deed, which M'Namara himself, by his answer, admitted had been extorted from the plaintiff by reproaches of ingratitude, and a threat to withhold from her all means of subsistence, it was stated to have been executed by her voluntarily, and with the warmest expressions of gratitude. The cause was represented as having originated in a shameful conspiracy between the plaintiff, her attorney, and a discarded steward of the defendant, to destroy his character; and the Court was stated to have decided the cause upon a strict rule established in Courts of Equity, that a trustee cannot take a conveyance from the party for whom he is a trustee, and not upon the particular circumstances attending the transaction, which were represented to be highly honourable to M'Namara; and the judgment, as reported, was a laboured panegyric on his virtues. So scandalous an attempt on the part of M'Namara * to impose on the public, to convert the proceedings of a Court of Justice into a vehicle of calumny, and to draw down the infamy which belonged to himself upon the heads of his victims, called for the severest animadversion; and, as counsel for Miss Purcell, I moved the Court, that M'Namara, and the person whom he had employed and paid to draw up the account, should be committed for a contempt of the Court.[1] The fact of their being the authors of the publication was clearly proved. I stated that I did not dispute the right that all persons had to publish the pro-

* M'Namara, who had been concerned in the course of his life in several duels, had vainly attempted during the hearing of the cause to intimidate Miss Purcell's counsel from doing their duty. Some years afterwards, having recovered from a very dangerous illness, he wrote a letter to a friend of mine, in which, after telling him how near dying he had been, he added, "but I was prepared to meet the event like a man of honour."

---

[1] See note, *infrà*, p. 176. — Ed.

ceedings of Courts of Justice: that I was sensible that it was highly important to the public that that right should be exercised, and that it was the best security we had for the pure and impartial administration of justice: that even when such publications were grossly inaccurate, if the inaccuracy proceeded merely from mistake or negligence, however injurious they might be to private individuals, they would not be a proper subject of punishment. But that the case was very different, when the account was published by one of the parties, with the manifest intent to vilify his opponents. I represented to him, in the strongest way that I could, the hard situation in which the suitors, witnesses, and solicitors in his Court must be placed, if he would not protect them against such libels. I pressed him to consider how much the preservation of the liberty of the press depended upon not suffering such an abuse of it to pass unpunished. I represented to him how much the offence was aggravated by the condition of the parties, who did not now even pretend that the account published was meant to be accurate; who attempted no apology, expressed no contrition, offered no atonement; but, already anticipating, as it were, their triumph over the Court, contended that they had done no more than they had a right to do, and pretty clearly intimated that they were ready to misrepresent the future proceedings of the Court, just as they had misrepresented the past. I called upon him to assert the honour of his situation; and I ventured to tell him that, although he would probably be disposed to disregard an indignity offered to himself, he should consider how much others, how much all his Majesty's subjects, were interested in his maintaining the respect due to the High Court, in which he presided. I added, however, that I knew it could not be necessary to enlarge on this topic; or to remind him of the importance and dignity of an office which had for ages been acquiring increased lustre, from the talents and virtues of the great men who had filled it, from the time of Lord Bacon to that of his immediate predecessor: and that there could be no doubt that as his office had become more honourable and dignified, in passing through the hands of the Somers, the Talbots, the Hardwickes, the Camdens, and his other illustrious predecessors, so it would be transmitted by him undiminished in splendour and dignity to his successor.* It was in my reply that I said this; and when I had concluded, the Chancellor immediately delivered his opinion. The Court was extremely crowded, for a good deal of interest and curiosity had been excited to see how he would conduct himself. He said that there could not be any doubt of the authority of the Court to commit in such a case; that the fact of M'Namara being the publisher was

* I did not act on this occasion spontaneously, but, as the counsel, and in conformity to the instructions of my client, Miss Purcell. I, however, pressed the matter very earnestly; and, at the time, I sincerely thought that the Lord Chancellor ought to have committed the offending parties. Having since had occasion to consider the subject of contempt of Court much more fully than I had then done, I greatly doubt whether I was right in that opinion; and whether, gross and flagrant as the misrepresentation of the proceedings of the Court in this case was, it ought not to have been left to be prosecuted as a libel.[1]

[1] See *infrà*, Apr. 5. 1810.—Ed.

clearly established; that the article was a gross mis-statement of the proceedings of the Court, and was manifestly printed for the purpose of exculpating the defendant in the public opinion, and of rendering odious his opponents; and that what he had said in delivering his judgment was shamefully misrepresented. After dilating on these topics at considerable length, and raising an universal expectation of the only decision which it was supposed possible could follow such a speech, he added, that, though this was certainly a case in which the Court might commit the offenders as for a contempt, it still remained to be considered whether, in the exercise of the discretion which the Court must necessarily have in such a case, it ought to do so; and that, exercising that discretion, he should certainly not commit them.

Foreseeing that the Chancellor might be afraid upon such an occasion to act on his own authority, I had, in the course of my reply, suggested that possibly, in so flagrant a case as this, it might be most expedient for the Court to direct that all the papers should be laid before the Attorney-General, for him to consider whether he would file an information against the offenders. The Chancellor, after declaring that he would not commit the parties, said he should take time to consider whether he would order that the papers should be laid before the Attorney-General. The next morning, however, he sent for the solicitor of Miss Purcell to his house, and told him that he thought that enough had been done in bringing the complaint before the Court, and that it was his wish that the matter should not be pressed any farther: that if it were pressed, he should determine as to the Attorney-General being applied to; but that he was desirous of not deciding it, and he added, that till he had heard my reply, he had made up his mind to do nothing upon the complaint. The solicitor, with a very proper degree of firmness, said that he could not abandon the complaint, but that his Lordship must do with it whatever he thought proper. This conduct of the Chancellor, to a person not well acquainted with his character, must seem incomprehensible. For myself, I have no doubt that it has not proceeded from regard to M'Namara, but merely from the fear of losing or endangering that vulgar popularity which he values a great deal too highly.

The Chancellor was so sensible of the loss of reputation which he has sustained by this, that about ten days after, upon a complaint against a man and his wife for a publication relative to the proceedings of the court in a lunacy *, he immediately committed them and their printer to the Fleet, although the case was much less flagrant than that of M'Namara.

Meeting of Parliament.

Dec. 15th. The new Parliament met; Abbot chosen Speaker.

19th. The Session of Parliament opened by the speech delivered by the commissioners in the King's name.

* See *exparte* Jones, 13 Ves.

1807.

Jan. 7th. A debate in the House of Commons on the late negotiation for peace.

Real estates to be made assets to pay simple contract debts.

10th. I have been thinking, for some time past, of bringing into Parliament a Bill to make the freehold estates of persons who die indebted assets for the payment of their simple contract debts. The law, as far as it affords satisfaction to a creditor out of the property of his debtor, requires great amendment. There seems no reason why the *whole* of a debtor's real estate should not be *extended* in his life-time, instead of a *half*, according to the present law of executions: nay, why the estate, or a sufficient part of it, should not be sold, instead of the creditor receiving the profits only till his debt is paid; nor why money in the funds, and debts due to the debtor, should not be made applicable by compulsory process to the payment of his debts; nor why copyhold estates should not be liable to judgments and executions, and be assets after the debtor's death. It should seem that it would be right even to make the estate tail of a debtor assets to pay his debts. As he has the power to acquire the absolute dominion over the property, and to charge it with his debts, it seems very reasonable to proceed as if he had done what he could, and as an honest man ought to have done, to satisfy his creditors. These are objects, however, which cannot be accomplished hastily; and to attempt them all at once would make it impossible, with the dread of innovation which prevails at present, to succeed in any of them. I have determined, therefore, to attempt only to make the freehold estates of debtors, after their deaths, applicable to the payment of their debts. No rational opposition can be made to this. Lord Ellenborough, however, to whom I have mentioned my intention, and who highly approves of it, tells me that I shall meet with great opposition, particularly from country gentlemen and men of landed property, who will be alarmed at the idea of subjecting real property to any charges from which it is now exempt.

I thought it proper, therefore, before I proposed a measure which may be made by Opposition a subject of clamour, to speak to Lord Grenville about it. I accordingly called on him to-day; and he said that he saw no objection to the measure. He then told me that he wished me very much to consider what had been suggested by the select committee of the House of Commons in 1799, respecting the consolidating the four Welsh circuits into one, and appointing a greater number of judges of the Courts in Westminster Hall.* He said that the circumstance which had induced him to turn his attention to this subject was, that the present vacant office of Welsh judge had been offered to three different gentlemen, all of them properly qualified to discharge its duties, who had all declined it; the salary being so inconsiderable, as to

Welsh judges.

* Twenty-seventh Report of the Committee of Finance, &c. Vide Burke's Speech on his Plan of Reform in 1780, p. 31. and 32.

make it by no means expedient for them to give up the business which would be incompatible with their holding the office: that, as no man fit for the office would accept it in its present state, there was nothing to be done but either to increase the salary, which under the present circumstances of the country ought to be avoided if possible, or to adopt some such plan as was suggested by the committee: that it might be thought an object to preserve the patronage of so many offices, but in his opinion that ought not to have any weight in a matter of so much importance to the public.

General register of deeds.

He then talked to me on the subject of a General Register of Deeds throughout England. He had before directed a number of papers on that subject to be laid before the Attorney-General and me. I stated to his Lordship the difficulties which it appeared to me that the subject presented. A Register on the plan of those in Middlesex and Yorkshire* seems to be of little use. The substance of the deed does not appear in the Register; or any thing more than the date, the parties' names, the description of the lands, and the names and places of abode of the witnesses. The memorial, too, must be executed by one of the parties to the deed, and attested by one of the subscribing witnesses to the deed, which is attended with much inconvenience, makes it often impossible, after a distance of time, to register deeds, and has no utility. What is most important is, that the object and substance of the deed should appear on the Register; but to

* Stat. 7 Anne, c. 20.; 2 Anne, c. 4.; 6 Anne, c. 35.; and 8 Geo. 2. c. 6.

effect this, is extremely difficult. To insert a transcript of the whole deed, considering the shameful length to which conveyances are drawn out by the persons who prepare them, would be attended with enormous expense; and yet a mere abstract of the deed may, quite unintentionally, be extremely inaccurate; and if an accurate abstract were made necessary to a valid registration of a deed, a most abundant source of litigation would be opened between different incumbrancers, who would contend for priorities, on the ground that deeds were to be postponed as not having been properly registered. I stated to Lord Grenville that I had not been able to suggest any mode of removing this difficulty. He said that it might be the duty of the officer to make the abstract, and all that should be required of the parties to entitle them to the benefit of their deeds, of entering conveyances, should be to produce their deeds to be registered. The objection to this seems to be, that it would occupy many persons in the office to abstract all deeds which were brought to be registered, and it would be attended with great expense, and probably would be very carelessly done. Lord Grenville asked me if I knew any person who might be advantageously consulted on the subject, which gave me an opportunity of mentioning John Bell; and he desired that I would request the Solicitor of the Treasury to lay all the papers before Mr. Bell, to consider what plan would be most likely to attain the object. I consider it as no inconsiderable service that I have rendered the public, when I have introduced a man of such knowledge, talents, and zeal for the public good as Bell, to be employed on such occasions.

28th. I moved, in the House of Commons, for leave to bring a bill into Parliament, to make freehold estates assets to pay simple contract debts. The motion was agreed to, and appeared to be very well received by the House.

Bill to make freehold estates assets to pay simple contract debts.

I had before sent a copy of the Bill to Lord Ellenborough; and I, last night, received a note from him, in which he says, "I cannot help thinking that the simple contract creditor should have his remedy by action against the heir and devisee, as well as the specialty creditor;" (for, as I have drawn the Bill, freehold estates are to be assets for simple contract debts, to be administered only in Courts of Equity). He adds in his note, "As so very great a change in the law will be effected by the proposed Bill, if it should pass, I think the judges should have an opportunity of considering it before it is introduced into Parliament. If the Bill commenced in the Lords, as bills of this nature used formerly to do, it would, I believe, be referred to the judges in the first instance*, as a matter of course, to report their opinion thereupon; and, though the proposed Bill originates in the Commons, where no such reference can be made, it would still be expedient to obtain their opinion individually respecting the alteration meant to be effected, and to leave the Bill, in that view, for their consideration a reasonable time before it is

Judges how far to be consulted before alterations are proposed in the law.

* See upon the subject a curious passage in a tract of Lord Hale's on the amendment of the laws, published in Hargrave's *Law Tracts*, p. [273].

brought in. In the hurry of Term I have not yet had time to attend to it as I ought. The general principle of subjecting real estates to the demands of simple contract creditors I much approve." I understood from this note that Lord Ellenborough wished me to defer my motion. As I knew, however, that if the measure were much delayed no interest would be taken about it, I determined to persevere; and I wrote Lord Ellenborough an answer, saying that, having given public notice of my intention, I had gone too far to allow of my postponing the motion; and I added, "with respect to consulting the judges individually, before a Bill is brought into the House of Commons, if that be necessary, or even proper, it is very obvious that no person in my situation can with propriety propose any alteration of the law; because, to devote the time which would be necessary for such a communication with the judges would be quite incompatible with his unavoidable occupations, or, I should rather say, with the discharge of the duties of his situation." I had besides (though I did not think it necessary to mention it to Lord Ellenborough) another objection to such a proceeding. It appears to me a most unconstitutional doctrine, that no important alteration can be made in the law, unless the judges are first consulted on it. If they are to be consulted, of course their opinions are to be followed; and consequently, if they, or if only a majority of them, disapprove of any proposed alteration in the law, it must be abandoned. They would be to be considered like the Lords of Articles formerly in Scotland; or like a fourth member of the Legislature, who are to have something like what has been called the initiative in legislation ; a power of preventing any proposed measure not only from passing into a law, but even from being debated and brought under the view of Parliament ; and this important power, too, exercised not ostensibly, and as public men, with all the responsibility which belongs to the discharge of any public duty, but with the indifference and carelessness which necessarily must attend such private communications.

29th. As I find that Lord Redesdale has said to a person who communicated it to me, that he shall oppose the Bill if it gets into the House of Lords, on the single ground that it has not been communicated to the judges before it is proposed to Parliament ; that there may not be a pretext for not discussing the merits of the Bill, I have this morning sent a copy of it to each of the judges. I do not ask them their opinions of it ; I shall probably not hear from any of them upon it ; and, whether they approve or disapprove of it, I shall bring it into the House.

The Princess of Wales.

The affair of the Princess of Wales is at last terminated, but not very satisfactorily to any party. The King referred the whole matter to the Cabinet ; and he has, by their advice (advice given after long and mature consideration), sent a written message to the Princess, saying that he is satisfied that there is no foundation for the charges of pregnancy and delivery ; but that he sees with serious concern in the depositions of the witnesses, and even in her Royal Highness's own letter to him, written by way of defence, evidence of a deportment unbecoming her station, or something to that effect (for, having heard it read but once, I have not been able to recollect the expression). In the message, as originally framed by the Ministry, it was, "His Majesty sees with concern and disapprobation," but the King, with his own hand, struck out the word "disapprobation," and substituted "serious concern."

Abolition of the Slave Trade.

Feb. 5th. *Wed.* The question of the second reading of the Bill for the abolition of the slave trade was carried in the House of Lords by a majority of 64; the numbers being for it 100, against it 36. This measure had always been rejected in the House of Lords during the administration of Mr. Pitt, notwithstanding all the zeal he professed on the subject, and the very great personal and ministerial influence which he possessed in that House.

My little girl was last month seized with a very dangerous fever, which lasted twenty-one days. Having read in Dr. Currie's book of the happy effects produced in many cases by the application of cold water in fevers, I asked Dr. Pitcairn, who attended her, whether it would not be advisable to try it. He said he thought it certainly would; that it might be of great service, and could do no harm; but that the prejudice against it in London was so strong, that he never ventured to recommend it. Cold water was accordingly applied to her, and I have no doubt that it saved her life; the delirium ceased the moment after it had been applied, and all the symptoms of her fever became milder.

18th. The second reading of the Bill to make

freehold estates assets to pay debts came on to-day in the House of Commons. The Master of the Rolls (to whom I had sent a copy of the Bill before I moved for leave to bring it in, and to whom I had mentioned my intention before I sent him the copy, and who had never stated any objection to it whatever to me) opposed it, on the ground that there was no pressing necessity for the measure; that a simple contract creditor, not having stipulated that the debt should be paid by the heir of the debtor, there was no reason to give him what he had not contracted for; and that, as the heir was affected by it, it was unjust to give it to him: that it was contrary to the Statute of Frauds, because it would affect land by means of parol evidence, and without writing; and on some other grounds of equal solidity. Some other members opposed it, particularly Mr. Canning, who saw in it an attempt to sacrifice the landed to the commercial interest, a dangerous attack made upon the aristocracy, and the beginning of something which might end like the French Revolution. It is not worth while to put down my answer to the Master of the Rolls. Canning spoke after me, and therefore I had no opportunity of answering him. They did not divide the House.

Bill to make freehold estates assets.

23d. I had the satisfaction of speaking in the House of Commons upon the second reading of the Bill to abolish the slave trade, and of speaking with great success; at least I was told by a great many persons that I made a considerable impression on the House. The question was carried by a majority which exceeded the expectations of the

Abolition of the Slave Trade.

most sanguine. The numbers were, 283 for the Bill, and 16 against it.

An innocent man executed for a mutiny, of which he was convicted by a court-martial.

A case has been lately laid before the Attorney-General and me, by direction of the Lords of the Admiralty, to consider of the expediency of prosecuting for a libel the printer of a weekly newspaper called the *Independent Whig;* which has brought some facts to our knowledge that demand the most serious attention. A sailor of the name of Thomas Wood was tried by a court-martial at Plymouth on the 6th of October last, on a charge of having been concerned in the mutiny and murders which were committed on board the Hermione. It was in September, 1797, that the mutiny took place; and the prisoner being only, as was supposed, of the age of twenty-five when he was tried, could not have been more than sixteen when the crime was committed. The fact was proved but by a single witness: that witness, however, who was the master of the Hermione, swore positively that the prisoner, who, he said, at that time bore the name of James Hayes, was the very man whom he remembered on board the Hermione; and that he saw him taking a very active part in the mutiny. Notwithstanding the positive oath of the witness thus identifying the prisoner, yet, as the witness said that he had never seen the prisoner since, and as the appearance of a man generally changes very considerably in the nine years which elapse between the ages of sixteen and twenty-five, little reliance could be had on such testimony. It was, however, the only evidence in support of the prosecution. But what was wanting in the evidence for the

Crown, was supplied by the prisoner's defence. It was delivered in, in writing, and was, in truth, a supplication for mercy rather than a defence. The following passage contains the whole substance of it: — "At the time when the mutiny took place, I was a boy in my fourteenth year. Drove by the torrent of mutiny, I took the oath administered to me on the occasion. The examples of death which were before my eyes drove me for shelter amongst the mutineers, dreading a similar fate with those that fell, if I sided with or showed the smallest inclination for mercy;" and then follow entreaties for compassion on his youth, and a declaration that he had not enjoyed an hour's repose of mind since the event took place. The Court found him guilty; he was sentenced to be hanged; and on the 17th of October the sentence was executed. In the mean time, his brother and sister, who were in London, heard of his situation, and made application at the Admiralty. They insisted that their brother was innocent; that he was not even on board the Hermione, but was serving as a boy in the Marlborough, at Portsmouth, at the time the mutiny took place; they procured a certificate of this fact from the Navy Office, and transmitted it to Plymouth, where it arrived previous to the execution. The guilt of the prisoner, however, appeared so manifest from his own defence, that no regard was paid to the certificate, and the execution took place. This proceeding was animadverted on in the *Independent Whig*, in several successive papers, with very great severity. The members of the court-martial called upon the Lords of the Admiralty to punish the author of these libels; and in consequence of this, they were laid before us. The Attorney-General suggested, at the consultation, the propriety of making some inquiry into the fact before the prosecution was instituted. We neither of us entertained any doubt of the man's guilt; but yet the Attorney-General thought that it would be advisable, to be able to remove all possible suspicion upon that point. An inquiry was accordingly set on foot by the Solicitor of the Admiralty; the result of which was, that the man was perfectly innocent, and was at Portsmouth on board the Marlborough when the crime was committed in the Hermione. He had applied to another man to write a defence for him; and he had read it, thinking it calculated to excite compassion, and more likely to serve him than a mere denial of the fact. The Attorney-General prevented any prosecution of the printer.

Bill to make freehold estates assets.

March 11th. The question of receiving the report of the Bill for making freehold estates assets to pay simple contract debts, came on to-day in the House of Commons. The Master of the Rolls and Mr. Canning had intimated to me that they meant to oppose it on the third reading only; and no debate was expected in this stage of the Bill. Colonel Eyre, however, the member for Nottinghamshire, there being an extremely thin house, thought proper to oppose the Bill. Amongst other things, he said that my bringing in such a measure might be ascribed to my hereditary love of democracy. A short conversation, rather than a debate, took place: in the course of it, notice having been taken of what Colonel Eyre had said, he made a kind of apology, aud expressed himself sorry to have said anything which might hurt my feelings. It became indispensably necessary for me to say something of myself. I very shortly answered the objections made to the Bill; and then said that "it was quite unnecessary for the honourable gentleman to have made the apology which he had done. Nothing that he had said had given me the least pain. I wondered that he had thought it worth while to inquire about the ancestors of a person so obscure as myself; but the information he had received was so erroneous, so little applicable to me, that nothing uttered under such a mistake could cause me a moment's concern; that I had never heard that any persons from whom I was descended had ever concerned themselves much about politics; that all that I knew of them was that, living in affluence under the French monarchy till the Edict of Nantes was revoked, and by a breach of public faith they were no longer permitted to worship God in the way they thought most acceptable to Him, they had preferred giving up the possessions which they had inherited to making a sacrifice of their consciences; and, that they might enjoy religious liberty, had sought the protection of an English monarch, and had left their posterity to trust to their own exertions for their support."

Probable change of administration.

15th. I dined with the Chancellor. He talked with me a good deal about the misunderstanding which has arisen respecting the Bill depending in the House of Commons, to enable Catholics to serve in the army and navy. It seems that the administration are likely to go out upon it. He tells me that he was himself an enemy to the Bill; but that he agrees entirely with the rest of the Cabinet on the point which is now in difference between the Ministers and the King.

18th.* Lord Howick, in the House of Commons, declared that the Bill would not be proceeded with; and, upon a question being asked, he declared that, though he was still in office, he understood that his Majesty was taking measures for forming a new administration.

Bill to make freehold estates assets.

The question of the third reading of the Bill to make freehold estates assets, came on to-day in the House of Commons; and, after a pretty long debate, was rejected by a majority of 69 to 47. The Ministers gave themselves no trouble to support it; and many persons who sincerely wished well to it, and who had paid me compliments upon it, and thanked me for bringing it in, stayed away, either supposing that the Bill was in no danger, or, though they approved the measure, not thinking it worth while to give themselves much trouble about it. The enemies to the Bill, on the other hand, made a point of attending; and, just before the division was expected, there flocked into the House almost all the most forward members of Opposition, all of them, indeed, except Perceval (the late Attorney-General), who had spoken for the Bill on the second reading, and who now stayed away, occupied probably in assisting to arrange the new administration,

* Query — Whether the first of these declarations was not made on the 17th, and the second on the 18th.

in which he is to have a high office. The principal opposer of the Bill was the Master of the Rolls, who, in a long, studied, and elaborate speech, exerted all his powers to throw it out. His arguments were all technical, and such as I could not have conceived could have satisfied himself. He said that justice was in such a case entirely out of the question; expediency was all that was to be considered. He spoke of the injury that would be done to the innocent heir-at-law, and of the heir's right to the real property of his ancestors, as that which ought not to be disappointed by the claims of creditors. He talked, too, of the dangers of innovation; of the mischief of enacting any law without considering all the consequences to which the principle upon which the law proceeded would lead. My reply to him was, perhaps, in some parts of it, more severe than it should have been: amongst other things, I said that I was surprised and lamented to hear some of the propositions which he had stated; and the rather, as coming from one who was the only person that appeared amongst us invested with the robes of magistracy.

19th. The Chancellor gave Piggott and me a long account of a very curious conversation he had yesterday with the King*; I should rather say of a long speech he made to the King. When he went in to his Majesty, and had told him that the Recorder's report was to be made, he says that, though it is contrary to all Court etiquette to speak on any

* This, though communicated very confidentially, he afterwards repeated to almost all his friends, and sometimes in large companies at dinner.

subject which the King has not first mentioned, he proceeded somewhat to this effect: — He said that he was about to do what he believed was very much out of order, but he hoped that his Majesty would excuse it, in consideration of the very extraordinary conjuncture in which the country was placed; that he was sensible that, when he first entered into his Majesty's service, his Majesty had entertained a prejudice against him; that he was quite satisfied that that prejudice was now entirely removed; and that his Majesty did him the justice to believe that he had served him faithfully; that upon the measure which had been the original occasion of the present state of things (meaning the Catholic Bill, as it has been not very properly called), he thought, both religiously and morally, exactly as his Majesty himself did; that, however, after what had passed, it appeared to him that the Ministers who had signed the minute of Council * could not possibly, with any consistency of character, retract it; and that to give a pledge not to offer advice to his Majesty upon measures which the state of public affairs might render necessary, would be, if not an impeachable offence, yet at least that which constitutionally could not be justified. He then said that he thought it his indispensable duty to represent to the King the situation in which he stood; that he was on the brink of a precipice; that nothing could be more fatal than to persevere in the resolution, which his Majesty had formed, of dismissing his Ministers; that the day on which that resolution was announced in Ireland would be

* The Chancellor was not one of them.

a day of jubilee to the Catholics; that they could desire nothing more than to have a Ministry who were supported by all the talents and weight of property in the country, go out upon such a measure: that he ventured to tell his Majesty that, if he proceeded with his resolution, he would never know another hour of comfort or tranquillity. The King, he says, listened to all this without once interrupting him; that he could observe, however, by his countenance, that he was greatly agitated; and when the Chancellor had concluded, the King said to him, "You are a very honest man, my Lord, and I am very much obliged to you;" and this was all. The Chancellor thinks that he has made a great impression, and half flatters himself that the King will retract his resolution. The fact, however, is, that his Majesty saw Lord Howick after the Chancellor, and perseveres most firmly in his determination of forming a new Administration.

Master of the Rolls.

21st. I received a letter to-day from the Master of the Rolls, complaining of my conduct towards him in the late debate; and I have written him an answer, which I shall send to him, apprizing him what it is that I think I had great reason to complain of in his conduct, and what I meant certainly to resent. He has used me most unkindly; and I think has acted in a manner unworthy of himself: but I have no desire to be at enmity with him, or indeed with any man.

Change of administration.

25th. All the Cabinet Ministers having been yesterday required to attend his Majesty to-day, and deliver up the seals of their offices, did so; except the Lord Chancellor, who is to retain the great seal till this day se'nnight, when the King will again return from Windsor. The King, understanding that there were some causes which had been argued, but in which the Chancellor had not yet pronounced his decrees, desired him to remain a week longer in office, that he might finish the business of his court.

The Ministers had determined not to resign, but to be dismissed from their offices.

I am still Solicitor-General ; but I shall continue such only till my successor is appointed.

I have some satisfaction, now the Ministers are out, in reflecting that I have never asked them for a single favour. There was one thing which I very much wished for ; and it is such a trifle, that I take for granted that if I had asked Lord Moira (the Master of the Ordnance) for it, it would have been done for me immediately. It was only to get my brother's youngest son into the Military Academy at Woolwich. However, I did not ask for it ; and, to the poor boy's great disappointment, it is not done.

The new ministry consists of the Duke of Portland, First Lord of the Treasury ; Lords Hawkesbury and Castlereagh, and Canning, Secretaries of State ; Lord Chatham, Master of the Ordnance ; and Perceval, Chancellor of the Exchequer.* This is all, I believe, that is yet settled. Perceval is also to be Chancellor of the Duchy of Lancaster. It was intended that he should have this office for

* In addition to these, it soon afterwards appeared that Lord Camden was to be President of the Council ; Lord Westmoreland, Privy Seal ; Lord Eldon, Chancellor ; and Lord Mulgrave, First Lord of the Admiralty.

life; but, this intention having got abroad, Henry Martin[1] yesterday gave notice of a motion for to-day in the House of Commons, to address the King, not to grant for life that, or any other office which has been usually granted at pleasure.

The motion was made, and the address carried by a majority of 208 to 115.

26th. Lord Howick in the House of Commons stated very fully all the circumstances which had led to the dismissal of himself and his colleagues. In the House of Lords, Lord Grenville did the same thing; and a very long debate ensued. The most remarkable circumstance in it was, Lord Melville taking a part in it, speaking from between the Duke of Cumberland and Lord Eldon, on the bench appropriated to the Ministers. The Duke of Cumberland placed himself at the head of this bench, probably to proclaim to the world, that he is the person who has brought about the change of administration.

Lord Melville.

Mr. Brand has given notice of a motion, upon the dismissal of the. Ministers, for Thursday, April 9th.

Both Houses adjourned over the Easter holydays to Wednesday the 8th of April. This adjournment will enable the new Ministers to strengthen themselves very much; every exertion will no doubt be made in the interval to gain over as many members of parliament as possible.

29th. Went to Ealing and stayed there till April 3d.

[1] The late Master in Chancery. — Ed.

Lord Erskine.

April 1st. Lord Erskine delivered up the great seal, and it was given to Lord Eldon.

Two days before Lord Erskine parted with the seal, he appointed his son-in-law, Edward Morris, a Master in Chancery. Sir William Pepys was prevailed on to make a vacancy by resigning. This is surely a most improper act of Lord Erskine's. He ought to have considered himself as out of office last Wednesday. Morris, though a very clever and a very deserving man, has no knowledge in his profession of that particular kind which is necessary to qualify a man to discharge the duties of a Master. This is a matter which will draw reproach on the whole administration; though, in every other department, they have more scrupulously, as I understand, abstained from making any promotions.

Lord Melville.

Lord Melville was to have been sworn of the Privy Council to-day, and was actually summoned for the purpose. An excuse however was made on the pretence of his being unwell, and he was not restored to the Council.

The cry of No Popery.

The new Ministers are, and have been, doing all they can to excite a cry in the country against popery; and to use religion as an instrument to favour their ambition. Perceval, who by accepting his office, has vacated his seat, tells the electors of Northampton, in his advertisement to them, that he doubts not, that they will not think the worse of him, for having on this occasion quitted his profession, and accepted his new office: that he shall not have forfeited their good opinion "in consequence" (these are his words) "of my coming forward in the service of my Sovereign, and endeavouring to stand by him at this important crisis, when he is making so firm, and so necessary, a stand for the religious establishment of the country." He then goes on to say that to do this is a duty in the people as well as in the Sovereign.

The Duke of Portland, it seems, who is Chancellor of the University of Oxford, wrote to the University, to desire that they would petition Parliament against the [Catholic] Bill.

The Duke of Cumberland, Chancellor of the University of Dublin, wrote two letters to that University, for the same purpose; and in the last of them, very plainly intimated that it was the wish of the King that this should be done. Henry Erskine, who does not make any scruple of repeating his own jokes, told me that he had just been saying to the Duchess of Gordon, that it was much to be lamented that poor Lord George did not live in these times when he would have stood a chance of being in the Cabinet, instead of being in Newgate.

7th, *Tu.* I dined at Lord Howick's, with a large party of the late Ministers and their friends. They are very sanguine as to carrying, by a considerable majority, Mr. Brand's motion. The Prince, however, has declared that he takes no interest about it; the motion being of a nature which much affects the King personally.

8th, *Wed.* Lord Melville was sworn of the Privy Council.

Mr. Brand's motion.

9th, *Th.* Mr. Brand made his promised motion in the House of Commons; which was, for the House to resolve something to this effect: "that it was contrary to the first duties of the responsible ministers of the Crown, to give a pledge that they would not offer advice to his Majesty on any subject of national concern." If it had been carried, it would have been followed by other resolutions; "that to advise his Majesty to dismiss his Ministers, because they refused to give such a pledge, was subversive of the Constitution;" and "that the persons who had given such advice, or who had come into office upon any such pledge, expressed or implied, were not deserving of the confidence of the House of Commons;" and then "that the resolutions should be carried up to the King." The debate was a very extraordinary one. Perceval declared that the King had no advisers in the measure; that this proceeding was in truth to arraign the conduct of the King personally; and to call him, as he said, to answer personally at the bar of the House. Canning, after the most fulsome adulation to the King, said that he had made up his mind, when the Catholic Bill was first mentioned, to vote for it, if the King was for it, and against it, if the King was against it. Every art was used to interest persons for the King. His age was repeatedly mentioned, his pious scruples, his regard for his coronation oath, which, some members did not scruple to say, would have been violated, if the bill had passed. Canning endeavoured to allure men to his party by very gross expedients. He talked about the King's remarkably good health and promise of long life, and the uncommon force and soundness of his understanding. He said very distinctly that, if the question were lost, the Ministers would not go out, but that they should appeal to the people: he meant undoubtedly that they should dissolve the parliament. The question was lost, and the order of the day was carried, by a majority of 32; 258 for the order of the day, 226 against it.

Our party were so little aware that they should lose the question, and it was so difficult in so full a House to ascertain the numbers in it, that during the division while we were locked out in the lobby, we supposed ourselves the majority by about 20; and in consequence of it, notice was given to the members present, that it was intended to proceed with the other motions on the same day, at the meeting of the House, it being then past six in the morning.

I spoke in the course of the debate; and, amongst other things, I said that for the exercise of every branch of the prerogative, I conceived that some persons were responsible as the advisers of the Crown, even for the choice of Ministers: that the King might by law make whom he pleased his Ministers; that he might call into his councils, and honour with his confidence, men whom the House of Commons had declared were unworthy of their confidence; that he might call into his councils a man of whom the House had resolved that he had committed a gross violation of the law, and a high breach of duty (in this, of course, I alluded to Lord Melville), and that he might do this while such a resolution was yet standing on the Journals of the House; but that the Ministers who advised such a measure were deeply responsible for it. That, though such a case would be greatly mitigated by the person having afterwards been tried and acquitted, yet not, if he had been acquitted in such a manner that not one of his numerous and powerful friends had ventured to move to have the resolutions expunged; and that when he went to seat himself in the other House, he could not look on the countenances of those who were sitting near him and opposite to him, but that, by that necessary association of ideas which is inseparable from our nature, he must have the words "*guilty upon my honour*" resounding in his ears. This provoked some very angry observations from Sir P. Murray, the member for Edinburgh, and a near connexion of Lord Melville's.

My speech upon the whole was a very bad one, and was by no means favourably received by the House. I felt mortified and chagrined to the utmost degree. I have this Session, upon some occasions, particularly on the Slave Trade, and in my reply to the Master of the Rolls on the Assets Bill, spoken with very great success, and met with very great applause. I have received compliments without number, and some very extravagant ones; but all the gratification which my vanity may have had upon those occasions would be much more than compensated for by one tenth part of the mortification which the coldness and the appearance which I thought I plainly discovered of the House beginning to be tired of me, have given me. One or two expressions in my speech, which I think were very foolish, have haunted my memory ever since I sat down. It will be long, I think, before I shall venture to speak again.

11th, *Sat.* Plumer received his patent as Solicitor-General, and was sworn in, and therefore I now cease to hold that office. I shall now renew my attendance at the Rolls, which I quitted on being appointed Solicitor-General.

13th. Debate in the House of Lords on the transactions which produced the change of administration. One of the most remarkable things in it was, that Lord Erskine, speaking of the King's repugnance to give his consent to any Bill in favour of the Catholics, because he conceived that it would be a violation of his coronation oath, after showing how little foundation there was for such a notion, said [1], that it should be remembered that, by the coronation oath, his Majesty swore to govern his people according to the laws and customs of the realm; and that to require a pledge of his Ministers not to give him counsel on any subject was manifestly contrary to the constitution, and the laws and customs of the realm: to say, therefore, that the King and not his advisers were the authors of this, was to say that he had undoubtedly broken his coronation oath. No notice was taken of this by any of the Peers who spoke after him. In this debate, and in that which took place in the House of Commons, the grossest adulation to the King has been shown; and the most

[1] See Hansard's Parliamentary Debates, vol. ix. p. 362. — Ed.

servile doctrines have been maintained: at the same time, however, nothing can have a greater tendency to democracy than that the personal conduct of the King towards his Ministers should become a subject of public debate.

15th, *Wed.* Debate in the House of Commons on Mr. Lyttelton's motion, expressing the regret of the House on the late change in his Majesty's councils. The motion was rejected by 244 to 198.

Freehold estates of traders to be assets for payment of their debts.

20th, *Mon.* A few days after the Bill to make freehold estates assets was rejected, I gave notice of a motion for leave to bring in a Bill for the same purpose, but confined to persons in trade. I have since brought in the Bill; and it was this day, in the House of Commons, read a third time and passed. Many of the objections which were made to the former Bill are applicable to this, — that it is an innovation; that it is to affect land without evidence in writing; that it holds out a delusive credit, &c. &c. There has not, however, been a single word uttered in opposition to the Bill in any stage of it. Country gentlemen have no objection to tradesmen being made to pay their debts; and, to the honour of men in trade, of whom there are a good many in the House, they too had no objection to it.[1]

Dissolution of Parliament.

26th, *Sun.* Parliament, it seems, is to be prorogued to-morrow, and then immediately dissolved. It was understood that a dissolution was to take place; but it was not supposed that it would be before the end of May and the regular close of

[1] This Bill passed into a law in the first Session of the next Parliament. It is 47 Geo. 3. c. 74.—Ed.

the Session. An immediate dissolution, it seems, was decided on, last Friday; though it has been kept a profound secret till this morning. The object, no doubt, is to take advantage of the cry of No Popery, which has been raised in some parts of the country; a cry so senseless, and, upon this occasion, so destitute of any facts to warrant it, that it could not but be felt that if the dissolution were postponed for some weeks, it might have wholly died away.

27th, *Mon.* Parliament was this day prorogued. The Lords Commissioners' speech does not affect to disguise, how necessary it was not to lose a moment, in order to obtain the benefit of the unfounded clamour which the Ministers have industriously raised. "His Majesty," they say, "is anxious to recur to the sense of his people, while the events which have recently taken place are yet fresh in their recollection;" and afterwards they say, "His Majesty trusts that the divisions naturally and unavoidably excited, by the late unfortunate and uncalled-for agitation, of a question so interesting to the feelings and opinions of his people will speedily pass away." Alluding to the supposed restraint imposed on the King by his coronation oath, they say, "His Majesty feels that, in resorting to this measure, he affords his people the best opportunity of testifying their determination to support him in every exercise of the prerogatives of his Crown, which is conformable to the sacred obligations under which they are held, and conducive to the welfare of his kingdom, and to the security of the Constitution." A part of the speech which cannot but excite disgust in the mind of every man, is that in which it is said, "His Majesty has directed us most earnestly to recommend to you, that you should cultivate, by all means in your power, a spirit of union, harmony, and goodwill amongst all classes and descriptions of his people." What detestable hypocrisy!

Sale of seats in Parliament.

I shall procure myself a seat in the new Parliament, unless I find that it will cost so large a sum, as, in the state of my family, it would be very imprudent for me to devote to such an object, which I find is very likely to be the case. Tierney, who manages this business for the friends of the late administration, assures me that he can hear of no seats to be disposed of. After a Parliament which has lived little more than four months, one would naturally suppose, that those seats which are regularly sold by the proprietors of them would be very cheap; they are, however, in fact, sold now at a higher price than was ever given for them before. Tierney tells me that he has offered 10,000*l.* for the two seats of Westbury, the property of the late Lord Abingdon, and which are to be made the most of by trustees for creditors, and has met with a refusal. 6000*l.* and 5500*l.* have been given for seats with no stipulation as to time, or against the event of a speedy dissolution by the King's death, or by any change of administration. The truth is, that the new Ministers have bought up all the seats that were to be disposed of, and at any prices. Amongst others, Sir C. H——, the great dealer in boroughs, has sold all he had to Ministers. With what money all this is done I know not, but it is supposed that the King, who has greatly at heart to preserve this new administration, the favourite objects of his choice, has advanced a very large sum out of his privy purse.

This buying of seats is detestable; and yet it is almost the only way in which one in my situation, who is resolved to be an independent man, can get into Parliament. To come in by a popular election, in the present state of the representation, is quite impossible; to be placed there by some great lord, and to vote as he shall direct, is to be in a state of complete dependence; and nothing hardly remains but to owe a seat to the sacrifice of a part of one's fortune. It is true that many men who buy seats, do it as a matter of pecuniary speculation, as a profitable way of employing their money: they carry on a political trade; they buy their seats, and sell their votes. For myself, I can truly say that, by giving money for a seat, I shall make a sacrifice of my private property, merely that I may be enabled to serve the public. I know what danger there is of men's disguising from themselves the real motives of their actions; but it really does appear to me that it is from this motive alone that I act.[1]

May 9th. After almost despairing of being able to get any seat in Parliament, my friend Piggott has at last procured me one; and the Duke of Norfolk has consented to bring me in for Horsham. It is however but a precarious seat. I shall be re-

[1] See *suprà*, p. 127.—Ed.

turned, as I shall have a majority of votes, which the late committee of the House of Commons decided to be good ones; but there will be a petition against the return, by the candidates who will stand on Lady Irwin's interest, and it is extremely doubtful what will be the event of the petition.

R. elected for Horsham.

10th, *Sun.* I went down to Horsham. The election began on Monday the 11th, and was not over till the 12th, though the numbers polled were only 44 for Major Parry and myself, and 29 for the other candidates. But the taking down, by the poll clerk, of the description of every burgage tenement from the deeds of the voters, was a very long operation. I came away Monday night, and before the election was over.

12th. The terms upon which I have my seat at Horsham will be best explained by a letter I wrote to Piggott to-day after the election was over, and which I am glad to keep a copy of. It is (at least so much of it as relates to this subject) in these words: "Though there is no danger that I should have misunderstood you, yet it may be as well just to say, while it is fresh in both our recollections, what I understand to be the extent of my engagement. If I keep the seat, either by the decision of a committee upon a petition, or by a compromise (the Duke and Lady Irwin returning one member each, in which case it is understood that I am to be the member who continues), I am to pay 2000*l.*; if, upon a petition, I lose the seat, I am not to be at any expence." Nothing has been said respecting the possible event of my vacating by accepting an office; but I take for granted that, in that case, I should be re-elected. It is an event certainly very unlikely to happen, for a change of administration (without which it cannot happen) is not likely to take place during the King's life.

June 9th. I received an application from the prisoners in the King's Bench Prison, to present, in the approaching Session of Parliament, a petition from them to the House of Commons, praying that a revision may take place of the law between Debtor and Creditor.

Imprisonment for debt.

10th. I answered their letter; and, as I shall be glad to remember hereafter what I wrote to them, I insert a copy of it in these memoranda:—"Sir, if the persons who have the misfortune to be confined for debt in the King's Bench Prison are desirous that I should present their petition to the House of Commons, I will certainly do it. I had much rather, however, that it should be presented by some other person. It has been suggested, though without any authority from me, that I had it in contemplation to bring a Bill into Parliament to remove the defects of the present laws respecting Debtor and Creditor; and my presenting the petition might give some countenance to that idea. I should be extremely sorry to give any countenance to it; for it would only have the effect of adding to the many misfortunes which those who are in confinement already suffer,—that of entertaining hopes and encouraging expectations which could only end in disappointment. I have no intention whatever to bring in a Bill on the subject. I think the law, as it at present stands, very defective and very oppressive. I have long thought it so; but I have not been able to discover the proper remedy for those defects, and for that oppression. Under these circumstances, I much wish to decline presenting the petition; but if I am required to do it, I will certainly present it; though my presenting it will be followed by no other motion from me, than that the petition may lie on the table. I am, Sir, your most obedient, &c. To Mr. John Bell, King's Bench Prison." When I said in this letter that I had not been able to discover the proper remedy for the present defects in the law, I did not go on to say, though it is the fact, that I intend to employ my first leisure in endeavouring to find that remedy. I have little hope, however, that I shall be able to suggest any thing that will have any chance of being permitted to pass into a law. It seems best, therefore, not to give any hint of my intentions.

Meeting of the new Parliament.

22d. Parliament met. The Speaker chosen.

26th. The Session opened by the King's Speech. Lord Howick in the Commons, and Lord Fortescue in the Lords, moved an amendment to the Address, censuring the late dissolution of Parliament. The numbers upon the division were, in the Lords, for the amendment 67, against it 160; in the Commons, for the amendment 155, against it 350.

27th. The prisoners in the King's Bench having sent me their petition, and again requested that I would present it, I this day presented it to the House of Commons, stating, at the same time, that it was not my intention to take any other step on it, than to move that it might lie on the table; which motion I accordingly made.

29th. I this day moved for, and obtained, leave to bring in a Bill to make the freehold estates of traders assets to pay their simple contract debts; the Bill which I had carried through the House of Commons in the last Parliament having been lost in the Lords by the late dissolution.

Committee to inquire into the public expenditure.

30th. The question upon the revival of the committee to inquire into the public expenditure, came on to-day in the House of Commons. Perceval proposed a list of members to form the committee. Nineteen members of the former committee, which consisted of twenty-four, had been returned to the present Parliament. Of these nineteen, six, some of them the most active and useful members of the committee, were omitted in Perceval's list; two others were properly left out, one as being in office, and the other (Sir H. Mildmay) at his own request, because his conduct, in a bargain made with government, had come into question; and thirteen new members were proposed. The substituting new members in the place of the six unexceptionable members of the former committee was strenuously opposed by all the members and friends of the late administration; and, upon the question whether Sharp, who was of the old committee, should be appointed, or Leycester, whom Perceval proposed, the House divided; for Perceval's motion 244, against it 149. Perceval artfully introduced his motion by stating several instances of the late Ministers having created new places, or given improperly pensions, as a reason why there ought not to be upon a committee who were to inquire into improper transactions of that kind so many friends of the late Ministers. The true object of this was, manifestly, to divert the attention of the House from the real question; and in a great degree it had that effect. The debate consisted principally of personal attacks and recriminations. I said a few words in the debate; but I avoided all those topics, and endeavoured to impress the House with the importance of satisfying the Nation, that the inquiries begun in the last Parliament were meant to be seriously prosecuted in this; and of removing the suspicions upon this subject, which, from what passed at many of the late elections, it was evident had gone abroad. Ministers had endeavoured to put all other business depending in Parliament as nearly as they could in the exact state in which it was when the dissolution took place. With respect to this committee alone, they sought to depart from that line of conduct; though the inquiries prosecuting by this committee were generally considered as the most important business depending in Parliament, when it was dissolved. It was so considered by the Ministers themselves, since they had advised the King to advert to it in his speech, and to recommend the revival of the inquiries in the new Parliament; and I observed that persons who had already sat upon the committee, and had their minds occupied with the subject, and had seen and heard the witnesses, must necessarily be better qualified to go on with their researches, than men who were new to the business.

Of all the facts stated by Perceval against the late administration, there is only one that appears to me to be of any importance; but that, I think, cannot be justified. It seems that a grant was made of a pension to Lord Cullen, a Lord of Session and Justiciary in Scotland, of 400*l.* a year, with a reversionary pension of 200*l.* a year to his wife. Lord Cullen's pension, it seems, was intended to be for life, but by mistake was made to depend on the King's pleasure. The grant had been promised by the Duke of Portland when he was in office; and Lord Cullen's fortune was extremely small, and a part of his salary as a Judge had been assigned to trustees to pay his debts; but this, in my opinion, affords no excuse for the measure. The grant of a pension to a judge for life is not by law prohibited, but is surely contrary to the spirit of the Constitution. If the King may grant pensions for life, he may, in substance, give unequal salaries to the Judges, as a reward for those who are most subservient to the wishes of his ministers.

Pension to Lord Cullen, a Scotch judge.

July 13th. I said a few words in the House of Commons, in support of Whitbread's Bill, for establishing schools for the education of the poor, in all the parishes in England. It was upon the second reading of the Bill. The question was carried, but the Bill will certainly be lost. Many persons think that the subject requires further consideration, and a more matured plan; but I am afraid a much greater portion of the House think it expedient, that the people should be kept in a state of ignorance.

Education of the poor.

17th. A Bill which I brought into the House of

Bill to abolish a privi-

lege of Members of Parliament, defendants in equity, injurious to other suitors.

Commons, to alter the practice of courts of equity in suits in which Members of Parliament are defendants, this day passed the House of Commons. The sole object of the Bill is to dispense with the necessity of the plaintiff delivering to the defendant, if he be a person having privilege of Parliament, an office copy of the Bill, at the time when he is served with a subpœna to appear to and answer the Bill. The expense of these office copies has, by means of stamp duties on law proceedings, become very considerable. It is true that if, at the conclusion of the cause, the defendant is ordered to pay the costs of the suit, a member of Parliament, who is a defendant, in the end pays the expense of the copy, which at the commencement of the suit was delivered to him: and in all such cases, the only inconvenience suffered by the plaintiff arises from the advance he is obliged to make, and the not being reimbursed during the time that the cause is going on; which is, unfortunately, in suits in equity, generally a long period of time. A man must be richer to be able to file a bill against a member of Parliament than against any other individual. There are, however, in courts of equity, some cases, where by the rule of the court, no costs are given on either side: there are others, where, without such a general rule, the court in its discretion does not think fit to give costs on either side; and there are many more cases, in which the plaintiff being worn out by delay and expense, is unable to prosecute his suit to a hearing, and therefore no costs can be given. In all these cases, Members of

Parliament are relieved from the ordinary costs of a suit, and that at the expense of their opponents; and in the last class of cases, it is often this double expense, thrown on the plaintiff, which greatly contributes to render him unable to prosecute his suit to a hearing. This inequality of expense is the more to be complained of, because the party having privilege of Parliament is generally more opulent than the man he contends with; and because it is principally occasioned by the stamp duties, which are imposed by Parliament. As far as relates to these copies, Members of Parliament, when they increase the stamp duties on law proceedings, tax the whole community except themselves. It has been suggested, that it would be an improvement of the practice of courts of equity, if in all cases the plaintiff were obliged, on filing his Bill, to deliver an office copy of it, at his own expense, to the defendant. That is not my opinion; but, even if it were, still, as long as the practice remains such as it is with respect to other suitors, it ought to be the same with respect to Members of Parliament. We can never hope that the defects which exist in the administration of justice will be reformed, if they are never known to, or felt by Members of the Legislature, on whom alone it depends that they should be reformed. The Bill is confined to Members of the House of Commons; as it appeared to me to be open to much objection, that a Bill to take away the privileges of Peers should have its origin in the House of Commons. I trust, however, that, when the Bill gets into the House of Lords, some Peer will move to insert as an amendment of it, the words "Peers of the realm, or Lords of Parliament."

Lord Cochrane's motion for an account of the places and pensions held by Members of Parliament, their wives, or children.

Lord Cochrane, one of the Members for Westminster, moved (July 7.), in the House of Commons, for the appointment of a committee to ascertain what places and pensions were held by Members of the House, or their wives or children. Perceval affected to have no objection to the object of the motion, but proposed to obtain it, by having an account stated of all places and pensions granted by Government, with the names of the persons by whom they are held. This, he said, would supply the information which was desired, but in a less invidious manner than by confining the inquiry to Members of Parliament. No person could fail to see that this was suggested, as an indirect mode of entirely defeating the object of Lord Cochrane's motion. It would be long before the account could be made out; and the names of Members of Parliament, their wives and children, would lie unknown or unobserved, in a long list of placemen and pensioners. The House divided on the question; and, as might be supposed, there was a great majority for Perceval's amendment; ninety to sixty-one. I voted in the minority. I know of no good reason why there should be any concealment as to the places and pensions, which are held by Members of Parliament or their near connexions. On the contrary, there seem to be the strongest reasons why the truth on this subject should be known; on the one hand, as it may lead to a reform of a very great evil, that of the increasing influence of the Crown over the determinations of Parliament, by means of the places and pensions which are distributed amongst the members of the House of Commons; and on the other, as it will restrain and reduce to their just standard those dangerous exaggerations on this subject, which are becoming every day more prevalent. That all public men are corrupt, and that the true interests of the country are disregarded in an unceasing struggle between contending factions for power and emolument, is an opinion spreading very fast through the country. No man has contributed so much and so successfully to propagate this opinion as Cobbett, the author of a weekly political paper; which, being written with great acuteness, and with great energy and vigour of style, has obtained a very wide circulation. This writer, who set out with being a zealous supporter of Government, and a furious enemy to republicanism, now every day maintains opinions which manifestly tend to establish the wildest democracy. His favourite doctrine is, that no man in place should be eligible to Parliament. He does not conceal his eager expectation of an approaching revolution, in which I have no doubt that he hopes himself to act some very conspicuous part. Although his opinions on most important subjects have undergone a total change, yet whatever opinion he entertains he advances with all the confidence of infallibility, and without regard to its consequences. He is an enemy to all foreign trade except the slave trade, of which he has always declared himself the champion. He has again and again recommended a national bank-

Cobbett.

ruptcy, as a measure the most expedient; and, keeping in view these great objects, and that revolution which he expects, he has for a long time determined, as a means of accomplishing his object, to destroy all confidence in every individual who has ever taken any part in public affairs. This he endeavours to effectuate by the grossest misrepresentations of their actions and their words. The only man he at present commends is Sir Francis Burdett, the member for Westminster, now the theme of his most exaggerated panegyric, but once the object of his bitterest invectives. But this Sir Francis Burdett is only an instrument whom he makes use of for the present; and whose reputation, when he finds it no longer subservient to his designs, he will, with his accustomed arts, destroy. Many persons suppose that this man has no object, by the indiscriminate attack which he makes on all parties, but to increase the sale of his paper. I am well satisfied that he has much higher views. Windham, from personal knowledge of this vain and ambitious man, has formed, I am told, the same opinion as that which has been with me the result of reading his publications. He has not mentioned me more than once or twice, and then rather with praise than censure: the horror, therefore, which I entertain of his disposition and designs, cannot have been provoked by any personal enmity.

Irish Insurrection Bill.

27th, *Mon.* The Irish Insurrection Bill [1] was

[1] This Bill was brought into the House of Commons on the 9th of July, by Sir A. Wellesley (now Duke of Wellington). It gave a power to the Lord Lieutenant to proclaim disturbed counties; and

read a third time and passed. A long debate on the Bill for enlisting the army from the militia had preceded it; and it was not till past three o'clock in the morning that this important measure of the Irish bill was entered on. Several amendments were moved, on receiving the report; and amongst others, one to limit the duration of the Bill to one year; but they were all rejected. Consequently the Bill stands as it went through the committee; and is to continue in force for two years, and to the end of the then next session of Parliament. It was five o'clock in the morning before the question upon the third reading was put; on which question alone, could the justice and policy of the measure be discussed; for, on the second reading, an understanding had prevailed on all sides, that the Bill should go into a committee, that it might be seen how far it could be altered or mitigated, before its merits were debated. The debate which now took place, was such as might have been expected at such an hour, when every body was tired and exhausted; and it lasted but a short time. Mr. Grattan spoke for the Bill: he had voted for the shorter period of its duration, and for all the mitigations which had been proposed; but yet he declared that such as the Bill was, he thought it a necessary measure;

---

authorised magistrates to arrest persons who should be found out of their dwellings between sunset and sunrise; and required that persons so arrested should be tried at the Quarter Sessions. A bill was brought in at the same time to oblige all persons in Ireland to register their arms; and authorising magistrates to search for arms. Both these Bills became law; the former is the 47 Geo. 3. sess. 2. c. 13.; the latter the 47 Geo. 3. sess. 2. c. 54.—Ed.

and he said that to his knowledge, there was a French party in Ireland. His arguments, or rather his assertions, or, to speak still more accurately, his authority, had great weight, and determined many, who had come to the House intending to vote against the Bill, to go away without dividing. Amongst these were Lord Milton, Ward (Lord Dudley's son), Ponsonby (the nephew of the late Irish Chancellor), and Dillon. For myself, the measure appeared to me to be so impolitic, so unjust, and likely to produce so much mischief, that I determined, if any person divided the House, to vote against it. Sheridan did divide it, on the question that the Bill do pass, and I found myself in a minority of 10, including the tellers, against 108. The 10 were, Sheridan, Lord William Russell, Daly, Colonel Talbot, Piggott, Henry Martin, Abercromby, Sharp, P. Moore, and myself. I did not speak upon the bill: that it would pass, whatever might be said against it, I could not doubt; and I therefore thought that to state my objections to it could have no other effect than to increase the mischief which I wished to prevent. What triumphant arguments will not this Bill, and that which is depending in the House for preventing the people having arms, furnish the disaffected with in Ireland! What laws more tyrannical could they have to dread, if the French yoke were imposed on them? What worse could they endure than to be exposed to domiciliary visits; to have their houses broken open in the dead of night; and to see insolent superintendents forcing their way into every bedchamber, to see that none of the family are from home; and to have those, who at such a season shall be absent, without being able to produce witnesses to prove that it was on some lawful occasion, subjected to transportation as felons to New South Wales? Can it be expected that men will be so blindly attached to a bondage thus cruel and degrading, as willingly to shed their blood in defence of it?

To adopt such a measure, at a moment like the present, appears to me to be little short of madness. Unfortunately the measure had been in the contemplation of the late Ministry. They had left a draft of the Bill in the Secretary of State's office; and they were now ashamed to oppose what some of them had themselves thought of proposing. The Attorney and Solicitor General of Ireland had approved of the bill; but Piggott and myself had never heard that such a matter was in agitation till it was brought into the House by the present Ministers.

Bill to abolish a privilege of members, as defendants in equity.

The Bill which I brought into the House of Commons, to dispense with the necessity of delivering office copies of bills in equity to members of Parliament who are defendants, passed the House of Lords without any alteration.* The operation of it was confined to Members of the House of Commons; because I thought that the Lords might take offence at any act, which was to abridge their privileges, originating with the Commons; but I had no doubt that, when the Bill got into the House of Lords, some peer would move, as an amendment, that it should extend to

* See the Act, 47 Geo. 3. sess. 2. c. 40.

the members of that House, as well as of the House of Commons. And, in truth, such an amendment would have been moved by Lord Holland; but we found that the Bill so altered would meet with opposition, and would probably be lost; and I thought it better to do the little good that was allowed me, rather than, by attempting too much, fail of doing any thing. As the Bill stood, no peer could with decency oppose it; for, if the Commons chose to part with their privileges, what pretext could any peer find for resisting it? and the bill did accordingly pass without opposition. The Chancellor has since told me, that the Peers must through shame pass a Bill to the same effect as to themselves, in the next session.

Education of the poor.

Aug. 6th. Whitbread's Bill for establishing parochial schools was read a third time, and passed the House of Commons. No opposition was given to it now, but it had been strenuously opposed in former stages; and it is probably suffered to pass the Commons, because it is well known that it will be rejected by the Lords. That such country gentlemen (so they are usually called) as —— and —— should oppose such a measure, might be expected: that a writer like Mandeville should have been a warm enemy to giving instruction to the mass of the people, is natural; and perfectly agrees with his great maxim in politics, that private vices are public benefits: but

Windham.

that a man so enlightened as Windham[1], and having upon many subjects such just notions,

[1] See *infrà*, May 1st, 1810.—Ed.

should take the same side (which he has done most earnestly), would excite great astonishment, if one did not recollect his eager opposition a few months ago to the abolition of the slave trade. It has been said, that when it is proposed to communicate knowledge to the lowest classes of society, it is very important to be informed what knowledge it is intended to give them; and that we should be very sure that they will not be taught errors, both in religion and politics, instead of truths. But what is proposed is, not to give knowledge to the poor, but to qualify them to acquire it: it is by teaching them reading, writing, and arithmetic, to give them means, which they do not now possess, of acquiring and communicating ideas, and of exercising their minds. If man be distinguished from the rest of the animal creation by reason, surely to improve that faculty, and to supply it with materials to work on, is to render him, whatever be his station of life, more perfect. If we could give our species a new sense, we surely would not withhold it from them. To enable men to read and write is, as it were, to give them a new sense. We cannot prevent those who are in the lowest ranks of life having political opinions; and few men would venture to avow that they would prevent it if they could. The question, then, is, whether it be better to let persons in inferior stations acquire their notions of politics and political economy from their companions, or from men of a juster way of thinking and more cultivated understandings — from ignorant clowns, or from writers of merit. The alarm lest false notions in politics and religion should spread throughout the country with a facility of acquiring knowledge, proceeds upon the false supposition that, if discussion were left free, error would be likely to prevail over truth. The danger of seditions and insurrections has been talked of; as if the most ignorant nations were not the most easily misled, and the most prone to tumults. Sir Francis Bacon, who had as well studied mankind, both in history and by observation, as Mr. Windham, says "Citra omnem controversiam, artes emolliunt mores, teneros reddunt, sequaces, cereos, et ad mandata Imperii ductiles. Ignorantia, contrà, contumaces, refractarios, seditiosos. Quod ex historiâ clarissime patet, quandoquidem tempora maxime indocta, inculta, barbara, tumultibus, seditionibus, mutationibusque maxime obnoxia fuerint," *De Augm. Scient.*, lib. i.; *Bacon's Works*, vol. iv. p. 25.

Irish arms Bill.

7th. The Bill to prevent improper persons in Ireland from having arms was read a third time, and passed. I had concurred with others in endeavouring in the committee to mitigate some of its severities but without success. I voted against the Bill; but, for the same reasons as I have given with respect to the Insurrection Bill, I did not speak upon it. Although this, as well as the other Bill, was a measure intended to have been adopted by the late Ministry, I found myself in not quite so small a minority as before: the numbers were, for the Bill[1], 79; against it, 34.

[1] Five members of the preceding administration were in the minority, viz. Lord Henry Petty, Sheridan, Windham, Sir Arthur Piggott, and Sir S. Romilly.—Ed.

The Reversion Bill.

10th, *Mon.* The Bill to prevent the Crown from granting places in reversion, which was depending in the House of Lords at the dissolution of the last Parliament, had been brought into the present Parliament by Mr. Bankes, the chairman of the Finance Committee, and went through the House of Commons without objection from any quarter. In the House of Lords, upon the second reading, it was opposed by Lord Melville and Lord Arden; of whom the latter enjoys a most lucrative office, that of Registrar of the Admiralty Court, granted to him while it was in reversion, with a second reversion to his brother, Perceval, the Chancellor of the Exchequer. Not one of the Ministers, except the Lord Chancellor, was present. He, together with Lord Redesdale, Lord Melville, and Lord Arden, voted against the Bill; and it was thrown out.[1] Bankes immediately gave notice of a motion upon the subject; and this day he moved accordingly that the House should address the King not to grant any office in reversion, before the end of [six] weeks after the meeting of the next session of Parliament. The Ministers did not oppose it, and the motion was carried unanimously. Perceval's reason for not opposing it, and the excuse he offered for Ministers in having been absent when the Bill was discussed in the House of Lords, was a singular one. It was, that he and his colleagues thought the measure one of

[1] On the ground that a bill of so much importance ought not to be decided upon in so thin a House, Lord Holland moved that the debate should be adjourned till the next day, which motion was lost by a majority of fifteen to nine; and the Bill was then rejected without a division. — Ed.

very little importance; that it would neither do the good which was expected from it by its partisans, nor prove so injurious to the prerogative as was represented by its enemies. A strange account this, surely, of the conduct of an administration! If good is not to be expected from the measure, and considerable good too, it is an unnecessary and therefore an improper interference with the prerogative! Men who entertain such opinions respecting the prerogative as Perceval and his colleagues have always professed, cannot consider such a measure as indifferent. The truth is, that the King's friends, as some men affect to call themselves, consider it highly objectionable. Mansfield, the Chief Justice of the Common Pleas, is loud in his censures of it, and most anxious that it should not pass into a law. I hardly recollect any public measure on which he has manifested more eagerness, unless it were on Lord Melville's trial, that that nobleman should be acquitted.

Considering only the King now on the throne, the Bill will certainly diminish his power; but, if we extend our view beyond the individual to the kingly office, it must necessarily enlarge and strengthen his authority. The lucrative offices which are in the gift of the Crown may be considered as a large fund, affording the means of rewarding public services, or of gratifying royal favour.* The giving an office in reversion is always

* This reasoning is applicable principally to sinecure offices. With respect to offices to which duties are attached, they ought not to be granted in reversion; because the person to whom they are granted, though well qualified to discharge the duties of the office when the grant is made, may have become unqualified for it by age or infirmity, before the office comes into possession. For this reason alone, it has

a most wasteful and prodigal application of that fund. In this respect, the case of monarchs is exactly the same as that of private men. A thoughtless and spendthrift heir who sells his reversionary interest, has not a sixth part of the advantage which he would derive from his property, if he waited till the prior interest was determined, and his reversion had become an estate in possession: and just the same is it with a prince who suffers his goodness to be abused in the inconsiderate distribution of places in reversion. At the time when the reversionary place is granted, the present value of it is very inconsiderable; and as such it is made the reward of no very signal service, or is given as a token of no extraordinary favour; but, when the place comes to be possessed in present enjoyment, it is that which might well have been granted as a recompence for the most essential services, or the most meritorious conduct. The grantee of the office, glad, as is the natural disposition of mankind, not to be loaded with too great a debt of gratitude *, considers what was given to him, not what he enjoys; and ascribes the greatest part of the emoluments which he possesses, and which are yielded to him by the public, to his

---

been held by our Courts of Justice, that the King could not by law grant in reversion a judicial office. (See Auditor Curl's case, Co. Rep. vol. xi. p. 4.) The same reason applies to every office to which duties belong, though not with the same force; the administration of justice being the most important of all duties.

* Lord Hale, in an imperfect tract on the amendment of the law, published in *Hargrave's Law Tracts*, p. 280., proposes not only the prevention of grants of offices in reversion in future, but the resumption of such grants already made, and the substituting pensions to the holders of such offices, in lieu of their salaries; and he adds, "neither the King nor the people would be losers by it."

own good fortune in having survived the person whom he found in possession of the office, rather than to the gracious beneficence of his royal master. If we forget the interests of the Crown to regard only the personal advantage of the Prince who happens at present to wear it, we may well suppose the prohibition of all such grants to be injurious; but if we regard the Crown, not as an estate for life, but as a permanent inheritance, no doubt surely can be entertained upon the subject. I say nothing of the interests of the people, because I cannot think that, upon this point, they are at all different from those of the Crown.

Ireland.

13th. Sheridan moved a resolution in the House of Commons respecting Ireland. The purport of it was, that Parliament would, early in the next Session, take the state of that part of the empire into its most serious consideration. The motion, it is hardly necessary to say, was lost. The minority, which voted for it, was 33; the majority, which rejected it, 76.[1]

Parliament prorogued.

14th. On this day the Parliament was prorogued. The Royal Assent was given by commission on the same day to many different Bills; amongst others, to the Bill which I had brought into the House of Commons, to subject the real estates of traders who die indebted to the payment of their simple contract debts. The Bill was put off from day to day, till the very last hour at which it could pass, by the Lord Chancellor; whose doubting and fluctuating mind considered again and again, whether some unforeseen inconvenience, which he knew not how to represent to himself, might not possibly

Bill to make freehold estates of traders' assets.

[1] Sir S. Romilly voted in the minority. — Ed.

attend it in practice. At one time he was strongly disposed to throw it out, thinking it too late in the Session to consider sufficiently so important a measure, as he was pleased to call it. He one day sent for me into his room at Lincoln's Inn Hall, and showed me two clauses which he had drawn, and which he proposed to add to the Bill, and asked me what I thought of them. They were so obscure, that, after reading them repeatedly, I found myself, very reluctantly and with great shame, obliged to ask him what the object of them was. He explained to me that they were intended to enable the heir of a trader who should die seised of a real estate more than sufficient to pay his debts, to sell part of the estate, leaving the rest to answer the demands of creditors. Without this explanation, I certainly never should have collected, from the words of the proposed clauses, that that was their object. The Bill, as it stood, did not prevent the heir from selling the whole of the real estate, and gave the creditors no power of following it in the hands of a purchaser; such clauses, therefore, were altogether unnecessary. I satisfied the Chancellor of this, and he gave up his clauses; and at last suffered the Bill to pass just as it came up from the Commons, with the addition of a few words only, to prevent its being so construed as to destroy the distinction, which now prevails in courts of equity, between legal and equitable assets. *

* Query.— Whether there was such an addition [1]; and see the Act, 47 Geo. 3. sess. 2. c. 74. Such an addition would certainly have been unnecessary.

[1] No such addition was made; the Act is in the same words as the Bill when first introduced.— Ed.

Lord Redesdale had opposed the Bill in some of its stages; and, what seemed very strange, considering that he was a decided enemy to the first Bill which I brought into the House of Commons, he moved in the committee to leave out the words confining the operation of the Bill to traders, and to make it apply generally to the freehold estates of persons of all descriptions. The reason he assigned was, that it would open a great field for litigation, to ascertain whether a man was, or was not, at the time of his death, a trader within the Bankrupt Laws. But as he was an enemy to the measure altogether, his real object perhaps was to have the Bill thrown out upon its being returned to the Commons, which it infallibly would have been if the amendment had been carried.

While the Bill was depending in the House of Lords, it occurred to me more forcibly than it had ever done before, that a bad use might possibly be made of the Bill, by having recourse to the expensive proceedings of a Chancery suit, in cases where a trader had died seised of a very small real estate; and, in order to obviate this evil, I suggested to the Chancellor to amend the Bill, by restraining its operation to cases where the real estate of the trader was of the clear yearly value of 10*l.* or upwards. But, upon further reflection I thought that this would rather have a tendency to increase than to diminish expensive litigations. It would in many cases be made a question, whether the deceased debtor's estate was of that value; and, as we see continually in Chancery, witnesses would be examined, at an expense greater than the whole value of the estate, to prove what its real value was. The Chancellor concurred in this objection, as he had before concurred in the proposed amendment; and the Bill, as passed, extends to all the freehold estates of traders, without any limitation in point of value. It will occasion undoubtedly some improper suits; but that is an evil which admits of no other remedy than a reform of the Court of Chancery. There are already improper suits to compel the administration of the *personal* estates of deceased debtors; but no person can imagine that the proper remedy for this evil would be to exempt personal assets from the payment of debts.

21st. I left town for the long vacation, intending to pass it at Cowes in the Isle of Wight with my family.

Answering cases professionally.

I have some cases which I have been unable for some time past, during my close attendance in court, to answer; and these I very reluctantly take with me into the country; but I am determined not to let any fresh cases be sent after me. If I were to suffer this, I should have full occupation, and occupation of a kind extremely disagreeable to me, during the whole vacation. The truth is, that, for the last two or three years, I have declined, as much as I well could, the giving of opinions. It is so important that one's opinion should be right (for in many cases it has the effect of a decision to the parties, and in others it involves them in expensive litigations); and at the same time it is so difficult, in the state of uncertainty which the law is in, to satisfy one's mind upon many questions put to one; and, in many cases, it must depend so much upon the particular mode of thinking of the judge before whom the question may happen to be brought, what the decision will be, that I have long found this to be the most irksome part of my profession.

Manner of passing my time in the Isle of Wight.

Oct. 16th. On this day I quitted the Isle of Wight. The time I spent there was passed very happily. For the last five weeks my excellent friend Dumont was with us, and added much to the pleasure of our society. If the state of public affairs had been less alarming, I might have reckoned this vacation among the happiest periods of my life. A letter which I wrote to Dumont to invite him to join us, gives so correct a picture of my situation at Cowes, that I shall perhaps hereafter have great pleasure in recollecting it; and will therefore preserve a copy of it.

Dear Dumont, Cowes, Aug. 25. 1807.

We arrived here last Saturday; and, though so short a time has elapsed, I seem to be quite settled here, and am enjoying what seems to me like perfect leisure. Not that I have yet really got rid of all business. To escape from town as early as I have done, I was obliged to encumber myself with a few remaining cases; but I shall very soon have answered them, and then shall have nothing to do all the day but to amuse myself with the books I have brought with me, to stroll about the country or sail upon the sea, and admire the cheerful and varied scenes with which this neighbourhood abounds. My only business, if business it can be called, is, that I have undertaken to be William's preceptor for an hour or two every day, lest he should forget, while he is here, all that the Abbé Buchet has taught him. I never enjoyed this kind of life more than at the present moment. The hot weather we have had in town, the ten hours a day which I have been almost uninterruptedly passing for some weeks in the Court of Chancery, the House of Lords, and the Rolls, with the addition of now and then a very late night in the House of Commons, had given me a most ardent longing for the country; and I am now almost satiating myself with its delights. I hope to enjoy, for some weeks at least, the greatest of earthly blessings, — the most perfect calm and tranquillity, in a beautiful country, and with those who are dearest to me in the world. Who knows but this may be the last summer of my life, in which it will be permitted to me to have such enjoyments! What is passing abroad, and what is passing at home, affords us but a melancholy prospect; and a man with but a little foresight, and only a slight attention to what he sees, even though he be not either of a very gloomy or a very timid disposition, must think that this country will be fortunate indeed if it is not soon involved, and perhaps for a very long period, in turbulence and disasters. These, however, are reflections which I endeavour to banish from my mind; and, as nothing that I can do can avert any of the misfortunes which threaten us, I indulge myself in enjoying the good that is still, and perhaps will not long be, within my reach.

You talked of paying us a visit; nay, I think you promised us one. I hope you will not fail to keep your promise. Come and see how tranquil, how uniform, and how happy a life we lead &c. &c.[1]

Soon after writing this letter, I found for myself some occupations not mentioned in it, and which were to me a source of great enjoyment. I began to put down in writing some observations on my present situation in life, and my future prospects; in the course of which, I indulged myself with passing in review some projects for the public benefit, which there seems no probability indeed that I shall ever realize. But the mere contemplation of them, though only a kind of delusive vision, afforded me so much delight, that I cannot think my time was ill spent; and though the paper is but an imperfect fragment[2], I mean to preserve it, as there is a

[1] The letter proceeds thus: — Ed. " Come and partake of our happiness. I should rather address myself to your generosity, and say, come and add to it, for your society will very greatly add to that happiness which is already ours. We can give you a bed-chamber; one that is small indeed, but yet so pleasant, that if you should wish any part of the day to be quite by yourself, you will not, I think, have any objection to make your bed-chamber your study. At any rate pray let us hear from you, and without delay. We think of staying here perhaps till the middle, but certainly till the beginning of October. Among the few books I have brought with me, are Bentham's yet unpublished pamphlet on the 'Reform of the Scotch Judicature,' and 'Bacon de Augmentis Scientiarum.' In Bacon, I have just met with a description of a class of writers who lived a little before his time, amongst whom I am afraid that, in some respects, our friend may be ranked. 'Verba licenter admodum cudentes nova et horrida, de orationis ornatu et elegantia parum solliciti, dum modo circuitionem evitarent et sensus ac conceptus suos acute exprimerent.'

" When you arrive here, inquire for Captain Hoskins', for that is the house we are living in. Anne desires to be particularly remembered to you."

[2] The paper here referred to, together with some others written with the same view, and under the influence of the same feelings, will be found at the end of Vol. III. — Ed.

possibility (though but a possibility) that it may at some future time be useful to me.

Criminal Law.

There were other projects to which I devoted some portion of my time at Cowes, which I have a better prospect of carrying into execution, and which I need not defer attempting to any distant period. I have long been struck with the gross defects which there are in our Criminal Law, and with the serious evils which result from our present mode of administering it. When I first went the circuit, which is now twenty-three years ago, some instances of judicial injustice which I met with made a deep impression on me; and I resolved to attempt some reform of the system, if I ever should have an opportunity of doing it with any prospect of success. It would give me great concern to have been some time in the House of Commons without making any such attempt; and yet my parliamentary life may now be hastening quickly to an end. There is a petition against my return, and it will be one of the first disposed of in the approaching session. What I have it in contemplation to do, however, compared with what should be done, is very little. It is only, in the first place, to invest criminal courts with a power of making to persons who shall have been accused of felonies, and shall have been acquitted, a compensation, to be paid out of the county rates, for the expenses they will have been put to, the loss of time they will have incurred, the imprisonment and the other evils they will have suffered: not to provide that there should be a compensation awarded in all cases of acquittal, but merely that the Court, judging of all the circumstances of the case, should have a power, if it thinks proper, to order such a compensation to be paid, and to fix the amount of it; a power similar to that which it now has under two acts passed in the reign of Geo. II.[1], to allow the expenses of the prosecution, and a compensation for loss of time and trouble to the prosecutor.

The only other object I had in view was to remove that severity in our law which has arisen from no intention of the Legislature, but altogether from accidental circumstances; and in all the cases of felonies made capital, according to the value of the thing stolen, and where, by the depreciation of money which has since taken place, that standard of guilt has become far different from what it originally was, to re-enact the laws, fixing the sums mentioned in them much higher, and according to the difference between the then and the present value of money. This ought long ago to have been done. As all the articles of life have been gradually for many years becoming dearer, the life of man has, in the contemplation of the Legislature, been growing cheaper and of less account. A stop ought to be put to that shameful trifling with oaths, to those pious perjuries (as Blackstone somewhere calls them), by which juries are humanely induced to find things not to be worth a tenth part of what is notoriously their value.

I occupied myself a good deal with these two objects, and in writing down the arguments by which I should endeavour to recommend them to the House, and the answers to such objections as

[1] 25 Geo. 2. c. 36. s. 11. and 28 Geo. 2. c. 19.—Ed.

appeared to me likely to be made to them. I drew, too, one of the intended Bills, that to provide a compensation for persons wrongfully accused; but, not having the statutes with me, I could not prepare the other Bill.

Upon quitting the Isle of Wight I proceeded with Anne to Bath, where her sister, Mrs. Whittaker, who was to have joined us at Cowes, and had set out on her journey, was stopped by illness, and was still confined when we arrived there on the 17th of October.

October 19th. I set out for Durham, leaving Anne at Bath, and intending to return for her and to accompany her to town.

Court at Durham.

23d. I held my sittings, as Chancellor, at Durham. The business, as usual, was very inconsiderable.

24th. I sat in an adjourned Court of Gaol Delivery, a Court which is continued by adjournments from time to time, from one assizes to another; and which the Durham justices had adjourned to the day on which I was to be there, in order that they might have my assistance in deciding on an application made to them by a prisoner, committed for a capital felony, to be admitted to bail. The offence was that of firing at a man with a gun loaded with shot, which is made capital by the statute [43] Geo. III. c. [58.] commonly called Lord Ellenborough's Act. Upon the circumstances, as they appeared in the affidavits, it was clear that, if the man had been killed, it would not have been murder, but only manslaughter. I therefore thought, although the Act is in this respect very defectively expressed, that the prisoner would, if the facts should appear the same upon his trial, be entitled to his acquittal, and that he ought to be bailed; which was accordingly done. If bail had not been accepted for this man, he must have remained in gaol for ten months; as the next assizes at Durham, where they are held only once a year, will not be till late in August. After having suffered an imprisonment of eleven months (for he has been above a month in prison already), it would have been declared by the verdict of the jury that he was not deserving of any punishment.*

After dining with the Bishop at Auckland, I went on and slept at Catterick Bridge. The next night, *Oct.* 25th, I slept at Chesterfield; the 26th, at Worcester; the 27th, at Bath. On the 29th I arrived in London. The next day, the 30th, the Lord Chancellor held his first seal before the Michaelmas Term.

* At the ensuing assizes in 1808 this man was acquitted.

1808.

Jan. 21st. Parliament met. A debate on the King's speech took place in both Houses; and, in the Lords, an amendment was moved by the Duke of Norfolk, to leave out of the Address those words which import an approbation of the expedition against Copenhagen. There was no division in either House, and not even an amendment moved in the Commons. It had been very industriously given out, for some days before the meeting of Parliament, that the Address would be very general, would be so framed as to pledge the House to nothing, and would not admit of any opposition. The members of the Opposition were deceived by these representations, and were unprepared to move an amendment, as they certainly ought to have done.

Meeting of Parliament.

23d. I dined to-day at Lord Erskine's. It was what might be called a great Opposition dinner: the party consisted of the Duke of Norfolk, Lord Grenville, Lord Grey, Lord Holland, Lord Ellenborough, Lord Lauderdale, Lord Henry Petty, Thomas Grenville, Tierney, Piggott, Adam, Edward Morris (Lord Erskine's son-in-law), and myself. This was the whole company, with the addition of one person; but that one, the man most unfit to be invited to such a party that could have been

Lord Erskine.

found, if such a man had been anxiously looked for. It was no other than Mr. Pinkney, the American Minister: this, at a time when the Opposition are accused of favouring America to the injury of their own country, and when Erskine himself is charged with being particularly devoted to the Americans. These are topics which are every day insisted on with the utmost malevolence in all the Ministerial newspapers*, and particularly in Cobbett. If, however, the most malignant enemies of Erskine had been present, they would have admitted that nothing could be more innocent than the conversation which passed. Politics were hardly mentioned; and Mr. Pinkney's presence evidently imposed a restraint upon every body.

Among the light and trifling topics of conversation after dinner, it may be worth while to mention one, as it strongly characterises Lord Erskine. He has always expressed and felt a great sympathy for animals. He has talked for years of a Bill he was to bring into Parliament to prevent cruelty towards them. He has always had several favourite animals, to whom he has been much attached, and of whom all his acquaintance have a number of anecdotes to relate, — a favourite dog, which he used to bring when he was at the bar to all his consultations; another favourite dog, which, at the time when he was Lord Chancellor, he himself rescued in the street from some boys who were about to kill him, under pretence of its being

* By a very strange good fortune this dinner never was mentioned in the newspapers.

mad; a favourite goose, which followed him wherever he walked about his grounds; a favourite mackaw, and other dumb favourites without number. He told us now that he had got two favourite leeches. He had been blooded by them last Autumn, when he had been taken dangerously ill at Portsmouth; they had saved his life, and he had brought them with him to town; had ever since kept them in a glass; had himself every day given them fresh water; and had formed a friendship with them. He said he was sure they both knew him, and were grateful to him. He had given them different names, Home and Cline (the names of two celebrated surgeons), their dispositions being quite different. After a good deal of conversation about them, he went himself, brought them out of his library, and placed them in their glass upon the table. It is impossible, however, without the vivacity, the tones, the details, and the gestures of Lord Erskine, to give an adequate idea of this singular scene.

Criminal Law

I have for the present given up the intention I had entertained, of bringing a Bill into Parliament to make some improvements in the Criminal Law. George Wilson has dissuaded me from it. He thinks that, unless I first consult the judges upon it, not only I am not likely to carry it, but I shall in all probability prejudice any attempts at improving the law which I may make at any future time, and under more favourable circumstances. A better judgment than Wilson's upon such a subject there cannot be, and I reluctantly submit to be governed by it. I cannot think of consulting the judges; I have not the least hope that they would approve of the measure; besides, before I could get their opinion on it, the petition may be decided against me and I may be out of Parliament.

[*Feb.* 1st.] Upon the third reading of the Bill to prevent granting offices in reversion, I said a few words to draw if I could from the Ministers their opinion on it; but without success, except that Perceval, as he had done formerly, said that he looked on the Bill with great indifference.

Lord Wellesley.

22d. The papers respecting Lord Wellesley's conduct in the affair of the Nabob of Oude, were this day to have been taken into consideration in the House of Commons. I spoke in support of a motion made by Creevey, that the papers should be referred to a committee to report upon them. Though the papers have been long printed, yet, as they are extremely voluminous, and as no statement has ever been made to the House which can assist any person who reads them, or direct his attention to any particular parts of them, they will never be read; and the House will decide upon the question in total ignorance of its merits. I have endeavoured to make myself master of the subject; and the conduct of Lord Wellesley appears to me to be unjustifiable. Creevey's motion was lost; and the debate on resolutions, afterwards moved by Lord Folkestone, was adjourned to a future day.

23d. At the particular request of the Bishop of Durham, I went into the Court of King's Bench upon the trial of his cause with Col. Beaumont.

The Horsham Petition decided against me.

26th, *Fri.* The Committee on the Horsham Petition, which had decided all the questions raised by the counsel in favour of the sitting members, on this day finally decided against them, upon a question of law, which had never been insisted on by the counsel for the petition, and which was quite incapable of being supported. The effect of it, however, is to exclude me from Parliament, and to put an end, certainly for the present, and perhaps for ever, to my political existence.

My election for Wareham.

March 26th. My absence from Parliament is not likely to be of long duration. Lord Henry Petty has had some conversation with Calcraft about one of the seats at Wareham; and though Calcraft knows how little I was to have given for my seat at Horsham, he says that that circumstance does not afford an insuperable objection to my being returned for Wareham.

April 1st. Piggott took occasion to speak to Calcraft on the subject of Wareham, and this morning informed me that I might have the seat for 2000*l.*, the sum which I was to have paid for Horsham; but that, though I was to pay no more, Calcraft would receive 3000*l.*; the remaining 1000*l.* being paid out of a fund which, till now, I did not know existed, and which has been formed, as I understand, by the most distinguished persons in Opposition, to answer extraordinary occasions. I was staggered at the first mention of this, and stated my objections to Piggott. He told me that he did not see how I could consider it as in any respect objectionable; that the principal persons of Opposition were very anxious that I should be in Parliament, and only regretted that I should be at any expense at all. I cannot, however, persuade myself to accept a seat upon these terms; and accordingly, in the evening, I wrote Piggott a note in these words: — "It is impossible to be more sensible than I am of the very kind and friendly part which you have taken for me. But, after reflecting on what was the subject of our conversation this morning, I feel a very great reluctance to consent to let the matter be arranged in the way that has been proposed. I am afraid that, after the matter is settled, I shall feel uncomfortable about it; and I had rather at once determine to be at all the expense myself. Do not ascribe this to any pretensions to an extraordinary degree of delicacy; I really have no such pretensions; but where one is in doubt, it is best to be on the safe side; and as it is only a pecuniary sacrifice that is to be made, it is a great satisfaction to be quite sure that one will not hereafter have cause to repent of what one has done. I must again and again thank you for your kindness to me, upon this, and upon former occasions."

The matter has been settled with Mr. Calcraft accordingly, and I pay the whole 3000*l.* myself.

14th. Sir Granby Calcraft, who sat for Wareham, vacated, by accepting the Chiltern Hundreds.

20th. I was this day elected. Though Mr. Calcraft has the entire command of the borough, he wished me to go down, which I accordingly did.

Criminal Law.

During the short time that I was out of Parliament, I regretted very much that I had made no attempt to mitigate the severity of the criminal law. It appeared to me that merely to have brought the subject under the view of the public, and to have made it a matter of parliamentary discussion, would, though my motion had been rejected, have been attended with good effects. On coming again into parliament, therefore, I determined to resume my original design. In the meantime, I had had some conversation on the subject with my friend Scarlett[1]; and he had advised me not to content myself with merely raising the amount of the value of property, the stealing of which is to subject the offender to capital punishment, but to attempt at once to repeal all the statutes which punish with death mere thefts, unaccompanied by any act of violence, or other circumstance of aggravation. This suggestion was very agreeable to me. But, as it appeared to me that I had no chance of being able to carry through the House a Bill which was to expunge at once all these laws from the statute book, I determined to attempt the repeal of them one by one; and to begin with the most odious of them, the Act of Queen Elizabeth[2], which makes it a capital offence to steal privately from the person of another.

May 18th, *Wed.* Having previously given notice of my intention, I this day moved for leave to bring in, first, a Bill to repeal the statute of Queen Elizabeth; and, secondly, a Bill for granting compensation, in certain cases, to persons tried for felonies and acquitted. To the first of these motions no

[1] Now Lord Abinger. — Ed.

[2] 8 Eliz. c. 4. — Ed.

direct opposition was given; but Mr. Herbert, the member for Kerry, talked about the danger of innovation, and the excellence of our Criminal Law; and, not opposing the motion, announced an intention of opposing the Bill. The other motion was resisted by Plumer, the Solicitor-General. I had declared that it was not my intention to propose a compensation in all cases; but to follow the model of the statute of 25 Geo. II. [c. 36.], with respect to the reimbursing to prosecutors the expenses of their prosecutions, and affording them a compensation for their trouble and loss of time; and to leave it to the Court by whom the prisoner is tried whether he should have any, and what, compensation. Such a law, Plumer said, would impose on the Judges a very difficult and odious task; and it would establish a distinction between acquittals with the approbation, and those without the approbation of the Judge, which he represented as very dangerous and unconstitutional. Sir Francis Burdett indeed, before Plumer, had stated the same objection; and I find that it is considered as a very serious one by many members of the House; which I confess much astonishes me. If the effect of a verdict of acquittal was to restore a man completely to his good name, and to send him with an unblemished character into the world, it would be very dangerous to give to the Judges any power of weakening such a certificate of innocence; but it is well known that, in practice, this is far from being the effect of an acquittal. So notorious is it, that men may be, and every day are acquitted, in consequence of some error of form or some de-

Compensation to persons wrongfully accused.

fect of evidence, that to have been tried is, in general, alone sufficient to destroy a man's character; and a poor wretch who issues forth from a prison will no where find employment, even though he may boast of an acquittal. That a man comes out of a jail is a fact which is plain and notorious; and who, in the case of a person in a state of the lowest indigence, will take the trouble to inquire into the circumstances of his case? The being able to produce a certificate of the Judge allowing his expenses would be decisive evidence of his innocence; the not producing such a certificate would only leave the party in the state in which all acquitted men are at this moment, that is, in a state in which it is doubtful whether they were really innocent or guilty.

Croker, an Irish Member, and Shaw Lefevre, once a lawyer, and now a country gentleman, also disapproved of the intended Bill; the latter, because it would impose a burthen on the county rates, the fund out of which I had proposed that the compensation should be paid. Perceval expressed great doubt about the measure, but thought that leave ought to be given to bring the Bill in; and leave was given accordingly.[1]

Poor Laws as to settlements.

May 19th, *Th.* Colonel Stanley, at the importunity (as he told me) of some of his constituents, has brought in a Bill to increase the difficulty of paupers acquiring settlements in parishes, by raising the yearly sum at which a tenement must be rented to gain a settlement to considerably more than

[1] The Compensation Bill was afterwards withdrawn.—Ed.

10*l.*[1], and the consideration for the purchase of a freehold estate which will confer a settlement to more than 30*l.* I opposed the Bill very shortly; and, availing myself of so favourable an opportunity, stated what mischievous effects had arisen from the law of settlements; and that, in my opinion, the most beneficial act upon the subject that could be passed, would be one to abolish the law of settlements altogether; and that the next best act would be, instead of increasing the difficulties of acquiring settlements, to render the acquisition of them more easy; as, by making a six months' residence, under any circumstances, gain a settlement. Many other persons spoke against the Bill, and it was rejected by a very great majority.[2]

Too great frequency of Oaths.

[30th,] *Mon.* In a committee of the whole House on the Local Militia Bill, I spoke against one of the clauses, which required a person drawn and paying the penalty to make oath that no one had contributed any thing towards enabling him to pay it. I endeavoured to impress, as forcibly as I could, upon the House, the mischiefs arising from the frequency of oaths which prevails in this country; how much it tends to make men think lightly of the obligations of an oath, and to increase perjuries. Windham and several other members also opposed it; and the clause was rejected.

Pensions to Scotch Judges who retire.

June 2d. I opposed so much of the Bill for giving pensions to retiring Scotch Judges as re-

[1] The Bill proposed to raise the yearly rent to 20*l.*; and the consideration for the purchase of a freehold estate to 100*l.* Hansard, vol. ii. p. 423.—Ed.

[2] The numbers were, in favour of the second reading of the Bill, 11; against it, 114.—Ed.

lated to Barons of the Exchequer. The truth is, that there is so little law business to be done by the Barons, that their offices are rather nominally than really judicial; and the consequence of giving them pensions, on their retiring from what may be considered as being already a sort of retirement, will be, that bargains will probably be made with persons who have an expectation of preferment to the bench, to pay them an annuity of such an amount that, added to the pension from Government, it will make the retiring judge's income just as large as it was before; and that persons, perfectly capable of discharging the very slender duties which belong to the office, will make way for others not at all more competent than themselves; and a very useless burden of expense will be fixed on the public.

Criminal law. Privately stealing from the person.

15th. The House went into a committee on my Bill to repeal the Statute of Elizabeth; and a pretty long debate took place upon it. Burton, the Welsh Judge, began it. He objected to the Bill as it was framed; it being simply a repeal of the Statute of Elizabeth, leaving the offence mere larceny, punishable with only seven years' transportation. He thought that the Judges ought to have power to inflict a much severer punishment, extending to transportation for life; and, unless this alteration were made in the Bill, he said that he should vote against it. He stated that the crime of picking pockets had become extremely common, and was increasing; and mentioned that at Chester, where he sits as judge, he had to try for this offence a great number of boys, who seemed to be educated to this way of life. This argument, that the crime was increasing, and that therefore there ought not to be any mitigation of the severity of the law, was also much insisted on by Plumer. It appeared to me, and I stated, that these were rather arguments for, than against the Bill. What better reason can be given for altering the law, than that it is not efficacious; and that, instead of its preventing crimes, crimes are multiplied under its operation? And if an alteration there must be, what can it be but to render the punishment less severe, but more certain in its operation? To add to its severity is impossible, since we already provide the same punishment for pickpockets and for murderers. Plumer observed that the utmost punishment which the Judges could inflict under the Bill as it stood, — namely, transportation for seven years, — was one of the most objectionable punishments that could be inflicted; that, when transportation was resorted to, it should be for a longer period, or for life; a seven years' transportation only rendering the criminal more hardened and depraved, and turning him loose, at the end of the seven years, a man more dangerous to society than he had ever been before. Upon this I observed, that if this were an accurate representation, some alteration in our punishments ought very speedily to be adopted; because, at present, three times as many offenders are transported for seven years as are transported for any longer period; and that it was an extraordinary argument for having recourse to punishments inordinately severe, that we had made a very injudicious choice of slighter punishments. I had, some time before, suggested to Abercromby[1] to institute an inquiry into the state of the colony of New South Wales, and the efficacy of that species of punishment; a task which it is impossible for me, occupied as I am, to undertake, without altogether abandoning my profession. Abercromby, who is always zealous in promoting objects of public utility, readily entered into my views; and he now took the opportunity, which this debate afforded him, of giving notice that he should, early in the next Session, move for a committee on the subject. I have the highest opinion of Abercromby, and think him likely to render most essential service to the country. He has a very enlightened mind, an excellent understanding, very just principles of political economy, an independent spirit, and a warm love of liberty; and he has the more merit, because all his connexions are Tories. If I do not mistake, his brother married a daughter of Lord Melville.

Preamble of the Bill to repeal the Statute of Elizabeth.

Amongst other parts of the Bill, Plumer objected strongly to the preamble; which, however, was nothing more than this. It first recited the Act of Elizabeth, and then went on in these words: "And whereas the extreme severity of penal laws hath not been found effectual for the prevention of crimes; but, on the contrary, by increasing the difficulty of convicting offenders, in some cases affords them impunity, and in most cases renders their punishment extremely uncertain. And whereas, the Act herein-before recited hath, by

[1] The late Speaker of the House of Commons, now Lord Dunfermline.—Ed.

the great diminution of the value of money, become much more severe than was originally intended." Plumer said that it was extremely dangerous to insert such abstract principles in Acts of Parliament, and to pronounce, by taking notice of the alteration which has taken place in the law by reason of the diminution in the value of money, a condemnation upon a great part of the law, as it at present exists, and is daily executed. Though I thought this a most futile objection, and that the preamble ought to stand, yet it was not of sufficient importance to risk the loss of the Bill. I consented, therefore, to its being struck out; and it was agreed that the Bill should be printed with Plumer's alterations and additions, and be recommitted on a future day.

Plumer told me that he had consulted several of the Judges, and that they approved his alteration of the Bill. He showed me a letter from Lord Ellenborough, in which he says that, if any alteration in the law were necessary, of which he was by no means satisfied, he was clearly of opinion that the Judges ought to have a power of transporting for life. This did not surprise me. I knew the severity of Lord Ellenborough's disposition, and had therefore avoided consulting him before I brought either of the Bills in. I thought it proper, however (considering the great civility which he has always shown to me), to make him some apology for this omission; and accordingly, in a letter which I wrote to him, I gave him the best reasons I could for it. His answer to me was in these words: —

"My dear Sir,

"I assure you that, if I had not received the favour of your note, I was not at all likely to have attributed the non-communication of your plan respecting the Criminal Law to any want of that attention and kindness which I have always experienced from you. Perhaps it was as well that you did not previously apprize me of your intentions, as you did not mean to communicate with the other Judges on the subject. I shall be happy to find your plan such as I may fully approve. If I should not, I shall, with great respect for its author, do that which my own impressions of duty may require of me upon the occasion; as you will of course expect and wish that I should. I remain, with great respect and regard, my dear sir, very sincerely yours, ELLENBOROUGH.

"Bl^ry^ Sq^re^, May 17th, 1808."

If any person be desirous of having an adequate idea of the mischievous effects which have been produced in this country by the French Revolution and all its attendant horrors, he should attempt some legislative reform, on humane and liberal principles. He will then find, not only what a stupid dread of innovation, but what a savage spirit it has infused into the minds of many of his countrymen. I have had several opportunities of observing this. It is but a few nights ago, that, while I was standing at the bar of the House of Commons, a young man, the brother of a peer, whose name is not worth setting down, came up to me, and breathing in my face the nauseous fumes of his undigested debauch, stammered out, "I am against your Bill; I am for hanging all." I was confounded; and, endeavouring to find out some excuse for him, I observed that I supposed he meant that the certainty of punishment affording the only prospect of suppressing crimes, the laws, whatever they were, ought to be executed. "No, no," he said, "it is not that. There is no good done by mercy. They only get worse; I would hang them all up at once."

Tax on alienation of property.

16th. The House went into a committee on the Bill for imposing new stamp duties. I opposed the new duty on all conveyances and assignments of property, the amount of which is to be in proportion to the consideration for the conveyance, on the ground that, as a tax on property, it was extremely unequal, since it would fall only on such property as the proprietors were obliged to sell; that it was a tax therefore on distress; that it would necessarily fall on the seller, because the buyer would allow for it, in calculating the price which it would be worth his while to give; that where estates were sold to pay debts, it would in many cases operate as an increase of loss to the creditors, it would be a deduction from the dividends they were to receive; that, when coupled with the auction duty, it was grievously oppressive; and that estates which men were compelled by distress or insolvency to sell, they were generally compelled to sell by auction. These were arguments which it is hardly necessary to say made no impression on the committee.

Tax on law proceedings.

The act imposes new duties on law proceedings;

particularly on warrants for attendances in the offices of Masters in Chancery. I intended fully to have resisted this, and to have stated the great injustice, and the mischievous effects, of imposing any taxes on judicial proceedings; but I lost the opportunity of doing it. Not imagining it possible that the Bill could pass through the committee in one night, I left the House about one o'clock in the morning. A very few of the clauses of the Bill had then been gone through, and almost every clause had given rise to a good deal of discussion; a great many clauses remained; and the tax on law proceedings, being only in the schedule, was last to be considered. The next morning, however, I found that Perceval, whose object it is to hurry through the business as much as possible, had resisted the postponement of the further consideration of the Bill, and had insisted on its going through the committee, which was done at three in the morning, when very few members remained in the House.

I should afterwards have objected to this tax, upon the third reading; but the Bill was read a third time, on a subsequent day, in a very thin House, at two o'clock in the morning, when no one expected that it would come on; though it is true that it stood, with a great many other Bills, as an order of the day. Many persons had clauses which they meant to propose; but not having the least intimation that, at such an hour, this Bill would be selected from among the other orders of the day to be hurried through, they were prevented from doing so.

Affairs of the Carnatic.

17th. The further proceeding on the question respecting the conduct of Lord Wellesley against the Nabob of the Carnatic was fixed for to-day. It had been fixed on Sheridan's account, who, after having again and again announced his intention of speaking on this question, had always deferred doing it. There were few persons in the gallery, and hardly more than forty members in the House. It was the two last of Sir Thomas Turton's series of resolutions which were to be disposed of. The first was put; Sheridan remained silent; no other member attempted to speak. The question was put; a division took place; and the motion was lost. The Speaker then proceeded to put the last question; the same silence prevailed; the votes on both sides were given; and the Speaker was just about to declare that the motion was rejected, when I got up. I had intended to speak in the course of the debate which was expected, but I had no thought of taking the lead in it; and nothing but my unwillingness to let the question be put, without stating the sense I entertained of the flagrant injustice which had been done to the Nabob, could have induced me to take the part I did. I was, however, very well master of the case, and was able to show very clearly the flagrant violations of law and justice which had attended every part of the proceeding.* None of the Ministers had opened their lips upon the sub-

* I had intended to have taken a part in the debates upon the transactions respecting the Nabob of Oude, and had read all the papers; but just before the question was discussed, the decision of the Horsham Committee put me out of Parliament.

ject; but, by observing on their unaccountable silence, I forced Lord Castlereagh to rise, and to enter very fully into Lord Wellesley's defence; and a wretched defence he made for him. Sheridan spoke, but not at any length; and the question was lost.[1]

Scotch Judicature appeals to the House of Lords.

21st. In the committee on the Scotch Judicature Bill, I resisted the clause which takes away appeals from the Court of Session to the House of Lords upon all interlocutory orders. The injustice of forcing suitors to go on with a cause till its final close, at great expense, and for many years to be spent in litigation, when a decision on an interlocutory question often decides the whole merits of the case, was so obvious, that I could not have thought it possible that such a provision could have received the approbation of any man accustomed to the proceedings either of an English Court of Equity or of the Scotch Courts of Justice. It had, however, it seems, the full approbation of the Chancellor. Upon my motion, an amendment was adopted, allowing the appeal upon interlocutory orders in all cases in which there is any difference of opinion in the Court.

Oyster stealing made felony.

22d. A Bill had been brought into the House to make the stealing of oysters from oyster fisheries felony, and was read a third time to-day. I opposed it, but without success. I thought the punishment too severe; and that, after what had been recently stated in the House, as to the inexpediency of transporting men for seven years for

[1] By a majority of 78; the numbers being for the resolution 97, against it 19.—Ed.

any offence, it was very unjustifiable to make that the punishment for new offences.[1]

Parliament prorogued.

July 4th. Parliament was prorogued. The Bill I brought in to take away the punishment of death for the crime of privately stealing from the person passed, with the alterations Plumer had made in it, into a law. It is the 48 Geo. III. c. 129. In the House of Lords it passed without opposition, and without a word being said upon it.

Privately Stealing Bill.

Aug. 20th. Being determined to enjoy as much as possible of the long vacation, I left town the first moment that the business of the Court of Chancery would allow me. The Chancellor sat this morning, and in the evening I left town, and slept at Salt Hill.

I passed the vacation almost entirely at Knill. G. Wilson and Dumont spent a great part of it with us, and accompanied us in a very delightful tour down the Wye. Dumont brought with him to Knill several MSS. of Bentham's, which he is translating and arranging, in order to publish them, as a continuation of the work of which he has already printed three volumes. One of them, a treatise on punishments, appears to me to have very extraordinary merit, and to be likely to be more popular than most of Bentham's writings, and to produce very good effects. I strongly exhorted Dumont to finish it without delay, and to publish it, if possible, in the ensuing winter; and

Bentham's Treatise on Punishments.

[1] On the same day, Sir S. Romilly opposed so much of the Copy Right Bill as secured to the libraries of the Universities and other public libraries copies of all newly printed books and books reprinted with additions; on the ground, that it was unjust to lay upon authors the exclusive burden of a contribution which was not for their exclusive benefit, but for the benefit of the public at large. — Ed.

he has promised to do so.* Since the work of Beccaria, nothing has appeared on the subject of Criminal Law which has made any impression on the public. This work will, I think, probably make a very deep impression.[1]

* It was afterwards published in July, 1811, in London, under the title of "Théorie des Peines et des Récompenses."

---

[1] The following letter from Dr. Parr was received in the vacation of this year. It refers to the two Bills brought into Parliament by Sir S. Romilly in the preceding session; one to abolish the punishment of death for the offence of stealing privily from the person, the other to give to the judges a discretionary power of granting pecuniary compensation to persons who had been tried for felony and acquitted. See p. 245. — Ed.

"Dear Sir, September 28. 1808.

"I read your wise and interesting letter with great eagerness and great satisfaction, and I thank you for taking the trouble to write it. Fearing that you might be absent, I applied to Lord Holland, who sent me a copy of the statute. It confirms all the fears and all the hopes which the debates had excited in my mind, and it lies open to all the objections which I had put to paper. My good friend, the last conversation which I had with Mr. Fox turned upon our penal code, and upon the testiness and responsibility of judges. Now, in something which I have printed about Mr. Fox, I could not fail to notice the fondness he had for trouncing your loquacious and quibbling brethren of the craft, and I was led to say a good deal of which he would have approved, in a note on our penal laws. I love them not, and I have not spared their principles, or the furred homicides who administer them. But all is done gravely, decorously, legally, morally, and sometimes, in obedience to the dictates of my own heart, even religiously. I have quoted our friend Jeremiah[a] (the prophet of the law) again and again; and, as you lawyers may look upon a parson as an intruder, I have often called in the aid of allies from our writers on jurisprudence, such, dear sir, as you read and approve, such as I understand, and such as the sable bigots in Westminster Hall detest or disregard. Well, out comes your statute, or rather the debate upon it. My heart was gladdened, and I made very large additions to the note. In plain truth, I have spoken my mind upon all the general principles which this occurrence suggested. I do not approve of the power given to the court in fixing the quantum of punishments. You could not avoid it. After all, your achievement was noble, and I hope you will follow it up. I was very desirous to know what you had been doing in the inchoate statute, and your letter has relieved me in part from the apprehensions

[a] Jeremy Bentham. — Ed.

Oct. 21st. Set out for Durham, and slept at Shrewsbury.

22d. Chester; saw the new court there, and the jail, built partly on the panopticon principle.

25th. Arrived at Durham.

26th. Held my Chancery sittings there.

30th. In the evening, arrived at London.

I felt, after a short and desultory chit-chat with the Solicitor-General. Come to our shop, say all the lawyers. Your prices, say I, are very high, your promises are big, your boasts are loud; but I can go no where else. Well you may be the venders of the wares, but I fear you are often the spoilers of them, and I am sure you are not fit to be the manufacturers. There are certain raw materials called good sense; there are certain arts in working them up called honesty and humanity; and here you are no dealers.

"My friend, I can very easily conceive that you would be teased upon details in carrying the other statute into execution. Who is to fix the quantum of pecuniary compensation? Who is to pay it when fixed? Here objectors will prate; but I am provoked at the doubts which have been started upon the principle. If the laws create the inconvenience to innocent men, common sense and common justice seem to require that the very same laws by which their sufferings are occasioned, and their innocence has been proved, should provide for them speedy and plenary redress. Lawyers and philosophers deride us poor ecclesiastics for our dogmatism, our bigotry, our ignorance, our subtleties, and our intolerance upon certain mysterious subjects; but I will wager my best and largest wig against Lord Eldon's, and my best Greek folio against Lord Ellenborough's Abridgment of the Statutes, if your brethren of Westminster Hall are not a match for the Convocation in England, the General Assembly in Scotland, and even the Conclave at Rome, in zeal about trifles, in attachment to dogmas, in faith in absurdities, in jealousy towards inquirers, and in a spirit of unrelenting persecution against all reformers. To be sure, you and five or six others whom I have the happiness to know, are illustrious exceptions to the general rule.

"By the way, I have opposed Dr. Paley for calling in question the wholesome adage, that "it is better that ten guilty men should escape than for one innocent man to swing."[1] I trust that you are a faithful believer in the old mumpsimus. I hope you will lay in a large stock of health and spirits during the vacation; and that, on the meeting of Parliament, you will co-operate with Sir A. Piggott in chastising Saint Perceval and Orator Canning for the Portugal convention. I beg my best compliments to Lady Romilly, and have the honour to be, dear sir, with the greatest and sincerest respect, your faithful friend and very obedient servant,

"S. Parr."

31st. In the morning, the Lord Chancellor sat at Lincoln's Inn Hall.

Bankrupt Laws.

Nov. and *Dec.* In the very few minutes that I have been able to command in the midst of business, I have been preparing a Bill to remedy some defects in the Bankrupt law, which I shall probably attempt to carry through the House in the approaching session.[1] The defects, and the proposed remedy for them, I have long and frequently reflected on.

Duke of Sussex.

Dec. 21st. I dined to-day with the Duke of Sussex: the party consisted only of Sir A. Piggott, Richards the King's Counsel, the Recorder of London, Dillon a Barrister, and Richards the Duke's solicitor. We dined at an hotel in Bond Street, where the Duke receives his visitors. The object of our meeting was that the Duke, who has been lately attacked in a number of anonymous publications, might state his case to us, and communicate to us a memorial which he has lately presented to the King. He had no advice to ask us; and there was no step to be taken by any of us. His Royal Highness said that he merely wished that we should be apprised of his situation.

Duke of Kent.

Dec. 28th. I this day, by the desire of the Duke of Kent, waited on him at Carlton House. He said that he wished to consult me, not professionally, but rather as a friend, on a point on which some difference of opinion existed amongst those persons whose judgments he most highly valued. A publication had very recently appeared by a person of the name of M'Callum, professing

[1] See *infrà*, p. 268.—Ed.

to state the persecutions which he, the Duke, had experienced at the hands of the Duke of York. It had been thought advisable that he should publish a disavowal of any privity in the publication; and he put into my hands a paper which had been drawn up for the purpose. All his friends, except his secretary Major Dodd, advised him to publish it; and he was desirous, in consequence of the Prince of Wales's recommendation, to take my opinion upon it. The paper which he gave me, and which he desired me to take home with me, and to consider at my leisure, was in these words:

"The Duke of Kent requests the Editor of the *Morning Post* to give insertion to the following paragraph: —

"Kensington Palace, Dec. 24th, 1808.

"Several pamphlets having recently appeared, in which my name has been mentioned with high encomiums, while those of several members of my family, and of various other individuals, have been noticed in terms of abuse; and having reason to apprehend (from the circumstance of several extracts and dates of two correspondences that took place between the members of his Majesty's government and myself in 1803 and the present year being quoted in different parts of them) that a belief is entertained by persons who are unacquainted with my real sentiments that I have sanctioned the publication of them; I feel it incumbent upon me, for the justification of my character to the world (although it is extremely repugnant to my feelings to be obliged thus to obtrude myself on the attention of the public), to adopt this mode of solemnly and unequivocally declaring that there is not the slightest foundation for so ungenerous a suspicion. At the same time, I conceive it right to avow that I certainly did give free circulation to the whole of the one correspondence alluded to, and to the substance of the other, accompanied by an extract of some of the most striking passages in it, and a memorandum of the dates, amongst my military friends, at the periods when they respectively closed; that being the only method left me of proving to them, and to every officer of the British army, (who, having served under me in North America, the West Indies, and the Mediterranean, had witnessed the manner in which I have ever strove to discharge my duty,) first, that I had spared no pains to obtain an investigation of my conduct at Gibraltar, when, after commanding in that fortress for a twelvemonth, I was recalled from my government, for the avowed purpose of rendering an account of the causes that had led to the mutiny; and, secondly, that, if I was not at my post, as I felt I ought to be, it was not for want of my making every possible exertion to return to it. But it never even once entered my thoughts that any part of the correspondence might one day or other appear in print; and still less that it would furnish materials either for the public commendation of myself or for the abuse of others. On the contrary, my opinion always has been that pamphlets of the nature of those alluded to could do no good, while they certainly have a tendency to produce much mischief; and, such being my sentiments, I should be the last man living to give a sanction to the publication of them."

It required but little consideration to determine against the publication of such a paper. The Duke told me, however, that he wished me to consider it maturely; and, if I was against the publishing it, to write him a letter saying that such was my opinion, and shortly to give my reasons in my letter, and to send it to him at Kensington Palace. He desired me too, to consider, whether, if this paper were not proper to be published by him, it might not be right for him to publish some other. He said that he should be governed entirely by my opinion; and that he wished to have a letter from me, to show to those of his family who were urgent with him to publish a disavowal of the pamphlet. The part of his family who were so urgent with him, were those who were most attached to the Duke of York. He begged that in the letter I would not mention the name of Major Dodd. I took my leave of him, and the next morning sent him a letter in these words:—

"Sir,

"Your Royal Highness having done me the honour to ask me what I thought of the propriety of your Royal Highness's authorising the publication, in some of the daily newspapers, of the paper which I have now the honour to return enclosed, I have given it the best consideration in my power; and I have read attentively the pamphlet to which it principally alludes. It appears to me, Sir, after thinking very anxiously on the subject, that it would not be by any means advisable that the paper in question should be published, or, indeed, that your Royal Highness should authorise the publication of any paper that could be written for the purpose of disavowing any knowledge of the pamphlet. Your Royal Highness, by condescending to take notice of the suspicion that it may have been with your Royal Highness's privity that the pamphlet has been published, would give a degree of weight, and importance, and publicity to that suspicion, which I am fully persuaded it has not at this moment obtained. The tone and spirit of the pamphlet must alone convince every rational man that it has never received any sanction from your Royal Highness; and no inference, to the disadvantage of your Royal Highness, can be drawn from the mere circumstance of the writer having had access to the correspondences which took place in 1803, and in the present year; since it is known that your Royal Highness did not make those correspondences matter of secrecy; and, consequently, it must have been impossible to prevent some copy of them getting into improper hands. If any paragraph upon the subject were to appear under your Royal Highness's name, it would necessarily have the effect of giving a very extended circulation and a considerable degree of weight to an imputation, which, as far as the public is concerned, I really believe, cannot truly be said at present to exist. It seems to me, Sir, that it must be some very extraordinary occasion indeed, that could render it expedient, even for a private individual, and much more for a person of your Royal Highness's exalted rank, to make such an appeal to the public as the paper would amount to; and, by that means, to expose himself to all the animadversions, inquiries, attacks, and provocations to further explanations, which such appeals seldom fail to produce, and which they may be said, in some degree, always to challenge; and I am most fully convinced that this is not such an occasion. I have the honour to be, &c. &c.

"Dec. 29. 1808."

I have heard nothing since from the Duke; but I believe he has abstained from publishing anything.

1809.

Jan. 19th, *Th.* Parliament met. It had been intended that it should meet on the Monday preceding, the 16th, and Parliament had been prorogued to that day, and a proclamation, that it would then meet for the despatch of business, published. But, upon the pretence that, if it met on Monday, many members would be obliged to travel on a Sunday, to the profanation of the Sabbath, a further prorogation for three days, to the 19th, was made.

Meeting of Parliament.

Lord Grenville in the House of Lords, and Ponsonby and Whitbread in the Commons, spoke in terms of strong censure of the conduct of Ministers; particularly of their military plans in Spain and Portugal, and their conduct towards America; but no amendment to the address on the King's speech was moved in either House.

Feb. 1st, *Wed.* I this day brought a Bill into the House of Commons to extend the benefit of the Lords' Act (the Statute 32 Geo. II. c. 28.) to the case of prisoners in custody for not paying money or costs ordered to be paid by Courts of Equity. The Lords' Act, with the extension it has received by the Statutes 33 Geo. III. c. 5. and 37 Geo. III. c. 85., enables debtors taken in execution for sums not exceeding 300*l.*, by giving up every thing they are possessed of to their creditors, to entitle themselves to a subsistence from the cre-

The Lords' Act extended to prisoners committed by Courts of Equity.

ditor at whose suit they are imprisoned, at the rate of sixpence a day, or, if this be not paid, to be discharged. These acts extend, however, only to legal, and not to equitable debts. To extend them to persons owing equitable debts, and imprisoned in form for a contempt of court, but in substance for not paying such debts, is the only object of the Bill. It will probably meet with no opposition. It has been observed to me by the Solicitor-General and by several other persons, that there are but few such prisoners. I do not at all know what their numbers are; probably they are very few, when compared with the multitude of debtors imprisoned under legal process, with which our jails are crowded; but, if I can procure liberty for only two or three persons every year, I shall be well satisfied.

This Bill passed through the House of Commons without opposition.*

March 1st, *Wed.* I moved for and obtained leave to bring into the House of Commons a Bill to alter the Bankrupt Laws; and on

Bankrupt Laws.

3d, *Fri.* I brought in the Bill, and it was read a first time, and ordered to be read a second time on the 29th instant.

The intention of the Bill is to remedy some of the principal defects in the Bankrupt Law. 1st, To provide for the proof of debts which cannot now be proved; such as debts due to sureties and to persons liable for the bankrupt.

* Nor did it meet with any opposition in the House of Lords. It received the Royal Assent on the 13th of March.[1]

---

[1] The Act is the 49 Geo. III. c. 6.—Ed.

2d, To prevent assignees keeping the bankrupt's estate in their own hands and employing it for their own benefit. 3d, To diminish, in some degree, the expense of proceedings under Bankruptcy. And 4th, To take from creditors the power which they now have, without appeal or control, of withholding from the bankrupt his certificate, and, by that means, exposing him to be perpetually imprisoned for not paying debts which it is impossible (unless he has committed a capital felony) that he should have the means to pay.

The Duke of York.

13th, *Mon.* This was the fourth day of the debate in the House of Commons on the conduct of the Duke of York.[1] It had lasted Wednesday, Thursday, and Friday last, till between two and three o'clock in the morning each day, and the further debate was adjourned to this day. I took part in this day's debate by supporting, in a speech of some length, Colonel Wardle's motion for an address to the Crown to remove the Duke from the command of the army.

[1] The conduct of the Duke of York in the disposal of commissions and promotions in the army was brought before the House of Commons on the 27th of January; on that day Colonel Wardle moved for the appointment of a committee to investigate the charges against the Duke, and on the motion of Perceval (Chancellor of the Exchequer), it was determined that it should be a committee of the whole House. The examination of witnesses at the bar of the House commenced on the 1st of February, and after having occupied twelve days closed on the 22d of February. On the 8th of March, the evidence was taken into consideration by the House, and a very long debate ensued, which was prolonged, by successive adjournments, to the 17th of March; and on that day a resolution, moved by the Chancellor of the Exchequer, acquitting the Duke of personal connivance with the corrupt practices, the existence of which had been fully proved at the bar of the House, was carried by a majority of 278 to 196. On the following day, 18th of March, the Duke of York resigned the command of the army, and on the 20th of March the House determined to proceed no farther in the matter.—Ed.

When Wardle first stated to the House the facts of which he had received information, and moved to refer them to a committee, scarcely any body imagined that he would be able to establish any of them by evidence. Indeed, there is great reason to believe, notwithstanding the proofs which in the sequel appeared, that the accusation would have proved wholly abortive, had it not been for the presumption and rashness of the Ministers. In their foolish confidence that no charge could be substantiated, and that they should serve the Duke by a public refutation of what they termed infamous calumnies, they insisted, contrary to Wardle's wishes, that the matter should be referred, not to a select committee, but to a committee of the whole House, in order that all the witnesses might be examined publicly.[1] It was obvious that such a proceeding must be most mischievous to the Duke. Though no violation of the law might be established against him, yet the mere exposing to the public that he, who was mistakenly supposed by most persons to be leading a moral, decent, and domestic life, was entertaining at great expense a courtezan, the wife, too, of another man, and a woman who had risen from a very low situation in life, could not fail to do him irreparable mischief in the public estimation. But, in the

[1] Mr. Perceval (Chancellor of the Exchequer) had moved, on the 27th of January, that the matter should be referred to a committee of the whole House, and his motion was supported by the two secretaries, Mr. Canning and Lord Castlereagh. In the course of his speech, Mr. Perceval said that "he would stake his reputation upon it, that it was impossible that, after the result of the inquiry, any suspicion even could attach to his Royal Highness." See Hansard's Parliamentary Debates, vol. xii. p. 196.—Ed.

course of the inquiry, from the bad management and unskilful conduct of the Duke's friends, new matter of a very criminal nature, which had never been stated by Wardle, presented itself to the House. Written evidence and documents, not known to be in existence either by Wardle or by the principal witness, Mrs. Clarke, were discovered, and produced by the witnesses who appeared for the Duke; and these did his Royal Highness more mischief than any thing that was said by the witnesses against him. It was established, beyond the possibility of doubt, that the Duke had permitted Mrs. Clarke, his mistress, to interfere in military promotions; that he had given commissions at her recommendation; and that she had taken money for the recommendations. That the Duke knew that she took money, or that he knew that the establishment, which he had set on foot for her, was partly supported with the money thus illegally procured by her, did not appear otherwise than from her evidence. She, however, asserted the fact directly and positively; and her evidence was supported, in many other particulars which seemed the most incredible, by such strong corroborations, that her immoral character, her resentment, and her contradictions, were not sufficient to render her evidence altogether incredible. There was not evidence sufficient to convict the Duke of the crimes imputed to him; but, undoubtedly, there was evidence sufficient to charge him with them; and it is to me matter of astonishment that any considerable number of members should be brought to concur in the resolution which Perceval has stated that he intends to move; namely, that there is no ground to charge the Duke, either with corruption, or with connivance at the corruption of Mrs. Clarke.

I took no part while the inquiry was going on, except that, upon the examination of Captain Huxley Sandon, who had suppressed a very important note in his possession, written by the Duke of York, relating to Captain Tonyn's promotion, I endeavoured, by some questions I put to him, to discover whether the note was not still in existence, and could not be obtained. Particularly, I asked him whether, if a messenger were immediately sent with him to his house, he would not be able to find it. He had begun by denying that the note existed; had then stated that it had existed, but was lost; next doubted whether he had not still got it; and at last admitted that it was safe at his house; and, being committed to the custody of the Sergeant at Arms, and sent in that custody to look for it, actually produced the note before the House rose. In another instance, too, I took some part in the proceeding; it was, to object to the House receiving the evidence of persons from the Post Office and the Bank, to prove, by a comparison of hands, that this note was not written by the Duke. My objection was overruled by the House; and, in the anxious desire which a majority of the House had to find any pretext for doubting the fact of the note being the Duke's, they agreed to receive this most dangerous species of evidence. In no Court of Justice, I believe, had it ever been even attempted to prove, *by a comparison of hands*, that a paper imputed to any individual was not his handwriting.

Entertaining a very strong opinion against Perceval's proposed resolution, and in favour of Wardle's address, I thought it my duty to express that opinion; and I did it to-day, to the best of my ability, and in a way which seemed to make some impression on the House. I knew very well that, in taking this part, I was not acting much more agreeably to the late than to the present Ministry; and that I was provoking the strongest resentment of all the persons upon whom my ever being in office must depend. The King took the strongest possible interest for the Duke. The Prince of Wales had, in a letter written to Adam, at the moment of the matter being first brought before the House, and which Adam showed me, stated that he considered an attack upon the Duke as an attack upon himself. It is true that, as the inquiry proceeded, and the Prince observed the very strong impression against the Duke which the evidence had made on the public, he withdrew his support from the Duke, and affected to remain in a state of neutrality. Still, however, there could be no doubt that he saw with great uneasiness the turn which the matter took, and that his neutrality arose only from an apprehension of drawing on himself some share of the popular odium, by seeming to espouse the cause of the Duke. That the Duke may himself, at one day, ascend the throne, is an event by no means improbable.

I had fully considered all this, when I determined not to shrink from my duty, and to give my most sincere opinion to the House. I and Henry Martin were the only lawyers in the House who spoke against the Duke. Amongst his advocates in the House were the Master of the Rolls, the Attorney-General, the Solicitor-General, the Lord Advocate, the Solicitor-General of Scotland, the Judge Advocate * (Ryder), two Welsh Judges (Burton and Leycester), and Adam and Leach. I ought, however, in justice to the profession, to observe that, as far as I have been able to learn, there was as great a majority of lawyers out of the House against the Duke as there was in the House in his favour.

There is nothing so injudicious as to talk, in the House of Commons, of a man's own disinterestedness. It is the topic which the House, with great reason, hears dwelt on with the most impatience. I thought, however, that I might, on this occasion, be allowed to observe, that my vote did not concur with my interest; and I concluded my speech with these words: "It has been observed by a learned gentleman (Burton) in this debate, at the close of his speech, that he has nothing to hope for or to fear on this side the grave. I cannot say the same thing. Not la-

* It was curious to observe, how many of the persons who argued for the Duke were men holding offices: besides those who are here enumerated, there were the Chancellor of the Exchequer [1], the two Secretaries of State [2], the Secretary at War [3], the Treasurer of the Navy [4], and one of the Paymasters. [5]

---

[1] Right Honourable Spencer Perceval.
[2] Right Honourable George Canning and Lord Castlereagh.
[3] Sir James Pulteney.
[4] Right Honourable George Rose.
[5] Right Honourable Charles Long.—Ed.

bouring under the same affliction that he does, and not arrived at the same period of life *, I may reasonably be allowed, for myself and for those who are most dear to me, to indulge hopes of prosperity which is yet to come. Reflecting, too, on the vicissitudes of human life, I may entertain apprehensions of adversity and of persecution, which perhaps await me. I have, however, the heartfelt satisfaction to reflect, that it is not possible for me to hope to derive, in any way, the most remote advantage from the vote which, on this occasion, I shall give, and from the part which I have thought it my duty to act."

I have been told by several persons that, after making such a speech, I must give up all hopes of ever being Chancellor. I am not quite sure of that; but of this I think I may be sure, that if ever, after the part I have now taken, I should be raised to that situation, it will not be in expectation that I shall act in it otherwise than as an honest man. It certainly is not probable that I should receive such a promotion; nothing perhaps can be more improbable; but if, contrary to all expectation it should happen, the promotion will be more honourable to myself, and more honourable to the person to whom I shall be indebted for it, than it possibly could have been if, upon this occasion, I had adopted a different line of conduct. It follows, from these observations, that I was not quite correct in saying that I could derive no possible advantage from the vote which I gave. This is perfectly true; but, when I used those expres-

* He is blind, without children, and near seventy years of age.

sions, I neither meant, nor I believe was understood by any one, to be speaking of such an advantage as I here allude to.[1]

15th, *Wed.* The debate was continued to this day, being in the whole six days; and, at five o'clock in the morning of Thursday, the 16th, the first division took place.

Mr. Bankes had proposed an address different from Colonel Wardle's, but yet for the Duke's removal. From the mode in which the questions had been put (viz. of an amendment to leave out the whole of Wardle's motion, except the first word "That;" and then an amendment, moved by Bankes, of that amendment), the first question put was in substance whether there should be an address or merely a resolution; and, all the supporters of both addresses united, the numbers were, for an address, 199; against it, 296.[2] Bankes's amendment being thus lost, the next question was on Perceval's amendment, which was, to strike out the whole of Wardle's address: for this question, the Ayes were 364, the Noes 123. The further

[1] The following extract from a letter of Sir Jas. Mackintosh, dated 15th Oct. 1809, refers to the part taken by Sir S. Romilly in the investigation into the conduct of the Duke of York.—Ed.

"'I envy Romilly neither his fortune nor his fame, though I am likely to be poor and obscure enough, but I do envy him so noble an opportunity of proving his disinterestedness. If his character had been in the slightest degree that of a demagogue, his conduct might have been ambiguous; but, with his habits, it can be considered only as a sacrifice of the highest objects of ambition to the mere dictates of conscience. I speak so because, though I trust that he will not lose the great seal, yet I am sure he considered himself as sacrificing it; and to view it in any other light, would be to rob him of the fame which he deserves.

"'I beg you to communicate, either directly or indirectly, to Romilly my sentiments on his conduct, and remember that my anxiety is not to do him any honour, but to do myself justice.'"

[2] Tellers included.—Ed.

consideration of the subject was then adjourned to Friday; and, on

17th, *Fri.* Perceval moved his resolution, that it was the opinion of the House that the evidence reported to it afforded no ground for the House to charge the Duke of York, in the execution of his official duties as Commander-in-chief, with the personal corruption alleged against him in that evidence, or with any connivance at the corrupt and infamous practices which are therein disclosed.

To this, Sir Thomas Turton moved, as an amendment, that, in the opinion of the House, there was ground to charge his Royal Highness with knowledge of the corrupt practices disclosed in the evidence. On this amendment, the numbers were, for it, 135; against it, 334. Perceval's motion then being put, the numbers were, Ayes 278; Noes 196.

I voted in the minority upon all these questions. The further consideration of the report was adjourned to Monday.

18th, *Sat.* The Duke of York this day resigned the command of the army.[1]

20th, *Mon.* Mr. Bathurst moved a resolution which he had before stated, on the conduct of the Duke of York; but his motion was got rid of by an amendment moved by Lord Althorp, and carried, in these words: "That the Duke of York having resigned the command of the army, the House does not think it necessary to proceed any farther

[1] The Duke of York was re-appointed to the command of the army by the Regent, in May, 1811.—Ed.

in the consideration of the minutes of the evidence, so far as they relate to his Royal Highness."[1]

29th, *Wed.* The Bill for amending the Bankrupt Law was read a second time, without any opposition; but Mr. Jacob, a merchant, announced some opposition to different clauses of it in the committee.

Parliamentary Reform.

My conduct respecting the Duke of York has procured me a letter from Major Cartwright, enclosing a list of stewards of a public dinner intended to be held at the Crown and Anchor Tavern by the friends of Parliamentary Reform. The letter, which is dated March 27th, begins in these words: — "Dear Sir, — The enclosed would not have been submitted to you at all, had you not, while others by their prostitution were rendering your profession hateful to the nation, redeemed its honour, and secured to yourself the public veneration, by a conduct that must have placed between yourself and the objects of an honest ambition a bar which never can be removed but by a truly public power. Believing, therefore, that, were you thus early to join the small rallying band of parliamentary reformers, it would add nothing to the strength of that bar of your own placing, while it might naturally be expected to augment the force which will one day be wanted to its removal, I am induced to express a hope that I may be allowed to inscribe your name," &c. Many arguments are then used to prove the expediency of such a measure, and

[1] A division took place upon the question, whether the word "now" should, as proposed by Lord Althorp, be inserted after the words "the House does not;" and it was decided by a majority of 235 to 112, that the word "now" should be omitted.— Ed.

the advantage which the writer supposed would result from having my name among the stewards. I was formerly acquainted with Major Cartwright, but for the last twenty-five years I have hardly had any intercourse with him. I returned him an answer in these words:—

"Dear Sir, March 28, 1809.

"I trust that I need hardly assure you, that my opinion on the subject of a reform of Parliament is not at all altered; but yet I cannot consent to be one of the stewards of the dinner which is to take place; nor indeed is it my intention even to be present at that dinner. Upon whatever questions come before the House of Commons, while I have a seat in it, I shall vote and speak as I think my duty and the good of the country require, without caring whom such a conduct may please or may offend. But I have a very great aversion to acting any conspicuous part, or putting myself forward in any way, out of the House, upon any public measures. I cannot think that there is any sufficient reason for my adopting, at the present moment, a different line of conduct from that which I have hitherto thought it right to pursue. The tenor of this letter sufficiently shows that I wish it to be considered as private and confidential; and I cannot conclude it without assuring you of the very great satisfaction it affords me to find that my public conduct has met with your approbation."

31st. I set out to-day, with Anne and one of my children, for Hastings, in Sussex, to recruit my strength with the sea air, after the fatigues I have lately undergone. We stayed there till the 10th of April.

Votes of thanks in popular meetings.

April 15th. If I were much delighted with what is usually understood to be popularity, I should lately have had great enjoyment. I have had voted me, together with Sir Francis Burdett, Lord Folkestone, Whitbread, and General Ferguson, thanks for my conduct upon the late inquiry respecting the Duke of York, in a great many popular meetings: amongst others, by the Livery of London, in their Common Hall; the Common Council of London; the inhabitants of Westminster; the inhabitants of Southwark; the freeholders of Middlesex; the Corporation and inhabitants of Nottingham; and the town of Norwich.* It has been necessary to acknowledge the receipt of some of these resolutions of thanks, when they have been formally communicated to me. My answer to the town-clerk of London was as follows: —

"Sir, Lincoln's Inn, April 15, 1809.

"I yesterday received your letter of the 8th inst., enclosing the resolutions of the Livery of London, in Common Hall assembled, and a resolution of the Common Council of the City of London. Nothing can be more gratifying to me than to find that my conduct as a Member of

* And soon afterwards by Sheffield, Worcester, Carmarthen, Reading, Liverpool, Lewes, Maidstone, Doncaster, Shaftesbury, Wycombe, Coventry, Berwick, Hampshire, Hertfordshire, Norfolk, Wiltshire, Bristol, Bolton, and Huddersfield. In all these places, and others, whose names I do not recollect, I was thanked by name. There were many other places which returned thanks to Mr. Wardle, and to the 125 who voted with him.[1]

[1] On the 15th March.—Ed.

Parliament, upon the late inquiry in the House of Commons, has met with the approbation of the Livery, and has been thought by the Common Council deserving of their thanks. Such flattering distinctions have not, however, had the effect of making me exaggerate to myself the merit which belongs to me. I am sensible that the only praise I can claim, is that of having done what I conceived to be my duty. Viewing the case in the light in which I saw it, I should have been highly culpable if I had taken any other part than I did. I shall think myself, sir, greatly obliged to you if you will have the goodness to express to the Common Council and to the Livery how grateful I am for the very high honours they have conferred on me."

My other letters, on the same occasions, were, in substance, pretty much the same as this. The resolution of the Livery would have justified, and might perhaps be thought to have called for, some answer as to what I intended to do in future, for it was in these words: — "Resolved, that they do highly approve of the conduct of Sir Francis Burdett, Lord Folkestone, Samuel Whitbread, Esq., Sir Samuel Romilly, General Ferguson, and the rest of the 125 honest and independent members who supported Mr. Wardle's proposition on the 15th of March, 1809; and trust that, uninfluenced by party or feelings of interest, they will support every measure calculated to remove abuses and root out corruption;" and I knew that it was much wished that the persons named in the Resolution should, in their answer, say something about the general system of corruption which is so prevalent. I determined, however, not to please them in this particular. The very persons who inveigh most bitterly against party are, in truth, making the conduct of the Duke of York, and the late proceedings which it gave rise to, the means of acquiring strength to a party which is becoming very formidable, and which, I have no doubt, makes the correction of abuses only a cover for promoting much greater designs.

Some of the Liverymen of London have agreed to have a public dinner, and to invite to it Colonel Wardle, and the other persons named in the City resolutions of thanks and approbation. Mr. Waithman, a common councilman, who has much distinguished himself in the City on the popular side, came, with three other gentlemen, to my house, as a deputation from the Livery, to invite me to the dinner; and, not finding me at home, wrote me a letter of invitation. I determined not to dine with them, thinking such a sort of public festival on such an occasion highly improper; and I therefore answered Mr. Waithman's letter thus: —

My Letter to Mr. Waithman.

"Sir, Russell Square, April 14th, 1809.

"The honour which the Livery of London, who intend dining together at the London Tavern, on the 21st inst., have done me of inviting me to their dinner, is one which is extremely flattering to me, and for which I am very grateful. It would give me the greatest concern, if my declining to accept their invitation could be construed by any one into a mark of disrespect to the Livery, or to any of the members of that most respectable body; but that, I persuade myself, must be impossible, when my reasons are known. I voted against the Duke of York, because I could not, as an honest man, vote otherwise. I thought it did not become me to give a silent vote upon such a question, and I therefore spoke as well as voted. Seeing the case in the light in which I saw it, to have acted otherwise than I did, I must have been base enough to have deserted my public duty upon a most important occasion, from the mean apprehension that to discharge my duty might be attended with personal disadvantages to myself. If there be much merit in not having been actuated by such unworthy motives, (which I cannot think, but if there be,) that merit I certainly may pretend to. But, though I consider the late proceedings in the House of Commons as being of the highest importance, yet I cannot think that the result of them is that which ought to be celebrated by a public dinner. So many persons, for whose opinions I have the utmost deference, think differently from me on this subject, that I cannot but very much distrust my own judgment. But it is by my own judgment that I must regulate my own conduct; and, with the opinion which I entertain, it certainly would not be proper for me to be present at such a dinner. I shall consider myself, Sir, as being under great obligations to you, if you will have the goodness to state to the gentlemen by whom you have been deputed, what my reason is for declining the honour intended me; and to say, that I decline it most reluctantly, and with most sincere regret; for no man can set a higher value than I do on the approbation and applause of the Livery of London.

"I am, Sir, &c.

"Robert Waithman, Esq." "S. R.

17th, *Mon.* Lord Folkestone moved for a committee to inquire into the corrupt disposal of offices in the State. The motion was rejected.[1] I happened to be absent.

Bankrupt Laws.

19th, *Wed.* The Bill to amend the Bankrupt Laws went through the committee. It had been committed on Friday, April 14th; but so many objections were made to so many clauses in it, that the further proceeding was adjourned to this day; and it was twelve o'clock at night before it was gone through. The principal, or I may say the only, opposers of the Bill were the Attorney and Solicitor General. They opposed most of the clauses, and suggested a number of difficulties; really, as it should seem, only to show their vigilance when any innovation was attempted. The clauses they principally opposed were, that to enable the proof of debts by sureties; that to enable a certificated bankrupt to be a witness for his assignees, though he has not released his allowance, and the surplus of his estate; and that which gives the bankrupt a power, after his creditors have refused to sign his certificate for two years, of appealing to the Chancellor. To the

[1] By a majority of 148; the numbers being, 178 against Lord Folkestone's motion, 30 in favour of it.—Ed.

second of these clauses * the objection insisted on, by both the Attorney and Solicitor General, was, that it broke in upon a principle of the law of evidence. It certainly does: and it is a principle I was very glad to break in upon. The executing releases, to make a witness competent, is a mere fiction. The release it is intended should be given up as soon as the cause is over, in which case it is a deception; or, if the transaction is real, the witness purchases the right of giving evidence; and he is considered as a disinterested and a competent witness, from the very circumstance which proves how deep an interest he takes in the cause. In the case of a bankrupt, this objection is stronger than in any other case, because a bankrupt who releases his allowance, releases all that he can lawfully have in the world. He consents to give up all he is possessed of, to be allowed to become a witness. The clause respecting certificates was opposed by them, principally on the common grounds, that we are a very humane nation; that creditors are more proper objects of compassion than debtors; and that the instances of indulgent creditors were very numerous, and those of oppressive and cruel creditors very rare. My experience does not justify this observation; but, without cruelty, the mere indifference and carelessness of the creditor about the fate of his debtor, whom he has once lodged in prison, is alone the cause of great suffering and misery. The indifference of the nation upon such subjects cannot be more strongly manifested than it was by the very

Evidence.

* This clause was struck out in the House of Lords.

thin attendance which there was upon this Bill. On the second reading, and on both days of the committee, the number of members who attended was not nearly sufficient to make a House; and any member who had chosen to count the House, or call for a division, might have delayed any further proceeding. The Bill, however, passed through the committee without one clause being rejected. One clause was added in the committee by the Solicitor-General, and another by Sir Charles Price, one of the City members, which are of little importance.

28th, *Fri.* The Bill passed in the House of Commons.*

Sale of seats in Parliament.

May 11th, *Th.* Mr. Madocks moved, to-day, in the House of Commons, that an inquiry should be made into the conduct of two of the Ministers, Lord Castlereagh and Perceval, in having procured a seat in Parliament for a Mr. Quintin Dick for a sum of money, and having afterwards endeavoured to influence his vote upon the inquiry respecting the Duke of York; and having, as he would not vote according to their wishes, intimated to him that he ought to give up his seat, which he accordingly did. All the members of the late administration opposed the motion. I voted for it, and was in a minority of 85 against 310. It was said that such things have been done by all administrations. It may be so; but it seems impossible that when the notice of Parliament is drawn to them, it should not condemn them. In this case, too,

* Certain alterations and additions were made in this Bill by the Lords, which were agreed to by the Commons, and it passed into a law. See *infrà*, p. 291.

the particular occasion on which the influence was exercised over the member, made it, in my opinion, a most aggravated offence. The very ministers who were charged with so exerting their influence, were among the foremost to observe, in the debate on the Duke of York, that the proceeding was purely judicial.[1] The offence, therefore, was no less than obliging a magistrate to resign a judicial office, because he was about to decide a cause as his conscience dictated, but as Ministers disapproved. The conduct of the late Ministers, considered merely with a view to their own interest, is highly impolitic. Nothing that could be proved against them will do them more injury in the public opinion than this screening of political offences, through fear of recrimination. The decision of this night, coupled with some which have lately taken place, will do more towards disposing the nation in favour of a parliamentary reform * than all the speeches that have been or will be made in any popular assemblies.

Lotteries.

12th, *Fri.* Perceval opened the Budget, and,

* Cobbett has since, in his exaggerating style, said of this decision and the debate which preceded it, "that it involved in it consequences of ten million times more importance to England than the fate of all the expeditions, all the armies, and all the fleets in the world; and that the charge and the decision should be printed in all Almanacks, Court Calendars, Books of Roads, &c., to be continually in the eye of the public." Cobbett's Register, May 20.

---

[1] The Chancellor of the Exchequer, in his speech, delivered on the first day of the debate, said,—"Upon such a charge, when once made against such a character, I cannot doubt but the House will feel it their indispensable duty to pronounce a direct, a decided, opinion. Is he (aye or no), upon the charge of corruption, guilty or not guilty? That is the question proposed to us,— the question from which we cannot shrink,—the question which we must decide." See Hansard's Parliamentary Debates, vol. xiii. p. 54.—Ed.

as a lottery was amongst his resources for the year, I followed Whitbread and Wilberforce in opposing it, on account of the misery and the crimes which lotteries produce.

18th, *Thurs.* The lottery came again under discussion. Whitbread, Windham[1], Wilberforce, and myself, spoke against it. The only persons who defended it were Perceval and Sir Thomas Turton: upon a division, the numbers were, for it 90, against it only 36. I was one of the tellers.

Perceval's plan is to have the lottery drawn in one day, which he thinks will prevent insurances; and he contends that it is from insurances alone that all the evils attendant on lotteries arise. This is calculated just for the present, and when a strong impression has been made on the public by the report of the Committee, to reconcile men to lotteries, by taking away some of their evils. In a few years, when the report is forgotten, we shall have lotteries again upon the old plan. Much evil arises from insurances, but not by any means all the evil which lotteries produce.

Criminal law.

26th, *Fri.* I moved, in the House of Commons, for returns of the number of persons convicted of offences from the year 1805, with their sentences; and the number transported to Botany Bay, from the first formation of the colony. At the same time, I gave notice, that I should, early in the next session, propose some altera-

[1] The two concluding sentences of Windham's speech, as given in Hansard's Parliamentary Debates, vol. xiv. p. 623., afford some ground for concluding that, although generally opposed to lotteries, he did not vote against them on this particular occasion.— Ed.

tions[1] in the Criminal Law, to lessen the severity, and increase the certainty of punishment.

Seditious meetings Bill.

June 9th, *Fri.* The Attorney-General[2] has had a Bill some time depending in the House of Commons, which he called a Bill to amend the Act of 39 Geo. III. c. 79. for the suppression of seditious meetings. He represented it as a Bill of little importance, which was merely to remove a doubt which he thought unfounded; and which would, in effect, only strike out of the Act a few useless and unmeaning words. He said a few words only to this effect when he introduced the Bill, and it was ordered to be read a second time on the 30th of May. Ponsonby, Lord Henry Petty, and all the members of the late administration were satisfied with this; saw no harm in the Bill, and meant to make no opposition to it. It struck me in a very different point of view. I thought it an extremely important bill, and I apprised the Attorney-General that I should oppose it on the second reading. Other business occupied the House till past 12 o'clock at night, and at that hour I represented to him that it was too late to begin a debate on such a subject, in which he very reluctantly acquiesced. The second reading was then put off from day to day; and on this day the Attorney-General said that, as the Bill was to be opposed, it was too late to carry it through this session, and he should therefore withdraw it, and

[1] These alterations were proposed on the 9th of February, 1810. See *infrà*, p. 309.—Ed.

[2] The Attorney-General (Sir Vicary Gibbs) had moved for leave to bring in this Bill, and had explained its object on the 18th of May. See Hansard's Parl. Deb. vol. xiv. p. 615.—Ed.

bring it on again in the next session. I cannot but consider this as a very essential service which I have rendered the country. I have, for a time at least, defeated a most insidious attack upon the liberties of the people.

By the 36 Geo. III. c. 8. s. 12. it was enacted that every house, not licensed by two justices according to that Act, in which lectures were given or debates had concerning public grievances or matters relating to the laws, constitution, government, or policy of the realm, and to which persons were admitted for money, should be deemed a disorderly house. The person opening or using the house was to forfeit 100*l.* for every time it was so used, and to be otherwise punished as the law directs in cases of disorderly houses; and the persons present at such lectures or debates were also declared to be punishable as the Act particularly directs. This was merely a temporary law. It was passed, indeed, at a moment of great political heat and ferment, when very numerous meetings had been recently held in the open fields to discuss such subjects, when many dangerous doctrines had been advanced in numerous publications, and when an attack had been made on the person of the King as he was going down to the House of Lords.[1] And yet, with all this, and with Mr. Pitt for Minister, the Act was only temporary; and it did not pass till after it had undergone long discussions[2], and till after there had been a call

[1] On the 29th October, 1795.—Ed.

[2] The Bill in question was brought into the House of Commons by Mr. Pitt, on the 12th November, 1795, and after being strongly opposed

of the House. Before this Act expired, the 39 Geo. III. was passed, which, after reciting the former Act, declares that every house not licensed as the Act requires, in which lectures were delivered or debates had on any subject whatever, or in which books or newspapers were lent to be read, and to which persons were admitted for money, should be deemed a disorderly house within the intent and meaning of the Act of 36 Geo. III. The Act of 36 Geo. III. had since expired; but the Act of 39 Geo. III. was a perpetual Act. If, therefore, the section which referred to the 36th was, as I think it was, merely an extension of that Act, these clauses had now expired; but if the words "within the meaning of the former Act" were nugatory and inoperative, as the Attorney-General insists they are, then the clauses in question, as well as the rest of the 39 Geo. III., are still in force. The Bill now brought in by the Attorney-General was to repeal these words. The Bill, therefore, if his construction of the Act were just, was useless, and would have no operation; and he stated its object to be merely to remove a doubt which he thought ill founded. But if that doubt were not ill founded, this was, in effect, a Bill to revive a law which had expired for nine years, and which imposed most vexatious restraints on the liberty of the subject, and on the diffusion of knowledge.

Welsh judges not to be members of Parliament.

12th, *Mon.* In the committee upon a Bill to increase the salaries of the English and Welsh

---

by Mr. Fox, Mr. Sheridan, Mr. Grey (now Lord Grey), Mr. Erskine, and Mr. Whitbread, it passed both Houses on the 9th December.—Ed.

judges, Mr. Bankes proposed a clause to declare that the Welsh judges should not be eligible to sit in Parliament. Thinking that such a provision would be attended with very good effects, I said a few words in support of it. It appears to me to be desirable that the judicial and legislative characters should, in general, be kept distinct. It certainly is not universally true, but yet, in general, a man is a worse judge for being a Member of Parliament, and a worse Member of Parliament for being a judge. That the Welsh judges may sit in Parliament, gives the King great influence over the deliberations of Parliament, not so much by means of the votes of the Welsh judges themselves, who hold their offices for life, as of the lawyers in the House who have the expectation of becoming Welsh judges. It is generally from that part of the profession which is in Parliament that Welsh judges are chosen. The English judges are generally chosen from the profession at large, and it is very seldom that the choice falls on a Member of Parliament. When a Welsh judge is to be appointed, it is not the man best qualified in the profession to fill the office who is looked for, but one best inclined and qualified to support the Minister in the House of Commons: his judicial qualifications are only a secondary consideration.

Sale of seats in Parliament.

The Bill which Mr. Curwen brought into Parliament, to prevent the sale of seats in Parliament, was this day read a third time and passed. It was carried by a majority of only 12; there being 97 for it, and 85 against it. I voted against it. When the Bill was first brought in, the Ministers were hostile to it, but had not the courage to oppose it openly; and after the Speaker had in the committee made a speech of very great effect in favour of the Bill, they found it indispensably necessary, in order to save their reputation with the public, that some such Bill should be passed. They have, however, struck out the clause which required an oath of the member, and which annexed the penalties of perjury to the taking such an oath falsely, and every other clause that could make the Bill effectual. With their alterations the Bill is, in truth, what Lord Folkestone[1] proposed to entitle it, "A Bill to secure the Purchase of Seats exclusively to Government." I could have no hesitation in voting against it.

Cruelty to animals.

13th, *Tu.* A Bill brought by Lord Erskine into the House of Lords, for preventing malicious and wanton cruelty to animals, and which passed that House with the dissent of only two peers (Lord Redesdale and Lord Stanhope), was this day debated in the House of Commons, on the question whether the House should go into a committee upon it. The Bill declared it a misdemeanor "maliciously and with wanton cruelty to wound, cut, maim, or otherwise abuse any horse, mare, mule, ass, ox, cow, sheep, or swine," and made the offence indictable as a misdemeanor, or punishable, upon conviction, in a summary way before a justice. The principle of the measure

[1] Lord Folkestone moved that the title should be "An Act for more effectually preventing the Sale of Seats in Parliament for Money, and for procuring the Monopoly thereof to the Treasury by the means of Patronage." There were 28 votes in favour of this motion, and 133 against it.—Ed.

was all that in this stage of it could be discussed; and I spoke in favour of the Bill. I contended that it was to be supported, not merely as a measure of humanity but of sound policy; that the Legislature had a right to prohibit those vicious habits which tended to make men bad members of society, and led to the commission of atrocious crimes; that habits of cruelty towards animals led to the exercise of cruelty towards human beings; that nothing could be more just than the observation of a very distinguished artist, who, more than any other of his profession, had devoted his talents to the cause of morality, and who, in tracing cruelty through its different stages, had represented it as beginning with taking delight in the sufferings of animals, and ending in the most savage murder; and that such a Bill as this might not improperly be entitled, a Bill to prevent the crime of murder. The Bill was carried; but not going through the committee on this night, the opposers of it, on the next day *, when no person imagined that there would be a division, again opposed going into the committee, not with speeches but by a division. Upon the division, in a very thin house, the Bill was lost; 27 for it, and 37 against it. Windham took the lead in the opposition.

Many persons objected to that part of the Bill which enabled justices to imprison offenders upon conviction in a summary way, without the intervention of juries; and, in this respect, the Bill, as it was drawn, gave too large a power to justices.

* Not the next day, but Thursday, June 15.: on the 14th there was no House.

They might imprison for a month; and, if they convicted, they must imprison for a week. I should have thought the Bill much better, if it had merely given to justices a power of imprisoning for twenty-four hours, or for any number of days not exceeding a week. So restrained, I should have very much preferred summary convictions, where the punishment would follow quick after the offence, to the slower and more expensive proceeding of an indictment and a trial before a jury. Those who are always extolling the Trial by Jury, forget how dearly it is often purchased. Those who are shocked at the idea of giving a justice of the peace power to imprison by way of punishment, forget that, in indictable misdemeanors, and in the case of poor persons who cannot find bail, justices have power to commit the accused till trial; that is, in most cases, for a longer period than the law would allow them to do as a punishment. For small offences, and in the case of persons in the lowest situations in life, a prosecution by indictment is, of itself, a grievous punishment. The power which the prosecutor alone has to remove the indictment by *certiorari* into the King's Bench, and that at any time, even just before the trial is expected; the fees which the defendant must pay before he can be permitted to plead that he is not guilty; and the acquittal fees which he must pay if he proves the truth of that plea, and the other expenses of a defence, are intolerable evils. I had it, indeed, in contemplation, to propose a clause in the Bill to exempt persons indicted under it from the payment of fees to the Clerk of Assize, or

Fees on pleading not guilty and on acquittal.

Clerks of the Peace, upon pleading not guilty and upon acquittal. But, being apprehensive that such an alteration might endanger the Bill when it went back to the Lords, I mentioned it to the Chancellor, and asked him whether he thought it would be objected to. He told me that by himself it certainly would not be objected to; but that Lord Ellenborough was extremely averse to every alteration in the fees of officers of courts, and very much alive to every thing that had a tendency to such kind of reforms; and that he could not, by any means, answer for Lord Ellenborough's not opposing the Bill, if it were so altered. Of course I gave up all intention of proposing such an amendment. But whatever may be thought of such fees in cases where they are already established, it should seem that no person could reasonably object to the Legislature's merely abstaining from adding to them, and declaring, when it creates a new offence, that such fees shall not be paid. The officers can hardly be heard to complain that their emoluments are not increased.

Bankrupt laws.

15th, *Thurs.* My Bill to amend the Bankrupt Laws was this day brought back from the Lords with alterations. Some of them are additions of so important a nature, that, if they are right in themselves, yet it cannot be right that they should become law, without passing, in both Houses, through all the regular stages of a Bill. These alterations being only proposed in a committee in the Lords, that House had little opportunity of considering them; and the Commons will have but one opportunity, that of the question being put, to agree to the Lords' amendments. This summary mode of legislating has been, upon this occasion, adopted by two of the most strenuous enemies to innovation, the Lord Chancellor, and Lord Redesdale, they being the persons who have altered the Bill in the House of Lords. The alterations were not even shown to me before they were proposed and adopted; and this, not from any incivility towards me (for the Chancellor always shows great attention and kindness towards me, and has sent me written observations on the Bill, which I have answered in writing), but from the Chancellor's habits of doubt and procrastination, which induced him to put off the consideration of the Bill from day to day, till it became necessary to hurry it through with great precipitation or to reject it. The alterations are so important, the effect of some of them so doubtful, and the mode of enacting them as law so objectionable, that I hesitated whether I should not abandon the Bill altogether; for, at this late period of the session, there is no alternative but that, or adopting every alteration which the Lords have been pleased to make. As, however, the Bill, even altered as it is, will in my opinion be a great improvement of the law, I have taken the latter course; and on

19th, *Mon.* After stating in the House the alterations which had been made in the Bill, I moved to agree to them. The motion was adopted without observation from any one, and the Bill has passed.[1]

[1] It is the Act 49 Geo. 3. c. 121.—Ed.

The appeal to the Lord Chancellor upon the certificate, if the creditors refuse to sign it for two years, has been struck out, and so has the clause which made a certificated bankrupt a competent witness without releasing his allowance and surplus. In the place of these are inserted a clause to alter the proportion of creditors necessary to assent to a certificate, from four fifths to three fifths in number and value; another to relieve bankrupts from the effect of covenants in leases before their bankruptcy; another, to enable the proof of annuity debts; and a fourth, to prevent commissioners from declaring dividends upon the admission of the assignees, and to compel them in all cases to take the account of the bankrupt's estate, before they can be allowed to declare a dividend. Additions have been made to other clauses; particularly that relating to sureties, which, I fear, as it is now framed, will give rise to many questions upon the construction and application of it, and will greatly increase that litigation which it was one principal object of my Bill to diminish. Amongst other alterations in this clause relating to sureties, the Lords have struck out the words which the Attorney and Solicitor-General contended for, and at last prevailed to have inserted, in the committee in the House of Commons. Neither of these gentlemen have taken any notice of this since the Bill came from the Lords.

The vacation.

21st, *Wed.* Parliament was prorogued.

One of my children had this summer a most dangerous illness, which very nearly proved fatal to him, and left him in a very reduced and feeble state. With a view principally of recovering his strength, Anne and I determined to pass the vacation somewhere by the sea. We accordingly fixed on Weymouth, and arrived there on the 18th of August, having left town on the 16th.

After having been at Weymouth somewhat less than a fortnight, we left all our children there except the eldest, and proceeded with him on a little tour into Devonshire, which we had long meditated.

Sept. 22d. We returned to Weymouth, and remained there till the 17th of October.

Soon after my return to Weymouth happened the duel[1] between Lord Castlereagh and Mr.

[1] The following note is written on a detached paper which did not originally form part of this Diary. — Ed.

"The publication of the letters which passed between these ex-ministers previous to their duel, has fully enabled the public to judge of their conduct in that transaction. The practice of duelling, as it has of late prevailed, is a great national evil; and though it is extremely difficult to find a remedy for it, yet that conduct is certainly in the highest degree criminal, which tends in any degree to render the practice still more common. When, indeed, a man has received some flagrant insult, and finds himself exposed, if he patiently endures it, to public contempt and scorn, and if he resents it, not only to a violation of the laws of his country, but to a profanation of the law of God — though it cannot, to those who have a true sense of the duties of religion, be doubtful how he should act, yet even the most austere piety must admit that his is a most trying and painful situation, and that he is well entitled, if not to indulgence, at least to pity. But very different is the case of those, who, without any insult offered to them, without the least imputation on their honour, merely because they have been deceived and offended by another, attempt to soothe their chagrin and mortification by the blood of their adversary. Unfortunately, of late years, instances of this latter kind have not been very rare. No example, however, has come within our knowledge, of a duel more unjustifiable than that which has taken place between these men, whose peculiar duty it was, as being entrusted with the government of the country, and as the favoured servants and confidential advisers of a moral and pious prince, to set an example of obedience to the law and respect for religion. Admitting every thing that Lord Castlereagh alleges, granting that Mr. Canning had basely deceived his Lordship,

Resignation of two of the secretaries of state.

Canning; the resignation of both those ministers; Perceval's application to Lord Grenville and Lord Grey, to join in an administration with himself and

---

had endeavoured to turn him out of office by a dark intrigue, and had afterwards suffered an experiment to be tried at an enormous risk of blood and treasure to the nation, which, if it succeeded, as it would make Mr. Canning's own place secure, was to remove all objection to his Lordship, but, if it failed, was to furnish new grounds for the removal of his pretended friend—admitting the private and public treachery of this proceeding, yet there was nothing in all this which any man of the most punctilious sense of honour could think required an appeal to arms. Nothing done, and nothing attempted had the least tendency to bring dishonour on Lord Castlereagh. His lordship is compelled, indeed, by way of giving some colour of excuse for his challenge, to pretend that, in some way or other, his honour was affected; and therefore he says, that, if his situation had been disclosed to him, he could not have submitted to remain one moment in office without the entire abandonment of his private honour. But his situation never was disclosed to him; his complaint indeed is, that it was not disclosed, and consequently his honour must have remained perfectly unsullied. Not only Mr. Canning had not dishonoured him, but, by withholding from him the knowledge of his situation, he had made it impossible that his lordship, by remaining in office, should be dishonoured. According to Lord Castlereagh, Mr. Canning had, it is true, deceived and wronged him; but into what a state must society fall, if, by the example of those men, of whose virtues and talents his Majesty forms a sufficiently high opinion to intrust the fate of his people to their hands, we are to be taught that it is incumbent on every man who has been deceived or injured, to wash out the wrong that he has suffered in the blood of the offender.

"But, if Lord Castlereagh's sending the challenge was reprehensible, the manner in which it was accepted by Mr. Canning was, if possible, still more deserving of censure. According to that gentleman, Lord Castlereagh was totally mistaken as to his conduct. 'His Lordship's letter,' he says, 'abounds with misapprehensions;' and yet he does not attempt to remove one of them. He does not undeceive Lord Castlereagh in any particular, but, on the contrary, he rejoices that his Lordship had misconceived the matter, because it afforded them an opportunity of fighting. No other sense can be put on his letter, in which he says that Lord Castlereagh has been led to send him a challenge because he is in a complete error, but yet that he cheerfully accepts his challenge. 'Having totally misconceived my conduct, you send me a challenge; I will not set you right, but your challenge I eagerly accept.' This is a language well suited to a rash youth who is ambitious of the reputation of a duellist, or to a person of doubtful character, who wishes to intimidate any man from saying what all men think of him; but who would expect to find it in the mouth of a Minister of State, of one who has lived to a mature age, and who has never been in danger of being stigmatized as a coward?"

Lord Liverpool; and the refusal of both those noblemen to communicate with him on such a subject. The letters which passed between them have been published in the newspapers. The proposal was probably not intended as an insult to Lord Grenville and Lord Grey. But surely no greater insult could be offered to any public men, than to suppose them so eager to be in office, that they would unite in an administration with persons whom they had constantly represented as having supplanted them in office by a dark and disgraceful intrigue, as having set up a false cry of danger to the Church, in order to excite the populace against them, and as having entered on their office upon the most unconstitutional principles. Even if they were dead to all sense of honour, and were regardless of every thing but their own interests, they could not have listened for a moment to such a proposal. The consequence would have been that, degraded in character, they would in a short time have been again dismissed through the intrigues of their colleagues, and could never have become again formidable to any administration, however constituted. Nothing, indeed, could contribute more effectually to destroy all confidence in all public men, than so base and unprincipled a coalition. Perceval says in his letter, that no idea existed in his or Lord Liverpool's mind, that, in forming such an administration as was to be proposed, any dereliction of public principle was necessary on any side. The meaning of this it is difficult to discover. The principles of the present and of the last administration being, on the most

Perceval's proposal of a coalition.

important points, in direct opposition to each other, either one side must have sacrificed theirs, or there must have been an abandonment of principles on all sides, and a sort of common understanding among them, that the only object on which they should be steadfastly intent should be the preservation of their places; and that, as for the difficulties of the State, they should satisfy themselves with just struggling against them from day to day, as they might happen to present themselves.

Oct. 17th. I set out for Durham.

22d. At Sydney Smith's, Heslington, near York.

23d. Arrived at Durham.

24th. Held my sittings at Durham, where the only business was one motion.

The jubilee.

25th. This was appointed by Government to be celebrated as a day of jubilee; it being that on which the King enters into the fiftieth year of his reign. I attended divine service in the Cathedral.

Sermon at Durham.

We had a sermon preached by ——. As was to be expected, it consisted of a panegyric on the King. He praised his Majesty with great propriety for his domestic virtues; but when he passed from the man to the monarch, and entered upon his Majesty's public merits, his theme was not quite so fruitful. Indeed, I had a good deal of curiosity to see how he would deal with it; for I doubt whether the history of mankind can furnish an example of a good man seated on a throne, who, in the course of a long reign, has done less for the happiness of any portion of his subjects than the present King. The first topic dwelt upon was, the making the Judges immoveable, even upon the demise of the Crown. This having been a measure recommended by the King himself, it is very just to give him all the praise of it. It is true that, after the Judges had been confirmed in their offices, they, by the law as it already stood, would have been immoveable during the remainder of his reign, and that it was therefore the abandonment of a prerogative which he could not himself exercise. Still the measure was a very good one; and the people ought to be grateful when a King grants them a benefit, even though it be only at the expense of his successors. The other public measures which the preacher dwelt upon, as entitling the King above other Princes to the affection of his people, were, the Grenville Act, the removal of the disabilities of those who are not of the established religion, the King's attachment to the Church, the Union with Ireland, and the abolition of the slave trade. I say nothing of any of these few Acts of Parliament, not of Royalty selected out of the transactions of half a century to form the grounds of such a panegyric, except that for the abolition of the slave trade. The gross adulation of ascribing the merit of that measure to his Majesty, excited in me a degree of indignation which I could ill restrain. That the King, who was always personally most adverse to the abolition of the slave trade; who, by those men in both Houses who have been usually called his friends, constantly opposed it; who, probably alone, counteracted the zeal of his Ministers, and actually prevented, for several years, the measure being carried; and who may be truly stated to have been the immediate cause of many thousands of human beings and their posterity having been doomed to the most cruel of all slaveries; — that he should have incense offered up to him as the destroyer of this abomination, and that by a reverend divine, a high dignitary of the Church, before a numerous audience, and in a place consecrated to the worship of the God of Truth, might really astonish even those who know to what excess of flattery priestly ambition will sometimes have recourse. Strange, indeed, as this is, it is not without example. In a Latin sermon preached by Dr. Bowyer Edward Sparke, Dean of Bristol, before the synod of Canterbury, in July, 1807, a few months after Lord Grenville's administration was dismissed, on account or under pretext of their having attempted to remove some of the disabilities to which the Catholics of Ireland are still subject — in this very sermon, preached professedly against the Catholics and against the dismissed Ministers *, those Ministers, whose greatest glory it was that, in opposition to the Court, they abolished the slave trade, — in this very sermon, the reverend preacher does not blush to call the King "Patriæ parens, Africæ ab immanissimâ corporum mercaturâ liberator." For this, amongst other services, this

Sermon of Dr. Sparke Dean of Bristol.

* He describes the Catholics as openly professing that faith was not to be kept with heretics, and assuming authority over Kings, "Quid," he says, "magis est periculosum quam ullam potestatem iis demandari qui (si sibi constare velint) Ecclesiam evertere, adeoque Reipublicæ perniciem struere aut saltem alterutri insidias moliri non desinerent."

courtly preacher has, in the present year, been raised to the Bishopric of Chester.*

This Jubilee is a political engine of the Ministers; and no doubt they would have derived great advantage from it, if the failure of their rash and foolish expeditions and their own despicable quarrels and intrigues, had not made so unfavourable an impression on the public. The King's popularity for many years past will probably appear to posterity, when they reflect upon the measures of his government, to be very unaccountable. From the beginning of his reign to the close of the American War, he was one of the most unpopular Princes that ever sat upon the throne: he is now one of the most popular; and yet in nothing is the character or spirit of his government altered. But the truth is that it is to the conduct of others, and to events over which His Majesty had no control, that all his popularity is to be ascribed. When the coalition between Lord North and Mr. Fox took place[1], the tide turned in his favour. A very general and very just indignation was excited in the public when they saw those two statesmen renouncing all their inveterate political animosities, and forming what seemed a confederacy against the nation, and when they saw them supported in this against the people by their own representatives in Parliament. The fatal effects of that measure have been long, and are still, felt; and it will probably hereafter produce still greater evils than

Causes of the King's popularity.

* In May, 1812, the Prince of Wales, as Regent, translated him to the Bishopric of Ely.

1 In April, 1783.—Ed.

any that have hitherto flowed from it. The King's joining the people on so important an occasion, against his Ministers and against the Parliament, laid the foundation of his popularity. Then followed an attempt upon his life by a maniac[1]; then the irregularities and dissipation of the Prince destined to be his successor*; next his own unfortunate derangement of mind[2], and the dread which the public entertained of the government which they saw about to take place, with the Prince for Regent, and for his Ministers the heads of the coalition, who had already claimed for him the Regency upon grounds the most unconstitutional; then his joyful recovery when it was least expected[3], which dispelled in a moment the gloom which hung over the country: and last of all, but which added tenfold strength to every motive of endearment to the King, the horrors of the French Revolution; the sufferings of the Royal Family, the debasement of the nobles, the confiscation of the property of the rich, the persecution of the clergy, the national bankruptcy, and all those various evils which it had produced, and which gave almost every description of persons who have any influence on public opinion an interest to adhere to,

* The joke of the demagogue Wilkes, who, being asked by the Prince, upon some occasion on which he had manifested his attachment to the King in a very extravagant way — "How long it was that he had been so loyal?" answered, "Ever since I have had the honour of being acquainted with your Royal Highness," conveys a very exact explanation of many a man's loyalty.

---

[1] Margaret Nicholson, on Aug. 2. 1786.

[2] In the autumn of 1788.

[3] The complete recovery of the King was announced to the two Houses on the 10th of March, 1789.— Ed.

and maintain inviolably, our established Constitution, and, above all, the Monarchy, as inseparably connected with, and maintaining everything valuable in the State.

Oct. 25. After Church, and after I had sat in Court, I went to Bishop Auckland, and passed the rest of the day there.

29th. Arrived in London; on the next day,

30th. The Lord Chancellor held the first seal.

I spent the leisure which this late vacation afforded me in writing some papers on Criminal Law. If I should not have occasion to state the substance of them in Parliament, I, perhaps, may publish them.

1810.

Jan. 22. Parliament met.

An amendment was moved in both Houses to the Address in answer to the King's speech. The amendment was lost, and by a much greater majority in the House of Commons than the Opposition had imagined to be possible. For the amendment, 167; against it, 263: majority, 96.[1]

Expedition to the Scheldt.

26th. Lord Porchester, in the House of Commons, moved that the House should resolve itself into a committee of the whole House to inquire into the conduct and policy of the late expedition to the Scheldt; and the motion was carried against all the exertions of the Ministers by a majority of 9. For it, 195; against it, 186. I took some part in the debate.[2]

Offices in reversion.

31st. Bankes moved for leave to bring in a Bill to make perpetual the Act for preventing the grant of offices in reversion, which will expire in less than five weeks. Perceval moved, as an amendment, that the Bill to be brought in should continue the Act only for a limited time. Bankes's original motion was carried without a division. I spoke in support of it; and, amongst other topics, insisted upon those which are to be found above in page 226.

1 Sir S. Romilly voted in the minority.—Ed.

2 In support of Lord Porchester's motion.—Ed.

There were three divisions to-day, upon the nomination of different members of the committee to inquire into the public expenditure; and the Ministers were in a minority upon each division.

Criminal laws.

Feb. 9th. *Fri.* I moved for and obtained leave to bring into the House of Commons three Bills, to repeal the Acts of 10 & 11 Will. III. c. 23., 12 Ann. st. 1. c. 7., and 24 Geo. II., which punish with death the crimes of stealing privately in a shop goods of the value of five shillings, and of stealing to the amount of forty shillings in dwelling-houses, or on board vessels in navigable rivers.[1]

[1] The following is a letter from Dr. Parr to Sir S. Romilly, on this subject:—Ed.

"My Dear Sir, Feb. 21. 1810.

"I thank you for informing me of your intended motion in Parliament, as it protected me from being misled by newspaper statements. I was very much interested by your speech; I heartily wish you success, and, as the ice is broken, I should hope that the minds of men will be prepared for further progress. It has often struck me, that the crimes of unhappy men in our own days are much less aggravated than they were formerly, and this circumstance I have remarked in my note. I wish you to take it into consideration, when offences have not increased in a number at all proportionate to our increased population, and when their malignity is less, the Legislature has been strangely employed in multiplying capital punishments. You would do well for the present in confining your plan of Reform to crimes unaccompanied by violence, and thus far Paley is with you. What can Windham mean by contradicting you about Paley? I agree with you that Paley is much overrated. 'Videt meliora probatque,' but, in a certain way of his own, and for certain purposes of his own, 'laudat deteriora.' He commends, it is true, the paucity of executions, but he avowedly and elaborately vindicates the number of laws which ordain capital punishment; and here it is that you and I censure the multiplicity of laws which cannot be enforced. I was very glad to see that you agree with me in lamenting that discretionary power which is so capriciously exercised by Judges. Nearly all your brethren will be against you; and this spirit of the fraternity is an additional reason with me for leaving as little as possible in their power. I am glad that you joined the Solicitor-General in checking the extension of capital punishment in a recent debate. But the technical reason which he assigned had greater weight with the House than with me, and perhaps yourself. I observe that your brethren seldom or never touch on those great and leading principles of jurisprudence, which Beccaria and Bentham have so well illustrated. As to public affairs, you and I

The Solicitor-General, with his usual panegyrics on the wisdom of past ages, and declamations on the danger of interfering with what is already established, announced his intention of opposing the Bills after they should be brought in.

March 12th. *Mon.* I published the substance of my speech of the 9th of February, in the form of a pamphlet, with this title, "*Observations on the Criminal Law as it relates to Capital Punishments, and on the Mode in which it is administered. By Sir Samuel Romilly.*" I incorporated in it a good deal of what I had written in the course of the vacation. [1]

---

cannot have the smallest difference of opinion about men or measures. From my old habits of intimacy with Mr. Windham, I suffered great pain upon seeing him so completely convicted of inconsistency, vanity, &c. by Cobbett, and by the editors of the *Morning Post* and the *Times*.

"Pray give my very best compliments and best wishes to Lady Romilly. My good friend, I shall make you smile by a little story. I have lately been employed in making my will. It so happens that I am very fond of silver plate, and have been lucky enough to receive many valuable presents in that way. I wish, and have directed it to be kept together. I have bequeathed it to my grandchildren, who are three in number, and if they should all die before they are of age, I have left it to my friend Sir Samuel Romilly, as a mark of my respect and regard. You have little chance of getting it; but you will not be displeased with me for thus putting down your name.[a] With great respect and regard, I have the honour to be, dear Sir, your friend and obedient humble servant, S. Parr."

[1] The following is a letter from Mr. Dugald Stewart to Sir S. Romilly on the subject of this publication. — Ed.

"My dear Sir, Kinneil House, June 28. 1810.

"I have yet to thank you for the very great pleasure I received from your observations on the Criminal Law of England. On every point which you have there touched upon, your reasonings carried complete conviction to my mind; and however unsuccessful they may have been in accomplishing your object in Parliament, I am satisfied that they must have produced a very strong impression on public opinion. I hope that nothing will discourage you from the prosecution of your arduous undertaking, in which you cannot fail to be seconded by the

---

[a] See *infrà*, *Parl. Diary*, May 15th, 1817.

Complaint of breach of privilege by John Gale Jones.

28th. *Wed.* Upon the inquiry in the House of Commons relative to the late expedition to the Scheldt, Charles Yorke[1], member for Cambridgeshire, enforced the standing order of the House for the exclusion of strangers. This excited great dissatisfaction in the public; and was made a subject of discussion in a debating society, which was in the habit of advertising, by bills posted up in the streets, questions to be debated amongst them, and the decisions which they came to. The question on this subject was, whether Mr. Yorke by this conduct, or Mr. Windham by a declaration he had recently made in the House on the liberty of the press, had committed the greatest outrage upon public feeling; and the paper announced that it had been on the Monday preceding, "unanimously decided, that the enforcement of the

good wishes of every man of common humanity, whose understanding is not altogether blinded by professional, or by political prejudices.

"I was more particularly interested in that part of your argument where you combat Paley, whose apology for the existing system I never could read without feelings of indignation. Indeed, I have more than once lost my temper in discussing the merits of that part of his book, with some of your countrymen, who were disposed to look up to him as an oracle both in politics and in morals. Your reply to him is, in my opinion, quite unanswerable.

"I have desired my bookseller to send to you a volume of Essays, which I have just published, and of which I request your kind acceptance. In the midst of your present occupations (of which I had lately a circumstantial detail from our friend George Wilson), I do not expect that you will have a moment's time to look into it. But you may, perhaps, find leisure to write me your opinion of it, during your autumn vacation.

"Is there no chance of your visiting Scotland this season? Mrs. Stewart and I are living at present about twenty miles west from Edinburgh, where I need not say how happy it would make us to receive Lady Romilly and you. We have both gained much in point of health since we retired to the country.

"I ever am, my dear Sir,
"Most sincerely yours,
"DUGALD STEWART."

[1] First Lord of the Admiralty, and a member of the Cabinet.—ED.

standing order ought to be censured as an insidious and ill-timed attack upon the liberty of the press, tending to aggravate the discontents of the people, and render their representatives objects of jealousy and suspicion." Mr. Yorke complained to the House of this paper; and on the 21st of February the House resolved, that John Gale Jones (who was brought to the bar of the House, and admitted himself to be the author of it), in having been the author of the paper, and caused it to be printed, had been guilty of a gross breach of the privileges of the House, and that he should be committed to Newgate. He was accordingly committed; and the Speaker's warrant of commitment recited that "the House had adjudged that John Gale Jones having written and caused to be printed a certain paper containing libellous reflections on the character and conduct of the House, and of some of the members thereof, was thereby guilty of a high breach of the privileges of the House." Sir Francis Burdett, member for Westminster, published in Cobbett's Weekly Register of last Saturday, 24th March, a letter addressed to his constituents, and an argument which purported to be in substance the same with one which he had delivered in the House, upon an unsuccessful motion made by him on the 12th, for Gale Jones's discharge. In these he insisted very strenuously, and with some offensive and very disrespectful language towards the House and the Speaker, upon the illegality of the commitment; the House not having, as he contended, any authority to imprison for such an offence. Complaint was made of this paper

Sir Francis Burdett.

yesterday in the House, and a notice given of a motion upon it for to-day (28th); and it was now moved by Mr. Lethbridge, member for Somersetshire (who upon all occasions voted with the Ministers, and who had preferred the complaint), that the paper was a gross and scandalous libel, reflecting on the just rights and privileges of the House.

It was very difficult to know how to deal with this motion, especially as it is understood that the Ministers mean that it shall be followed by a commitment of Sir Francis Burdett to the Tower. There is no saying to what fatal consequences such a measure may, with the present disposition of the public towards the House of Commons, lead; especially if the principal members in opposition to Government concur in it. The popularity of Sir Francis Burdett, on account principally of his conduct in the inquiry respecting the Duke of York, and of the opposition he has made to a prodigal expenditure of public money, is great, just in proportion as the House is low, in the public estimation. Being strongly impressed with the danger of any hasty proceedings on such a subject, and entertaining great doubt of the power of the House to punish such an offence, I supported to the best of my ability a motion which was made by Mr. Brand, to adjourn the debate till to-morrow se'nnight. The Ministers at first would not hear of this; and nothing could exceed the violence of Croker and other members who supported the original motion. Amongst others Sir Joseph Yorke, brother of Charles Yorke, said he had hoped that the question would have been carried by acclamation. When, however, late in the course of the debate, Wilberforce, Bathurst, and even the Master of the Rolls, recommended an adjournment, Perceval, fearful of being beaten, thought it prudent to give way; and the debate was adjourned accordingly.

Expedition to the Scheldt.

30th. *Fri.* The motion of censure of Ministers for their conduct in the expedition to the Scheldt was lost, and a complete exculpation of Ministers voted by the House by a small majority, considering how many members were present; 275 against 227 upon one question; 253 against 232 upon another, a majority of only 21.

Sir Francis Burdett.

April 5th. The adjourned debate on the complaint against Sir Francis Burdett was resumed in the House of Commons. All the lawyers who took any part in the debate, and all the friends and supporters of the late administration, concurred with the present administration in thinking the paper a breach of privilege, and that the House had a right to punish the author of it in a summary way: but they differed as to the proper punishment to be inflicted; the Ministers supporting a motion made by Sir Robert Salisbury for committing Sir Francis Burdett to the Tower, and the Opposition supporting an amendment moved by Adam, that he should be reprimanded by the Speaker. Upon the best consideration that I could give the subject, I thought that the House had no cognisance whatever of the offence, and I maintained that opinion at considerable length. I did not dispute the right of the House to imprison in

Privilege of Parliament.

all cases of breaches of privilege which obstruct its proceedings; such as resistance to the orders of the House or the warrant of the Speaker; a refusal to answer questions put to a witness, or prevarication in giving evidence; interruption of the proceedings of the House by disorderly behaviour; and publications on proceedings that are pending, with a view to influence votes. But I denied the power of the House to punish the publication of animadversions on the proceedings of the House, or on the conduct of its members, in matters which were concluded. With respect to these, I thought they ought to be left to the ordinary tribunals. If the House punishes, it makes itself accuser, judge, and party. The party accused has no opportunity of being heard; for, though the paper is read to him, and he is asked what he has to say in his defence, he is not, even where he is a member, allowed to hear the debate; and being left ignorant what construction his accusers put upon his words, he has no means of explaining them, and of showing that he did not use them in the sense imputed to them. He is deprived of a trial by his peers; he cannot have counsel to plead for him; there is no appeal from the judgment against him. All these disadvantages must, of necessity, be submitted to in the cases of breach of privilege which I have mentioned, because the House could not proceed to discharge its important functions, if it had not the power to overcome such obstructions. But these extraordinary and dangerous powers, as they are only to be justified by necessity, so are they limited by the same necessity. Instances, indeed, were produced, where the House had exercised the power of imprisoning in cases of libels on their past proceedings; but they were few, and mostly in very bad times. One case was that of Arthur Hall, in Queen Elizabeth's reign (in 1580); who, on a complicated charge of publishing a libel on some members, and for disobedience to the summons of the House, was fined, imprisoned for a time certain, and till he should retract his book, and besides expelled; and, of this case, Hatsell observes, that it is the only instance he had found, previous to the Long Parliament, of proceedings on a complaint of publications derogatory to the honour of the House. (1 Hatsell, 127.) Other instances, indeed, were produced; but, really, instances of extraordinary powers exerted and submitted to, cannot in such a case make law. If they could, the Houses of Parliament would have a right to punish by pillory and other ignominious punishments, and by a sentence to be kept to hard labour for life; for such punishments have been inflicted by the Houses. The case of the *King* v. *Flower*, indeed, is a direct authority by the Court of King's Bench in favour of such a power in the House of Lords as is now contended for; but it was a judgment pronounced with great intemperance, and is entitled to no weight. Two judges only were present; and one of them Lord Kenyon, who had, as a Peer, taken a very active part in the proceeding complained of. It was not surprising that none of the political friends with whom I usually act concurred with me upon this occasion. They had themselves, in former cases, so strongly contended for this power in the House of Commons, particularly in the cases of Stockdale and of Reeves, that they could not exercise an unbiassed judgment now. Lord Grenville was the Peer who, in the House of Lords, moved for the imprisonment and fining of Flower. The question for commitment to the Tower was carried at eight o'clock on Friday morning, but only by a majority of thirty-eight persons, in a pretty full House.[1] The doctrine I maintained on this occasion is certainly not very consistent with the power which I once, as counsel in the case of M'Namara, contended that the Court of Chancery possessed. That, however, was in truth a case where the publication related to a proceeding that was depending; and though the arguments I used were not confined to such a case, I had not then given the subject all the consideration which I have since done.[2]

Popular disturbances.

6th. *Fri.* Outrages have been committed by the populace, in breaking the windows of the persons who took most part in the debate against Sir Francis Burdett, particularly Perceval's, Sir John Anstruther's, the house which Lethbridge lived in, but which he has quitted, and many others.

7th. *Sat.* Sir Francis Burdett refuses to obey the Speaker's warrant, and declares himself determined to defend himself in his house. He has written a letter calling upon the Sheriffs of Middlesex to protect him.

8th. *Sun.* The Guards were called out last night to suppress the riots which took place. The Riot

[1] The numbers being for the original motion 190, against it 152.—Ed.
[2] See *suprà*, p. 176.—Ed.

Act was read, and several persons were wounded. Ministers have sent for troops from all parts of the country within one hundred miles of London. I understand that Sir Francis Burdett is acting by the advice principally of Roger O'Connor, Colonel Wardle, and Lord Cochrane.

9th. *Mon.* It having been at last determined that Sir Francis Burdett's house should be broken open, and that he should be carried by force to the Tower, this was accomplished this morning at eleven o'clock; and he was conveyed to the Tower under a strong military escort of cavalry and infantry. The soldiers were grossly insulted and attacked on their return; they fired upon the people, and several persons have been killed.

It had been reported that Sir Francis Burdett had resisted the execution of the warrant under my advice; and in several newspapers it was stated that I had been with him on Friday and Saturday. This report I contradicted to-day in the House; and declared, as is true, that I have had no communication with him directly or indirectly, and that I never was in his house in my life. I had given notice of a motion for to-day for the discharge of J. Gale Jones, but I was advised not to bring on the motion in the state of irritation in which men are at the present moment, and I have therefore consented to put it off.

Burdett's letter to the Speaker.

The Speaker laid before the House a letter from Sir Francis Burdett, declaring that he should resist the execution of the warrant, couched in very indecent and insolent terms, and manifestly written to provoke his expulsion from the House. The consideration of it is deferred till to-morrow.

10th. *Tu.* Perceval proposed a resolution, that Burdett's letter is a high aggravation of his former offence against the privileges of the House, and he admitted, as did Windham and several others who spoke in the debate, that he did not propose an expulsion, lest Burdett should be re-elected by the inhabitants of Westminster. I opposed the motion merely on account of the language in which it was couched. I expressed my sense of the gross impropriety of the letter, and I strongly reprobated Sir Francis Burdett's conduct; but I said that, not thinking the former paper an offence cognisable by the House, I could not vote the letter an aggravation of that supposed offence. I was very unwell, and obliged to go from the House, and after I was gone it was agreed that the word "aggravation," which I objected to, should be left out of the resolution; and it was unanimously voted that the letter was a breach of privilege, but that, Sir Francis Burdett being already committed to the Tower, the House would proceed no farther upon it.

Motion for the discharge of John Gale Jones.

16th. *Mon.* I moved that J. Gale Jones should be discharged from his imprisonment. I made this motion without any communication with Jones himself: and, as my only objects were to bring the House to some degree of moderation, and to relieve the individual from his punishment, the only ground upon which I asked for his discharge was, that the punishment which he had already suffered was sufficiently severe for the offence with which he had been charged; and this was, in the course of the debate, admitted by every body but Windham. Still, however, my motion was opposed by the Ministers. They said that the uniform practice of the House was to require a person imprisoned for a breach of privilege to petition the House for his discharge, and in his petition to acknowledge the justice of his sentence, and to express his contrition for his offence. I endeavoured to show the injustice of adhering to such a practice, by which a man is compelled publicly to profess what he probably cannot in his conscience agree to, and by which he is debased in his own estimation, and is made an instrument of his own disgrace. The Master of the Rolls supported my motion in an admirable speech, and voted for it. The Ministers, however, succeeded in rejecting it. The numbers were, for it 112, against it 160.[1]

[1] The following letter from Dr. Parr refers to Sir S. Romilly's speech on this occasion.—Ed.

"Dear Sir Samuel Romilly, April 19. 1810.

"I have read your speech about Jones, not only with the entire assent of my judgment to every principle, and every modification of principle contained in it, but with deep, serious, solemn sympathy for the pure and hallowed maxims of morality which you feel so strongly, which you have expressed so luminously, which you have applied so judiciously. If wisdom, if virtue, if patriotism, if a thorough knowledge of human nature, if an unfeigned and ardent solicitude for the preservation and increase of human happiness constitute a good speaker, a good citizen, and a good man, you, Sir Samuel Romilly, are that speaker, that citizen, and that man. Dear Sir, I do not know whether our religious creed may in all points be similar. But we do agree upon those great points to which the belief of all doctrines whatsoever ought to be subservient; and this agreement, founded as it is upon an honest use of our understandings, and directed to the happiness of our fellow-creatures, will make both of us equally acceptable in the sight of that Deity who is the ruler of all events and the searcher of all hearts. May he bless and preserve you and yours for ever. My scribe, who is a man of letters, feels, I am sure, the same admiration that I do of your last speech; and I have said two or three times with a sigh, "Oh that Mr. Fox had been alive to hear it." Yet it will be heard by wise and good men in our own and every successive genera-

17th, *Tu.* A remonstrance and petition from the inhabitants of Westminster assembled at a public meeting on the subject of Sir Francis Burdett's imprisonment, couched in the most disrespectful terms, was this day presented to the House of Commons; and, after some debate, was received and ordered to lie on the table. It will, of course, be in the Journals; and this is certainly not the last affront which, in consequence of the contest in which the Ministers have rashly plunged the House, they will have to receive and to record against themselves. These are the first fruits of this boasted vindication of the rights and dignity of the House of Commons.

Criminal Law.

May 1st, *Tu.* The report of the Bills to make an alteration in the Criminal Law, which I have brought into Parliament, came on to-day, when it had been agreed that the principle of them should be debated. I understood that two of them, those relating to stealing in dwelling-houses and on navigable rivers, were to be opposed by the Ministry; and as there was a very thin House, and I was by no means sure that they would not also oppose the third, that which relates to stealing privately in shops; and as I knew that, whether opposed or not, it would not be suffered to pass without a great deal of discussion, I thought it most prudent to take first the Bills that were certainly to

---

tion, and it has been heard and approved, and recorded by the greatest, wisest, and best of all Beings. Farewell.

"I am truly, and respectfully, and gratefully,

"Your friend,

"S. Parr."

be opposed; and I began with the Bill to repeal the Act which makes it a capital offence to steal to the amount of forty shillings in a dwelling-house. Windham was most strenuous in opposition to the Bill; not that he much disliked the Bill itself, but he disapproved of the doctrines I had maintained in my speech and my pamphlet, and therefore he opposed the Bill as part of a system which he considered as very erroneous and very dangerous. That in which I had given him most offence was what I had said in answer to Paley, whose reputation he said it was, in his opinion, a great national object to maintain.* The Attorney

* The following character of Windham, contained in a letter of Sir James Mackintosh, is very accurate:—

"Bombay, Oct. 16. 1810.

"The Eclipse Sloop of War is arrived at Madras. She left England on the 16th of June, and brings no news of consequence, but the death of Windham. He was a man of a very high order, spoiled by faults apparently small. He had acuteness, wit, variety of knowledge, and fertility of illustration, in a degree probably superior to any man now alive. He had not the least approach to meanness. On the contrary, he was distinguished by honour and loftiness of sentiment. But he was an indiscreet debater, who sacrificed his interest as a statesman to his momentary feelings as an orator. For the sake of a new subtlety, or a forcible phrase, he was content to utter what loaded him with permanent unpopularity. This logical propensity led him always to extreme consequences; and he expressed his opinions so strongly, that they seemed to furnish the most striking examples of political inconsistency; though, if prudence had limited his logic, and mitigated his expressions, they would have been acknowledged to be no more than those views of different sides of an object, which, in the changes of politics, must present themselves to the mind of a statesman. Singular as it may sound, he often opposed novelties from a love of paradox. These novelties had long been almost established opinions among men of speculation; and this sort of establishment had roused his mind to resist them, before they were proposed to be reduced to practice. The mitigation of penal law had, for example, been the system of every philosopher in Europe for the last half century, but Paley. The principles generally received by enlightened men on that subject, had long almost disgusted him as common-places; and he was opposing the established creed of minds of his own class, when he appeared to be supporting an established code of law. But he was a scholar, a man of genius, and a gentleman of high spirit and dignified manners."

and Solicitor-General and Perceval also opposed the Bill; but the Master of the Rolls supported it very warmly. He said that the law and the practice being so opposite to each other, one of them must be wrong, and he had no doubt that it was the law. That it was important in all countries that the law should coincide with public opinion, but more especially in this country, where public opinion had so powerful an influence, and where juries prevailed; and that in truth it appeared that there was amongst prosecutors, witnesses, juries, judges, and the Ministers of the Crown, a general confederacy to prevent the law being executed. Canning also spoke in support of the Bill. It was, however, lost by a majority of two, there being thirty-three against it, and thirty-one for it.[1] Amongst the thirty-three were no less than twenty-two persons in office; three Lords of the Admiralty, two Lords of the Treasury, two Secretaries of the Treasury, the Secretary of the Admiralty, Secretary of State, Secretary at War, Secretary for Ireland, an under Secretary of State, &c. &c. Very few of the members of Opposition were present. In general they wished well to the Bill, but not well enough to give themselves the trouble of attending upon it.

Having succeeded in their opposition to this

[1] Sir John Newport, the Master of the Rolls (Sir W. Grant), Mr. Canning, and Mr. Wilberforce, spoke in favour of it. Mr. Wilberforce ended his speech by saying, that "to the able and eminent lawyer who had undertaken this revision, and who had brought forward the Bill under discussion, he for one would declare, as he felt, the most unfeigned thanks; and he could not avoid adding the expression of his regret, that his honourable and learned friend was not in his benevolent undertakings more adequately supported."—Ed.

Bill, they declined any opposition to that which related to privately stealing in shops; and the report of that Bill was therefore received, and on Friday following (4th May) it was read a third time and passed.

The third Bill, that to take away capital punishment for stealing to the amount of forty shillings on board vessels in navigable rivers and upon wharfs, was postponed; though, for some time, Perceval and Ryder (the Secretary of State) eagerly insisted that the House should immediately proceed on it, it being then near one o'clock in the morning.

Returns of convicts to be laid before the House.

4th. I moved in the House of Commons for returns of convicts for the last five years, distinguishing the crimes for which they were committed, the crimes for which they were indicted, and the crimes of which they were convicted.[1] My object in this was, to have, as nearly as possible, an exact state of the Criminal Law, as it is executed. At the same time I gave notice that I should, early in the next Session, bring into Parliament a Bill exactly the same as that which was thrown out three days ago.[2]

1 No opposition was made to this motion.—ED.

2 On this occasion Sir S. Romilly alluded to the thinness of the attendance on the 1st of May, when one of the Bills was thrown out, in the following terms:—"On a question of this description, totally unconnected with party, I have to lament that any one should have thought it necessary to canvass for votes against it; and yet it is obvious that all the gentlemen in office then present voted against it. Of this I do not complain, though I must complain of the thin attendance in the House on that occasion. It is impossible, one would imagine, that gentlemen can be indifferent on a question in which the fate, and even the lives of seven or eight hundred fellow-creatures are involved. It has been said that many gentlemen friendly to the measure would have attended if they had known that the Bill was to come on. But I had given notice of the day in rather a full attendance; and I do think it

City of London's petition to the House of Commons.

9th. On a question in the House of Commons, whether a petition of the Livery of London voted at the Common Hall, respecting Sir Francis Burdett's commitment, should be suffered to lie on the table, I spoke and voted for it. The petition certainly was not couched in respectful terms. There was nothing, however, in it which in my opinion justified the rejecting it. I thought that the House ought to facilitate, as much as possible, the approach of the people to them with a statement of their grievances, whether real or imaginary; that, if the people were discontented, nothing was more desirable than that the appeals they made should be to the House itself; and that therefore the House ought not to examine very scrupulously the terms in which the complaint was expressed. The petition, however, was rejected.[1] A petition of the freeholders of Middlesex on the same subject, for which I had also voted, though I did not speak, was on a former day, in the same manner, rejected by the House.

Penitentiary Houses and transportation to New South Wales.

On the same day, I moved that an address should be presented to the King, to pray that he would give directions for carrying into execution the Acts of 19 Geo. III. and 34 Geo. III. for erecting Penitentiary Houses. I stated very fully the gross injustice that, in particular instances, had been

---

strange that the Highgate Archway or the Holloway Water Bills should obtain a fuller attendance than a measure of such vital importance."—Ed.

[1] By a majority of 92; the numbers being, for receiving the petition 36; against it 128. The petition of the freeholders of Middlesex was rejected by a majority of 81; 58 having voted for it, and 139 against it.—Ed.

done by transporting felons to New South Wales *, and I endeavoured to point out, as forcibly as I could, the mischiefs which resulted from that species of punishment, as well as from imprisonment on board the hulks and in common jails, where prisoners of every description are confounded together, and youths, imprisoned for their first offences, are compelled to associate with, and are exposed to be corrupted by, the most desperate and hardened thieves. Ryder expressed a strong inclination to assent to the measure, but desired me to postpone it for some time, that he might inform himself more fully on the subject. I therefore withdrew my motion, and gave notice of it for a fortnight hence.

Sir Francis Burdett.

10th. Retainers were offered me by Sir Francis Burdett's solicitor, in the actions he has brought against the Speaker, Sergeant-at-Arms, and Constable of the Tower, accompanied with a note from himself. I returned an answer declining the retainers, and stating that I had made it a rule with myself not to go out of the Court of Chancery into any other Court; and that besides I could not with propriety, as a member of the House of Commons, be concerned as counsel in any such actions; especially as it seemed probable that questions might yet come to be debated and decided on in the House on which the retained counsel of Sir Francis Burdett ought not to speak or vote.

* In August, 1801, forty convicts were transported who had only one year of their term of transportation unexpired at the time of their embarkation, and ten who had only nine months unexpired, though it is a nine months' voyage. I stated this amongst other facts. Note, that the Duke of Portland was Secretary of State for the Home Department when this flagrant injustice was committed.

Privilege of Parliament.

11th. The House of Commons took into its consideration the mode in which Sir Francis Burdett's actions were to be defended, on the report of a committee, which had been appointed to search for precedents and report their opinions. A good deal of discussion took place, and, as I differed from much of what was said, I thought it right to state my opinion. It was, that the privilege of Parliament is unquestionably a part of the law of the land, and is to be administered only by Parliament: that, in a case of privilege, Parliament alone has jurisdiction, but that courts of law have a right to determine whether the case be a case of privilege; that the House of Commons cannot call what it pleases breach of privilege, and imprison whom it pleases under pretence of breach of privilege. In answer to the objection, "that such an abuse of authority by a House of Parliament, as calling what had nothing to do with Parliament a breach of privilege, was never likely to happen, and was an extreme and imaginary case," I instanced what had happened at no remote period of time in Ireland, where the House of Commons voted agistment tithes to be a grievance, and all men who sued for them enemies to their country; and then proceeded to commit, or would have committed, all persons who brought suits for the recovery of tithes unjustly withheld from them. Much was said of the analogy of proceedings in courts of law for contempts, where, it was maintained, that if any Court committed for a contempt, no other Court could take cognizance of it, and that the Court committing was the sole judge what was a contempt. I denied this doctrine, and, as a proof of its not being law, I mentioned Bushell's[1] case in Vaughan's *Reports*, and the authorities there relied on by the Chief Justice. I requested the House to consider that, while we were contending for these privileges, and insisting that they were, in truth, the privileges of our constituents, we were at the same time contending for similar privileges in the other House of Parliament, who have not, either in theory or practice, the same common interest or feelings with the great mass of the people that we have; and I observed that it was much to be lamented that, while we alleged that these privileges were the protection of the people, they seem to feel them to be only a source of oppression; and that, in truth, whenever those who exercised despotic power, whether individuals or bodies of men, condescended to make any apology for their conduct, they always had recourse to that topic which is now so much in fashion in the House, that they exercised such power not for their own advantage, but for the good of the people.

The Ministers seemed more moderate than the Opposition, who talked about committing the attorney who had brought the action; but at last gave up that notion, and acquiesced in the proposal that the Speaker and the Sergeant-at-Arms should be at liberty to appear and plead to the

[1] In the case of Bushell, jurors were fined, and in default of payment were committed to prison, for finding a verdict in opposition to the direction of the Judge; but on a *habeas corpus*, brought in the Court of Common Pleas, the commitment was declared to be illegal, and the persons who had been committed were liberated. — Ed.

actions. After all, therefore, that has been said, the privileges of the House will come into discussion in the courts of law, and probably before a jury: and this indeed is one objection to the doctrine that has been maintained, that it does after all seem impossible to prevent courts of justice from holding jurisdiction on the subject.*

18th, *Fri.* The committee made a second report on the subject of Sir Francis Burdett's actions. It was however so incorrect, that the House resolved to recommit the report. I spoke on the subject, and observed on the report containing the precedents only on one side, particularly with respect to commitments for contempt by courts of law; and that if it was proper to go into that subject at all, which I doubted, they ought at least to state the cases on both sides, particularly Bushell's case in Vaughan's *Reports*, which they have passed over in total silence. The truth is, though I did not say so in the House, that the committee seem disposed to assert the most arbitrary and despotic power in courts of justice, down even to courts of Quarter Sessions, which they mentioned in their report; relying confidently that the courts of law, having as it were by this means a common interest in the subject, will uphold, in its utmost extent, the authority for which they are contending. In pretty intelligible terms they say, "Let us be tyrants in the House of Commons, and in return be as despotic as you please in your own courts."

* Sir F. Burdett's action was finally carried by writ of error into the House of Lords; so that, in the end, the Peers were called upon to decide upon the privileges of the House of Commons.

Reform of Parliament.

21st, *Mon.* Upon Mr. Brand's motion in the House of Commons for a Reform of Parliament, or rather (for such were the terms of it) for a Committee to inquire into the state of the representation, I voted in the minority. The motion of course was lost; the numbers were, for it 115, against it 234.

Thanks of the Livery of London.

24th, *Th.* I received from the Lord Mayor a copy of a resolution of thanks, voted to me by the Livery of London at a Common Hall held last Monday. It was as follows:—"Resolved, that the thanks of this Common Hall be given to the Right Honourable Lord Erskine, Sir Samuel Romilly, and Samuel Whitbread, Esq., for their able, constitutional, and independent conduct on all occasions; and particularly for the stand they have lately made, in favour of the dominion of the law, against arbitrary discretion and undefined privilege."* I returned an answer to the Lord Mayor in these words:—

"My Lord,

"I have the honour to acknowledge the receipt of your Lordship's letter, inclosing a resolution of the thanks of the Mayor, Aldermen, and Liverymen of London, voted to me in their Common Hall on Monday last. The honour they have conferred on me is in the highest degree gratifying to me. Though I have never courted popularity, I have always considered the approbation and applause of my countrymen as the

* I soon afterwards had thanks voted to me in some other popular meetings at Sheffield, Coventry, Nottingham, the borough of Southwark, &c.

best reward of the conscientious discharge of my public duty."

I have lately received invitations to public dinners of the Livery, and of the electors of Westminster, and have declined them.

Criminal Law. Bill to repeal the Shop-lifting Act.

30th, *Wed.* The second reading of the Bill to abolish capital punishment for the crime of stealing privately to the amount of five shillings in a shop, came on to-day in the House of Lords, on the motion of Lord Holland, who had taken charge of the Bill. It was rejected by a majority of 31 to 11; the Ministers having procured a pretty full attendance of peers, considering the advanced season of the year, to throw it out. Amongst these were no less than seven prelates; the Archbishop of Canterbury, the Bishops of London and Salisbury, Dampier Bishop of Ely, Luxmore Bishop of Hereford, Sparke the new Bishop of Chester, and Porter an Irish Bishop.[1] I rank these prelates amongst the members who were solicited to vote against the Bill, because I would rather be convinced of their servility towards Government, than that, recollecting the mild doctrines of their religion, they could have come down to the House spontaneously, to vote that transportation for life is not a sufficiently severe punishment for the offence of pilfering what is of five shillings' value, and that nothing but the blood of the offender can afford an adequate atonement for such a transgression. Lord Ellenborough, the Lord Chancellor, and Lord Liverpool, were the

Conduct of seven Bishops upon it.

[1] Vide *infrà*, April 2. 1813.

only peers who spoke against the Bill; and Lord Holland, Lord Erskine, Lord Lauderdale, Lord Lansdowne, and Lord Suffolk for it. Lord Grey voted for the Bill, but did not speak; Lord Melville and Lord Redesdale were among the silent voters against it. The argument principally relied on by those who spoke against the Bill was, that innovations in Criminal Law were dangerous, and that the present measure was part of a system to innovate on the whole criminal code. It was said that the House should consider, not merely the Bill itself, but the speculations in criminal jurisprudence of the author of the Bill: that he had been the author of the act, passed two years ago, to abolish the punishment of death for the crime of picking pockets; and that the consequence of abolishing that punishment had been a very great increase of the crime. So Lord Ellenborough and the Lord Chancellor took upon themselves to affirm the fact to be from information which they said they had received. But how, it may well be asked, and was indeed asked by Lord Lansdowne in the course of the debate, do they know that the crime has increased? All they can know is, that prosecutions are much more frequent than they were before the act passed; and this, instead of affording any argument against the Bill, proves its efficacy. It was stated, when the Bill was proposed, that the inordinate severity of the punishment appointed by law prevented those who had been robbed from prosecuting, and by that means procured complete impunity to the offenders. Take away, it was said, this most severe punishment, and you will have many more prosecutors. The punishment is taken away; many more prosecutions are preferred; and this is the very fact which these men, blinded by their gross prejudices, put forward as proof that the measure has been unsuccessful. It is, on the contrary, the strongest proof of its success; and would afford us a triumph, if we were capable of enjoying it, on the justness of our speculations. Lord Ellenborough said that there was no knowing where this was to stop; that he supposed the next thing proposed would be, to repeal the law which punishes with death the stealing to the amount of five shillings in a dwelling-house, no person being therein: and then he declared that that act it was which afforded security to the poor cottager that he should enjoy the fruits of his labour; and he pathetically described the situation of the poor, relying with confidence on the security the law afforded them for the scanty comforts which they were allowed. No person, however, has yet proposed to abolish this law; and it is not very easy to see what there is in common between the two laws, except the words "five shillings." However, whether similar or not, the law he spoke of was not brought under the consideration of the House by the Bill under debate. He spoke of transportation, the severest punishment which the Bill allowed to be inflicted on the offender, as one which had few terrors for those who violate the law, and described it as being considered by them, and, as I understood him, as being justly considered, as only "a summer airing by an easy migration to a

Lord Ellenborough's speech.

milder climate." The part, however, of his speech which appeared to me to be the most objectionable was that in which he said that he doubted whether the Judges had not erred by too much lenity; and that it was probably that fault on their part which had encouraged these attempts to alter the law. I am not here stating his words, for I cannot recollect them, but what he said was pretty much to this effect. The inference to be drawn from this is pretty obvious, that in order to discourage such attempts in future, and to deprive these lovers of innovation of one of their arguments, namely, that the practice of the law is on this subject at total variance with its theory, it may be right to enforce the law more rigorously. I may by this means (which God forbid) have been the cause of increasing the very evils which I am most anxious to diminish. I have, however, already had reason to suspect that this may be the case. I will mention one cause of this suspicion.

In the last month, and while my bills were all depending in the House of Commons, I received by the post a letter signed Step. R. Amwell, informing me that, in passing through Maidstone, the writer had learned that three men, all convicted for slight offences, had been left for execution by the Judge; and that one of them, of the name of Lawes, whose crime was that of stealing property of the value of 40*s*. in a dwelling-house, might be thought to have some claim to mercy, as a Bill was depending in Parliament to repeal in such cases the punishment of death; and requesting me to apply to the Secretary of State without delay, as the man was to be hanged on the morning following the day on which I should receive the letter. Immediately on receiving the letter, I hastened to Ryder, the Secretary of State, and put the letter into his hands; and he, without delay, transmitted it to Mr. J. Heath, the Judge by whom the prisoner had been tried, and requested him to inform him of the nature of the case. Heath's answer to the application (for Ryder sent it to me, and I preserved a copy of it) is in these words:—

"Sir,

"I have received and read the letter with the signature of Amwell, and by some passages I am confident that he wrote me a letter signed Amicus Curiæ, respecting Lawes. As to Lawes, he was guilty of house-breaking, and *most probably* of burglary, in the dwelling-house of Mary Wilkins, a widow woman, who carried on the business of a baker at Minster, and stole plate to the value of 20*l.* and upwards, to the best of my recollection. As house-breaking had been frequent in Kent, and no person appeared to give him a character, I left him for execution. Stephen Nicholes* was convicted of stealing two heifers, which the prisoner and his brother, who has absconded, pretended to have bought for 34*l.* They were driven from the close of a poor widow woman whose property they were, and slaughtered by the prisoner. The third is Peter Presnal, who was convicted of breaking the cottage of John Orpin, no person being therein, and stealing

Cases before Mr. J. Heath.

* According to the newspapers, Nicholes was only nineteen years old.

therein property of the value of 5*s.*; in fact, the things were of the value of 40*s.* It was proved that the cottage was broken whilst the prosecutor was absent at his labour, and all the valuable things were stolen by the prisoner. I consider this offence as the worst of all; because, if not checked, it would destroy all parsimony and frugality among cottagers. In truth, I tried at Maidstone ninety-nine prisoners; and, excepting one executed for murder, I only left the above three for execution, and not one of them could adduce a single witness to his character.

"I have the honour to be, &c.

"J. Heath.

"Bedford Square, April 4. 1810."

No respite was sent, and consequently the three men were hanged. It surely ought to be made generally known, that the not producing witnesses to the character of a prisoner leads, according to the practice of some of the Judges, to such important consequences. To me this was perfectly new.

Lord Ellenborough, in the course of his speech, said that the other Judges were of the same opinion as himself with respect to the inexpediency of passing the Bill. He did not say that *all* the other Judges were of that opinion, but what he said implied this. Upon which Lord Lauderdale observed that, though he could not doubt the fact, as the Chief Justice affirmed it, he did not know how to reconcile it with what he had heard the Chief Baron say but a few days before, at a committee of the Lords on the Bill for consolidating capital offences against the Revenue Laws into one Bill, namely, that he had found by experience that making these offences capital prevented convictions.

Case before Lord Ellenborough.

Lord Lauderdale told me that, soon after my pamphlet appeared, he had some conversation upon it with Lord Ellenborough; in which Lord Ellenborough told him that, though the instances were very rare, yet it sometimes became necessary to execute the law against privately stealing in shops; and that he had himself left a man for execution at Worcester for that offence. The man, he said, had, when he came to the bar, lolled out his tongue and acted the part of an idiot; that he saw the prisoner was counterfeiting idiocy, and bade him be on his guard; that the man, however, still went on in the same way; whereupon Lord Ellenborough having put it to the jury to say whether the prisoner was really of weak mind, and they having found that he was not, and having convicted him, left him for execution. Upon which Lord Lauderdale asked the Chief Justice what law there was which punished with death the counterfeiting idiocy in a Court of Justice; and told him that he thought his story was a stronger illustration of my doctrines than any of the instances which I had mentioned.

Two days after the Bill had been thrown out, the Duke of Gloucester told me that he did not know the day on which it was to come on, or he should have made a point of attending and supporting it.

June 5th, *Tu.* I renewed my motion in the

Penitentiary Houses.

House of Commons, for an address to the King to execute the acts for erecting Penitentiary Houses. Ryder, the Secretary of State, was as little prepared now as he had been before, and requested me to withdraw the motion, and early in the next session to move for the appointment of a committee to inquire into the effects of the punishment of imprisonment in Penitentiary Houses. The Solicitor-General supported this proposal, and said that many improvements might be suggested in the old plan of the Penitentiary Houses; and that it would be desirable at the same time to establish some regulations for the reform of the county gaols. I declined, however, to accede to this proposal, and persevered in my motion, which of course was lost, but not by a great majority — *52* to 69. As soon as the motion was disposed of, Bragge Bathurst moved, and the Ministers not opposing the motion, the House resolved, that "The House would early in the next session of Parliament take into consideration the means of most beneficially carrying into effect the acts of the nineteenth and thirty-fourth years of his present Majesty, for the establishment and regulation of Penitentiary Houses."

Berkshire petition.

6th, *Wed.* A petition voted at a very numerous meeting, by the freeholders and inhabitants of Berkshire, was presented to the House of Commons, on the subject of the imprisonment of Sir Francis Burdett and Gale Jones. Perceval objected to its being received, because it stated that the petitioners expressed their regret and alarm at the injury suffered by the people in the punishment inflicted on John Gale Jones and Sir Francis Burdett; it being, as he contended, disrespectful to the House, to state that what it had done was an injury to the people. I spoke for receiving the petition, and said, that to deny that petitioners might state that the subject of their complaint was an injury, was in truth to deny the right of petitioning; because it was only for the redress of wrongs that petitions were presented. The petition was however rejected by a large majority.[1]

Irish Arms Bill.

8th, *Fri.* Upon a question whether the Irish Arms Bill, which is a mitigation of the system established by the odious Bill passed two years ago[2], should have duration for two years, or only for one year, I voted in a minority of only 10 for the shorter period.

Criminal Law.

9th, *Sat.* The Bill for repealing the Act of George II., which makes stealing on navigable rivers a capital felony, stood as one of the orders of the day. But it being impossible to bring it on, because there were not forty members present, (and if I had attempted to go on with it, the House would have been counted out), I put off the third reading to next Wednesday, though without any hope of being able to bring it on then, or indeed on any other day during the short remainder of the present session, which it is understood is to close in a week or ten days from this time. For the last three weeks I have endeavoured every day to bring on the third reading of

Hurry and multiplicity of business in Parliament towards the close of a session.

1 For receiving the petition 36; for rejecting it 78.—Ed.

2 See *suprà*, pp. 219—221.; and pp. 224. 228.—Ed.

the Bill. But this has been impossible; the other business, the notices, and the orders of the day for business taken up by Government having always precedence, and lasting till two or three o'clock in the morning. The truth is, that the Ministers do not suffer Parliament to sit half the time which is necessary to do the business which comes before it, or which ought to come before it. Many important laws are not proposed, or cannot receive any discussion, because there is not time for them; and many Acts are passed full of objectionable provisions, because the persons who would oppose them, after having waited night after night in expectation of them, find, at last, their patience exhausted. And thus the Bills pass through their different stages at one or two o'clock in the morning, or later, just after the close of a debate on some interesting subject, when it is supposed that nothing of importance is likely to be brought forward. There have been for many days successively, above thirty orders of the day; and on one day, forty-two orders of the day and six notices of motions. Considering the Bill, therefore, as lost, and that I should have no opportunity but this of saying any thing upon it, I took notice of some of Lord Ellenborough's assertions in the other House; particularly of what he said respecting the increase of the crime of picking pockets, since it had ceased to be punishable with death.* I observed, too, on what Lord Ellenborough had said of my intention, as author of the Bill, to overturn the whole system of our law, or something to that effect; and I dis-

Criminal Law.

* Vide *suprà*, p. 332.

claimed any such intention. I said I could not admit that I less justly appreciated the excellence of our system of laws, because I could discover some imperfections in it, and because I was desirous of removing them, than those who, in their blind admiration, defended and extolled every thing which they found established: and I added, that it would indeed be extraordinary if I, who had passed my life in the study and in the practice of the law, who owed whatever little consideration I enjoyed in society to my supposed knowledge of the law, and who must be indebted to the same recommendation for whatever future advantages I might be looking forward to, should be disposed to destroy that system, or to bring it into contempt.

10th, *Sun.* Whitsunday. At Ingram's, Twickenham, and stayed till Wednesday, June 13th.

Bill to regulate the office of Registrar of the Admiralty Court.

14th, *Th.* Perceval has brought into Parliament a Bill to regulate the office of Registrar of the Admiralty and Prize Courts*, that most lucrative office, which, while his father was First Lord of the Admiralty, was granted in reversion to his brother, Lord Arden (who now enjoys it), and after his brother's death to himself. The regulations are not to take place till after the expiration of the existing present and reversionary interests; and no regulations would have been proposed, but for the reports of the Finance Committee. The Bill to-day underwent much discussion on the question whether the report should be received. I objected to the principle on which the regulations proceed. The Bill declares that the Registrar

* Vide *infrà*, June 19. 1812.

shall be entitled to only one third part of the fees of his office; and that the remaining two thirds shall go to, and make part of, the consolidated fund. Upon this, I observed that, where the fees of an office relating to the administration of justice were too large, the proper course to be taken was to diminish the fees for the benefit of the suitors, and not, as was here done, to continue the abuse, and to let the public in to share the spoil. The Solicitor-General, who was the only person who spoke after me, took no notice of this observation. I also observed that the Bill, as framed, seemed to sanction indirectly the Registrar's employing the money in his hands, belonging to the suitors, at interest, for his own private advantage; that I thought it extremely doubtful whether such an employment of suitors' money could be made legally for the benefit of the officer; that I was strongly inclined to think that it could not; and that, if the matter were only doubtful, it ought not to receive the indirect sanction of the Legislature, without full consideration and discussion. The clause which gave this indirect sanction was, upon Bankes's motion, omitted. Before this was done, however, the Solicitor-General defended it, and stated it to be clear that such on officer might legally make interest for his own benefit of suitors' money. He said that it was done constantly and notoriously by the Deputy-Remembrancer of the Exchequer. I stated that this was not known to me; upon which the Solicitor-General observed, that then I was the only person who did not know it. The fact thus publicly stated by the Solicitor-

Office of Deputy-Remembrancer of the Exchequer.

General, shows the urgent necessity of a reform of the office of Remembrancer of the Exchequer. The Deputy-Remembrancer is the person to whom all references are made, in the same manner as to the Masters in the Court of Chancery. Till his report is made, the money paid into court cannot be taken out; and if he may, in the mean time, employ it for his own benefit, he has the strongest motives for delaying his report. In Courts of Equity there are always large sums paid into court, which, from the difficulty and expense of prosecuting the suit to its final close, are never taken out. Who, in the Court of Exchequer, has the benefit of these sums? Are they handed over from Deputy-Remembrancer to Deputy-Remembrancer, forming a large fund always accumulating, to be employed for the benefit of the officer for the time being? or in what other way are they disposed of?[1] Is there not something of the same kind, too, in the Admiralty and Prize Courts?

Poor Laws.

A Bill was brought into the House by Mr. Lockhart, member for the city of Oxford, to alter the law of settlement of the poor, by making it necessary that, in order to gain a settlement by occupying a tenement, it should be of the value of 20*l.* a year, instead of only 10*l.*, as the law now stands. He proposed this measure upon the

[1] Although an order of the Court of Exchequer was made on February 17. 1747, directing that the Deputy-Remembrancer should receive the dividends of the money of suitors in Court, in order to apply the same for the benefit of the suitors pursuant to the orders of the Court, this was never acted on; and the Deputy-Remembrancer continued to receive the dividends for his own benefit until 1820, when the Act 1 Geo. 4. c. 35. appointed an Accountant-General for the Court of Exchequer, provided for the payment of salaries out of these dividends, and regulated the mode of disposing of the surplus. — Ed.

ground of the change which has taken place in the value of money since the reign of Charles II., when the present law was enacted; and that now men refuse to let poor persons tenements of 10*l*. a year, in order to prevent their gaining settlements.

As nothing, in my opinion, can be more oppressive to the lower orders of the people than the law of settlements, and nothing more mischievous than to increase the difficulty of acquiring settlements, and by that means to subject poor persons, who are obliged upon any temporary occasion to ask relief of a parish, to all the vexation and misery which attends their removal from the place where they and their families happen to be resident, I opposed the Bill. Whitbread and Horner also opposed it; and it being impossible, at this late period of the session, that a Bill which would be opposed in its different stages could pass, Lockhart gave it up.

Mr. Giddy, however, who defended the Bill, gave notice that he would, in the next session, bring in a Bill to the same effect as this, and to prevent obtaining settlements by purchase of lands, unless the consideration paid was much higher than 30*l*., the sum now requisite; and to prevent gaining settlements by residence on land which the party inherits, or has given to him, unless it be of a certain value. I said that, though I had no inclination to attempt to propose laws respecting the poor, such a notice afforded me a strong temptation to submit to the House a measure of a very different tendency—a Bill to make a six months' residence in a parish, under any circumstances, give a settlement; which I thought would be a very great improvement of the law.

Some reform in the practice of the Chancery of Durham.

I this day made a general order, as Chancellor of Durham, to correct the practice of the Court by diminishing the delay of its proceedings. I limited the orders, which may be had for time to answer a Bill, to two; the first for six weeks, and the second for a month. Till this time three orders might be had, for periods of time which amounted altogether to between four and five months. I ordered, too, that a defendant should be entitled to call on a plaintiff to speed his cause, or dismiss his Bill at the end of nine months, instead of waiting, as he must hitherto have done, till there had been two sittings of the Court; which, as the Court has for a considerable time past sat only annually, might be nearly two years. There is, and always must be, so little business in the Court, that it is hardly worth while to set about a complete reform of the practice. No solicitor would give himself the trouble of learning what the new practice was, for the sake of one or two causes he might institute; he would rather file his Bill in some other Court.

Reform of Parliament.

21st, *Wed.* Upon a Bill brought into the House of Commons, by Charles Williams Wynn, more effectually to prevent bribery at elections, which was meant only to be printed and then to lie over till next session, I took occasion to say something upon a reform of Parliament. I expressed my earnest wish that some measures of reform might be speedily adopted; and at the same time I observed, that a moderate reform appeared to me to be alone attainable, unless by such convulsions as every honest man must contemplate with horror.

Parliament prorogued. Sir Francis Burdett released.

June 22d. *Th.* Parliament was prorogued.

On the same day, and as speedily as news of the prorogation could be conveyed to the Tower, Sir Francis Burdett was set at liberty. He went away secretly in a boat, to the great disappointment and mortification of an immense multitude, which had assembled on Tower Hill and in all the streets through which it was understood that he was to pass in a procession, which persons calling themselves a committee of his friends had arranged. He did well not to appear in the triumphal cavalcade that was prepared for him; but he would have done much better if he had declared his intention beforehand, and if he had not suffered it to be imagined, as he did, till the moment of his departure from the Tower, that it was with his privity and approbation that the procession had been publicly announced.

July 25th. I received an invitation from the stewards of a dinner to be given at the Crown and Anchor Tavern, by some of the electors of Westminster, to celebrate Sir Francis Burdett's liberation from the Tower. I declined the invitation in a letter to the person who had been directed to write to me. My letter was this: —

"Sir,

"I shall be much obliged to you to inform the stewards appointed to conduct the dinner in commemoration of Sir Francis Burdett's liberation, that I think myself much honoured by their invitation, and that I am sorry I cannot accept it. My opinion on the commitment of Sir Francis Burdett is well known, as I have stated it more than once in the House of Commons. But, notwithstanding that opinion, I cannot think that the circumstance of Sir Francis Burdett being discharged from the Tower, because the House of Commons which placed him there is no longer sitting, is an event which can with any propriety be celebrated as matter of public triumph. Entertaining this opinion, though not presuming to censure those who think differently from me on this subject, I am under the necessity of declining the obliging invitation of the stewards."

August 19th, *Sun.* The Lord Chancellor having ended his sittings yesterday, I this day set out for Kinsham, in Herefordshire, where, with Anne and all my children, I purpose spending the whole of the vacation, except the time which will be occupied with my annual journey to Durham.

Sept. 15th, *Sat.* Set out from Kinsham for Durham.

Oct. 30th, *Tu.* Arrived in town.

I have done very little during the vacation besides taking exercise and endeavouring to lay in a good stock of health. I found it necessary to give about two hours every day to William's instruction. This, the answering a few cases which I had been obliged to defer answering during the business of the Court, correcting and adding a postscript for a new edition of my pamphlet on *Criminal Law*, preparing another pamphlet on the subject of transporting criminals to New South Wales *, and some very desultory reading for my amusement of such works as I happened to meet with at Kinsham, have been my only occupations.[1]

* Never published.

---

[1] Extract of a letter from Sir S. Romilly to Mr. Dumont, dated Knill, October 13. 1810: — Ed.

"I must with shame confess that you have discovered the true cause of my not answering your letter. Without having any thing which I am obliged to do, I find myself so much occupied, that I put off answering letters till I am almost ashamed to answer them. You, who have been here, have already as just a notion of our manner of living, and passing our time, as any description could give you. We are staying a week here, we have been a week at Cabalva, another fortnight we shall be at Kinsham, and then there will be an end of the vacation.

"I contrived to vary a little my tour to Durham and back again, and the weather being delightful, our tour was a very pleasant one. William's passion for mineralogy conducted us into the salt-works at Northwich in Cheshire, and into some lead mines in the neighbourhood of Richmond. From Richmond we went across the country to the western part of Yorkshire to Ingleton and Settle, and from thence through a most beautiful country to Wigan, in Lancashire. We then proceeded to Chester, and from thence made a short excursion into North Wales, and passed through the enchanting vales of Clydd and Llangollen. The recollection of those scenes has taken off a little from the beauty of the country I am come back to inhabit. Still, however, I find it beautiful; and, as I ride a great deal, I every day find out new spots to admire.

"I have been reading a good deal, but, like a very idle person, just every thing which came in my way — Dugald Stewart, Hume, Voltaire, Made. Roland, Burke, and a good deal of poetry. Amongst others the *Lady of the Lake*, and Crabbe's *Borough*. I do not at all agree to the judgment which has been passed upon Crabbe's poem. So far from being the worst of his poems, I think great part of it infinitely superior to every thing that he had before written. Much, it is true, of the *Borough* is very tiresome and languid, but the horrible story of Ellen Orford, the description of the condemned convict, and of the sailor who dies in the arms of his mistress, and many other passages, show more genius than any thing that has lately appeared. It is true that in general his subjects are extremely disgusting. I cannot however but think, that it is useful to compel that class of persons, among whom alone he will find readers, to enter with him into poorhouses and prisons, and inspect and closely examine the various objects of wretchedness which they contain. The *Lady of the Lake* is said to be inferior as a poem to Walter Scott's former productions, but really one hardly knows how to examine such compositions as poems. All that one can look for is to find beautiful passages in them, and I own that there are some parts of the *Lady of the Lake* which please me

31st, *Wed.* The Lord Chancellor held the first seal.

Parliament met.

The King's illness.

Nov. 1st, *Th.* Notwithstanding an order made by the King in council, on the 17th of last month, for farther proroguing the Parliament, His Majesty having, before he could sign the commission for proroguing it, been affected by a derangement of mind which incapacitated him for all business, it became necessary that the Parliament should meet: and, accordingly, both Houses met to-day. In the House of Commons Perceval stated the King's indisposition, said that it had arisen entirely from his anxiety for his daughter the Princess Amelia, and that his physicians entertained the most confident expectation of his recovery; and proposed an adjournment for a fortnight, and that there should be a call of the House. These propositions were adopted *nemine contradicente*. I was present, but although there was a pretty full attendance of the Ministers' friends, very few of the Opposition attended. Letters had been sent to all of the ministerial party to require their attendance; and it had been kept a secret from all others, till the day before the House was to meet, that the commission had not been signed.

In the Lords the same course was pursued as in the Commons.

---

more than any thing in Walter Scott's former poems. He has a great deal of imagination, and is certainly a very skilful painter. The meeting between Douglas and his daughter, the King descending from Stirling Castle to assist at the festival of the townsmen (though borrowed in a considerable degree from Dryden's *Palamon and Arcite*), and the guard-room at the beginning of the last canto, all show extraordinary powers of description. If he wrote less, and more carefully, he would be a very considerable poet.

2d, *Fri.* The Princess Amelia died.

15th, *Th.* The two Houses of Parliament met pursuant to their adjournment. The King, though better, not being yet capable of attending to business, a further adjournment for a fortnight was moved by Ministers in each House. No examination of the King's physicians by either House was proposed, nor was even any examination of them taken before the Privy Council (as had been done in 1788), laid before either House. In the Commons Perceval merely stated that he had been that day to Windsor and had seen his Majesty's physicians, and from them had ascertained that the King was in a state of progressive amendment; and, upon this, he moved the adjournment for a fortnight. Whitbread opposed so long an adjournment, but said that he should not divide the House. Sir Francis Burdett, however, declared that he should insist upon a division. As a division was to take place, I thought it right to state my reasons for dividing against the adjournment; I said that, in my opinion, no ground had been laid before the House for its putting it out of its own power to do anything for a fortnight, whatever might be the calamities which might befall the nation in the interval. That though it might be right, in the present state of the King's health, and if there should not be any considerable alteration in it, not to take any step for a fortnight, yet I could see no reason why we should make it impossible to take any step during such a period; that I saw no reason why we, who were the servants of the public, should not, while the nation was deprived of the executive power, meet and adjourn from day to day. Ponsonby spoke against the adjournment, but said that, for some reason, which to me was not very intelligible, he should vote for it. Most of the Opposition members and all the Prince of Wales's friends followed his example in voting. On the division, therefore, there were only 58 against the adjournment, and 343 for it. Some went away without dividing.

29th, *Th.* The two Houses met, this being the day to which they had adjourned. Yesterday and this morning the five physicians who are attending the King were examined before the Privy Council. The result of their examination was, that the King was incapable of coming to the Parliament, or attending to any kind of public business; and that there was a very great probability of his recovery, and at no distant period; but that the probable duration of his disorder could not be ascertained. This examination was laid before each House, and in each an adjournment for another fortnight was proposed by the Ministers. Ponsonby, in the House of Commons opposed the adjournment; and moved that a committee of the House should be appointed, to inquire into the cause of His Majesty not being able to meet his Parliament. There was a division on each question; for the adjournment 233, against it 129; — for appointing the committee 137, against it 230. On each question I voted in the minority, but I did not take any part in the debate.

Dec. 13th, *Th.* Both Houses met again today; and the King's disorder still continuing, it was resolved in each House that a committee should be appointed to examine his Majesty's physicians.

Examination of the King's physicians.

17th, *Mon.* The Committee made their report of the examination of the physicians, and it was ordered to be printed. The whole of the evidence, however, which the physicians gave, does not appear in the report. Several of the questions and answers were expunged by the committee before they made their report. Some of the most important facts so suppressed are, that the cause of the King's insanity in 1801 was the resignation of Mr. Pitt; and the cause of his insanity in 1804, the publication of the correspondence between the Prince of Wales and the Duke of York.

Proceedings of the House of Commons on the King's illness.

20th, *Th.* Mr. Perceval moved in the House of Commons the same three resolutions as were moved by Mr. Pitt in 1788: — 1st, that the King was prevented by indisposition from coming to his Parliament, and from attending to public business, and that the personal exercise of the royal authority was thereby for the present interrupted; 2dly, that it is the right and duty of the Lords and Commons to provide the means of supplying the defect of the personal exercise of the royal authority, in such manner as the exigency of the case may appear to require; and, 3dly, that for that purpose, and for maintaining entire the constitutional authority of the King, *it is necessary* to determine on the means whereby the Royal assent may be given in Parliament to such Bills as may be passed by the two Houses of Parliament, respecting the exercise of the power and authorities of the

Crown, in the name and on the behalf of the King, during the continuance of his Majesty's present indisposition. The two first resolutions were adopted by the House without a division. When the question upon the third was put, Mr. Ponsonby moved to leave out all the words except "That," and to insert, — "An address be presented to the Prince of Wales, requesting his Royal Highness to take upon himself, during the King's indisposition, the government of the realm, and to administer it, in the name and on behalf of his Majesty, under the style and title of Regent of the United Kingdom of Great Britain and Ireland." A long debate ensued, in the course of which I spoke for the amendment and against the original resolution. I endeavoured to point out the inconsistency there was between the second and third resolutions; — the second resolving that it was the right and duty of the Lords and Commons to supply the defect; and the third that it was necessary to have the concurrence of the Royal assent to the supplying that defect: in other words, that it was the right and duty of the Lords and Commons to do alone what they could not do without the permission of the Crown. There was the same inconsistency too between the third and the first resolutions; — the third declaring that the Royal assent was necessary, and the first that, from the King's indisposition, his assent had become impossible. I disapproved of proceeding by Bill, because it was pretending to have the King's assent, where in reality it was not, and could not be, given. I thought that proceeding by address was an open, manly, and honest way of doing that which was in substance to be done. It was avowing that the measure was the measure of both Houses alone; which it still would be, though the idle ceremony were to take place, of putting (by the authority of the two Houses) the King's Great Seal to a commission for giving his pretended assent to their own act. All Perceval's motions were carried. The resolutions were afterwards agreed to by the Lords.

Dec. 31st, *Mon.* Perceval moved in a committee of the whole House his resolutions, to offer the regency to the Prince of Wales, subject to certain restrictions. The restrictions were, to withhold from the Prince the power of creating Peers, except for naval and military services; the power of granting places or pensions for life, or during good behaviour, except in cases where by law they must be so given; and the power of removing or appointing the officers of the King's household, which latter power was to be given to the Queen. These restrictions were to last only a year, and for six weeks of the then next Session of Parliament. There were divisions upon the two first of these resolutions: upon the first the Ministers had a majority of only 24, and upon the second of only 19.

1811.

Jan. 1st, *Tu.* Perceval moved the resolution respecting the King's household, which had been postponed from yesterday. I opposed it; and a tolerably accurate statement of my speech appeared in some of the newspapers, the best of which was, I believe, in the *Times*.[1] The proceedings in 1788 had been relied on as a precedent which ought not to be departed from. It had been stated on the preceding day by Perceval and by several others, to be a precedent of the greater weight, because it had the authority of that great man Mr. Pitt. Among other observations which I made on that precedent, I said it did not acquire additional authority with me from being a precedent established by Mr. Pitt; that I was not among the worshippers of Mr. Pitt's memory; that he was, undoubtedly, a man of most extraordinary and splendid talents, but that much more, in my opinion, was necessary to entitle a Minister to the character of a great man; and that, with all the talents that Mr. Pitt possessed, and the great influence which he had so long enjoyed, I looked in vain for any acts of his administration by which he had increased the happiness or improved the condition of any portion of his fellow-

Mr. Pitt's reputation as a statesman.

[1] A better account of this speech is to be found in Cobbett's *Debates*.

subjects. I then said that, in 1788, Mr. Pitt could not be considered as a statesman pronouncing an impartial judgment on a great constitutional question; that he was deeply interested in the transactions of that time, and was desirous of retaining his power as long as he could, and of transmitting it (when he should be obliged to give it up) as much curtailed as possible to his successors. These observations were extremely unpleasant, as I had no doubt they would be, to many of my political friends.[1] A sort of compact was supposed by many persons to have been entered into never to say any thing disrespectful of Mr. Pitt's memory. I, however, have never entered into any such compact; and, though I would not wantonly attack the reputation of Mr. Pitt, yet I have often felt indignation when I have heard his praises sounded forth in the House of Commons by the very persons who had acted throughout his life in opposition to all his measures. Upon this occasion, Mr. Pitt's name was used as an argument[2], and I had no choice but, by my silence and acquiescence, to admit the force of the argument, or to attempt to give an answer to

[1] Mr. Wilberforce complained of these remarks the same night.—Ed.

[2] Mr. Perceval said, "I look to the authority of the period to which I have alluded (1788) with the greatest reverence. I recollect whose judgment, whose abilities, and whose character presided over the transactions of those days; and although I do not expect the unanimous concurrence of those who hear me in the opinion, I am nevertheless persuaded, that, from the circumstance of the plan being proposed after great deliberation by the illustrious individual by whom it was proposed, the general presumption of the country is so much in favour of following such a high authority in the present instance, that it is much more necessary for me to say why I depart from the plan of 1788, in any one instance, than why I adopt it in general." — Ed.

it; and the only answer to be given was, to show that his name was not entitled to all that respect which many persons were disposed to exact for it. Upon the question, the Ministers were left in a minority of 13.[1]

2d, *Wed.* The resolutions come to in the committee were this day reported and agreed to by the House. A long debate took place. At the close of it, Canning, who had been in the House the night before, and had spoken some time after me without taking the least notice of what I had said of Pitt, produced a laboured panegyric on Mr. Pitt, and an attack on me. The panegyric was decked out in the most gaudy attire, and with the most splendid ornaments, for which he had been twenty-four hours ransacking the wardrobe of his eloquence. I answered him with great calmness and command of myself; and observed, at the close of what I said, that if he had answered my challenge of the night before, and had in plain and simple language pointed out the acts which I had overlooked, — if he had shown me in what class of the community I might discover an increase of comforts and happiness, the effect of Mr. Pitt's talents, and to what part of the empire I was to look to read his history in a nation's eyes, he would have better served the memory of his friend than by all his laborious rhetoric.

Canning's attack on me.

No doubt, I must expect to be abused for what I have done, and probably by all parties; but I feel the most perfect satisfaction with the part

[1] The numbers were, for the amendment, 226; against it, 213; — majority against Ministers, 13. — Ed.

which I have on this occasion acted. The reputation of Mr. Pitt, and the system upon which he has acted, are inseparable; and his system cannot, in my opinion, be too strongly reprobated. It has produced the most mischievous effects, and is still producing them.[1]

[1] The latter part of the following letter from Dr. Parr has reference to Mr. Canning's attack on Sir S. Romilly:—Ed.

"Dear Sir,

"I entreat you and Sir Arthur Piggott to accept my very sincere and respectful thanks for your prompt and noble contribution to my chancel window; and with great pleasure and great pride shall I record your honourable names in my parochial register. You have both of you the praise of acting up to the spirit both of a heathen moralist and a Christian one. I remember a heathen who tells us ὠκεῖαι χάριτες γλυκερώτεραι, and Paul has bestowed just commendation upon the ἱλαρὸν δότον. I shall write a short letter of acknowledgment to Sir A. Piggott, but I beg of you to convey my thanks to him by word of mouth, when you see him. I shall direct my bookseller to get me Mr. Leach's publication, and I shall employ Mr. Horner, who is a less busy man than yourself, to give me some information about the connexions and pursuits of the Speaker. Exquisite is the delight I feel from your own speeches in the late interesting debates, and from the effect that they produced on every intelligent man with whom I have conversed. I was entirely with you on the question of privilege[a]; and perhaps I go beyond you in maintaining that the House of Commons has, upon no occasion whatsoever, the right of inflicting that which has the property of punishment. Great, doubtless, is the power it has of removing obstruction; and great ought to be that power; though, in the exercise of it, I firmly resist all circuitous construction. If you expel a member, the act of expulsion may be the removal of an obstruction, because he does not comply with rules, or because he has committed some offence which the laws punish, and the commission of which is inconsistent with those rules which you have prescribed for the qualification of members. Treason, perjury, theft, perhaps sedition, are punished by the laws only; but the offender is not punished by your House when you expel him. He has brought upon himself incapacity for staying there, by violating those conditions upon which you have declared that a member is qualified to have a seat in your House. In case of libel against the House, the punishment ought to proceed from the Courts of Law only, and there the penalty may be proportioned to the offence; and if the penalty should, under the authority of the laws, amount to pillory, the criminal becomes infamous, and of course is disqualified from remaining in Parliament. Such is my view of the question.

"My good friend, I never was so puzzled to get a ποῦ στῶ as I am for reasoning upon the principle which is to create a Regent by Bill; and as Lord Grenville is wary and fastidious in the use of terms, I am quite

[a] See *suprà*, pp. 314. *et seq.*

The Ministers were again beaten, but by a majority of only three [1], on the resolution respecting

astonished at his application of the word *Legislative* to that which is done by only two branches of the Legislature, and is therefore an inchoate and imperfect act. If there were no House of Commons, would he extend this term to any act of the King and the Lords? I hope that you will soon bring these tiresome and multiplied delays to a happy termination; and in the mean time I shall often say of the person who drives our State Chariot,

'Ipse rotam adstringit multo sufflamine consul.'

"I am sure Sergeant Lens would allow the propriety of the quotation.

"I now have an amanuensis, and therefore, while you sip your tea, you may amuse yourself with a good deal of my classical jargon. Have you seen Mr. Canning's critique in the Quarterly Review, upon *Gifford's Life of Mr. Pitt?* I am not satisfied with all his reasoning upon French affairs, though in many parts he has argued very well, and has well put together the best things which he has met in books, or which have occurred to him in the course of his own reflections. As a composition it has some demerits, but far more merit. But the metaphors are too numerous. They are sometimes far-fetched. They are pushed now and then even to excess, and I can describe them only by the word *ἀνθολογία*. If I were talking to Sergeant Lens, who cares more about Greek than you do, I should say that, in what Mr. Canning has borrowed, and in what he has written from himself, his work may be compared to what Salmasius calls the *corona pancarpia* of Meleager; and the Sergeant may find a beautiful series of verses on this subject, if he will turn his eye to page 55. in the *Notitia Poetarum anthologicorum*, in Tom Warton's republication of the *Anthologia Cephala*, published by Reiske. If the Sergeant, and Canning, and I were talking together, I should say, 'Mr. Canning, I very much honour you for your zeal and your gratitude towards Mr. Pitt, your friend and your benefactor; and in likening your elaborate critique to the verses of Meleager, I have given, or meant to give you, great praise. But when you employed twenty-four hours to cull all your flowers of panegyric, and brought your dainty chaplet hastily made up into the House of Commons, you must permit me to remind you and the Sergeant of something which you read when you were boys at Eton upon the στέφος sent to Rhodocleia. You plucked the flowers and arranged them with your own hands:—

ἐστὶ κρίνον, ῥοδέη τε κάλυξ, νοτερή τ' ἀνεμώνη,
καὶ νάρκισσος ὑγρὸς, καὶ κυαναυγὲς ἴον.

But the work was done with too little art. The materials were perishable. The occasion and the place were improper; and therefore bear in mind the concluding line—

ἀνθεῖς καὶ λήγεις, καὶ σὺ καὶ ὁ στέφανος.

[1] The numbers were, for the resolution of the Chancellor of the Exchequer as amended in the Committee, 217; against it, 214.—Ed.

the King's household, which Perceval endeavoured by an amendment to bring back to something resembling what he had originally proposed. By his amendment, the Queen was to have the power of appointing to offices in the household upon the happening of vacancies, but not to have the power of removal. I have gained much credit by my answer to Canning. The only merit of it, however, was, that it was given with much calmness and command of temper. This incident has given

---

"Your reply, dear sir, was quite irresistible; and if Canning had understood as well as you do the 'sedes argumentorum, in quibus lateant, ex quibus sint petendæ,' he must have seen that when Mr. Pitt's name was introduced by Mr. Pitt's admirers to give authority to Mr. Pitt's measures, you and every other opponent of those measures were completely justified in appreciating the *value* of that authority. If I were talking upon the subject with Sir Arthur Piggott, who prefers sense to rhetoric, and who thinks your integrity and patriotism quite as respectable as the loyalty of Mr. Pitt, I should say, that when Mr. Canning let loose his wit upon Sir Samuel Romilly, he forgot some precautions which a much wiser man than[1] himself or Mr. Pitt has suggested for the use of ridicule. 'Vitandum etiam, ne petulans, ne superbum, ne loco, ne *tempore alienum*, ne *preparatum* et *domo allatum* videatur, quod dicimus. Nam quidam ita sunt *receptæ auctoritatis et notæ verecundiæ* ut nocitura sit in eos dicendi petulantia.' Well, my friend, I have been talking about you to Messrs. Canning and Piggott. But what shall I say to you about yourself and your antagonist, the lively Secretary? Why, I will use that language which Mr. Canning knows to be true, and which he must with sorrow allow to be pertinent. 'Ingenium tu ejus ita laudas ut non pertimescas, ita probas ut te ab eo *delectari* facilius quam *decipi* putes posse.' After this recent and signal defeat, 'nunquam te ille opprimet consilio: nunquam ullo artificio pervertet, ita contra te ille dicet, quamvis sit ingeniosus, ut nonnullum etiam de suo ingenio judicium fieri arbitretur.' I am quite confident that Sir Arthur Piggott and Sergeant Lens would agree with me in applying all this learned *lingo* to your Parliamentary skirmish. I shall not apologise to you for putting my meaning into better language than I can find for it in vernacular phrase. I suppose that you now and then lay aside your briefs, and skim over a newspaper while Lady Romilly makes the breakfast for you, and therefore this letter may amuse you a little in the few moments of leisure which are granted to you. Pray give my very best compliments and best wishes to her Ladyship. I have the honour to be, dear sir, with great respect and great regard, your faithful friend and much obliged humble servant,

"SAMUEL PARR.

"Hatton, Jan. 7. 1811."

---

[1] Quinctilian.— ED.

rise to some very just observations on Pitt's administration, by Cobbett, in his paper of Wednesday, January 9.

Parliament opened.

15th, *Tu.* The Parliament was this day opened under a commission, to which the two Houses had directed the Great Seal to be put.

Objectionable clauses in the Regency Bill.

17th, *Th.* In the Committee of the House of Commons upon the Regency Bill, I objected to a clause, by which it was to be enacted, "that the Regent should be deemed and taken to be a person having and executing an office and place of trust within England, and should take and subscribe such oaths, and make and subscribe such declarations, and do all such acts as are required by law to qualify persons to hold offices and places of trust, and to continue in the same, in such manner as by the statutes are required, and under such pains, penalties, forfeitures, and disabilities as are thereby appointed." The ground on which I objected to this clause was, that it must have the effect of making the Regent a responsible officer. By law the King can do no wrong, and it is only his advisers, and the instruments by which he acts, who are amenable to the law. A Regent ought equally to be irresponsible. To subject him to punishment for any acts done by him in the exercise of the royal authority, would be entirely to alter the nature of the Constitution. Perceval said that he conceived the effect of this clause would not be to make the Regent responsible; but would leave the question whether he was responsible or not just as it would have been if there were no such clause. In this he is unquestionably mistaken. A man declared by statute to be executing a public office of trust must necessarily be answerable for a breach of that trust. Perceval then said that the clause had been inserted in this Bill because it was found in the Bill which had passed the House of Commons in 1789, and that the clause in that Bill had never been objected to. This is true; but that it never was objected to is not a little surprising; it seems to have been quite unnoticed. Perceval said besides, that the same clause was to be found in the Regency Acts of 24 Geo. 2. c. 24., and 5 Geo. 3. [c. 27.], and that, being in so many acts of this kind, it ought not to be hastily rejected. It is true, that such a clause is to be found in those Acts; and there can be no doubt, I think, that it was meant to make the persons who were described in such clauses, namely, the Regent and Council of Regency, responsible. The sovereign power there was to be exercised by the Regent and Council, not by a single individual; and the Council was to consist of all the great officers of State, the Chancellor, First Lord of the Treasury, First Lord of the Admiralty, Secretaries of State, Privy Seal, &c. They were their own ministers and advisers; and unless they were personally responsible, no person could be responsible for their acts. But the case of a sole Regent is very different. Some discussion took place, and at last it was agreed to postpone the clause till the rest of the Bill had been gone through.

The next day, *Fri.* 18th, Perceval proposed to leave out the clause, and in the place of it merely to require that, before the Prince entered upon the office of Regent, he should take the oath of allegiance, and produce a certificate of his having taken the sacrament. As he thus yielded to the objection I had made, nothing was said on any side.

Question whether the Regent will be a responsible officer.

Much doubt is entertained whether the Regent will be a responsible officer or not; and it is thought by some persons most prudent to leave that doubt unsolved. I cannot say that I am of that opinion. I cannot think it prudent to leave it for matter of future discussion what shall have been the nature of the Constitution under which we shall have lived. The Act empowers the Regent to use and exercise all authorities and prerogatives of the Crown. The perfection of the King in his politic capacity is one of his attributes — is a part of his prerogative. It may be asked, could not a Regent, who exercises authority in the name and on behalf of a King, be guilty of high treason towards the King? Is it clear that an attempt to dethrone, or, which is the same thing, to dispossess the Regent of his power would be treason? These are difficulties undoubtedly; but yet, with respect to all acts of government which the Regent must do as King, and with responsible instruments and advisers, it would be in the highest degree inexpedient that he should be himself responsible. If such a Regent would be responsible, undoubtedly the heir-apparent of the throne ought not to be appointed to the Regency. I have not however thought that it became me to force on, against the wish, as it should seem, of all parties, a discussion of these important points.

There were divisions upon some proposed alterations in the Bill with respect to the appointment of officers of the Household, and to confining the restriction respecting the creation of Peers to six months, in which the Ministers had majorities of 27 and 22.

Jos. Lancaster's schools.

19th, *Sat.* William Allen, the Quaker and chemist, called on me according to his own appointment, to speak to me on the subject of Lancaster's schools. A plan has been for some time formed for extending them to every part of the kingdom. Allen and Jos. Fox, who are the principal promoters of this plan, and who have generously made the greatest sacrifices of their time and property to promote it, think that it will be useful to have my name amongst the members of a committee for this purpose. As I think the object is one of the highest importance, I have willingly consented to be of their committee.

The Regency Bill.

21st, *Mon.* Upon receiving the report of the Regency Bill, another attempt was made to diminish the restrictions to be imposed on the Regent with respect to the household. I supported this on the ground that the Bill, as it was framed, was not a fair and honest execution of the resolutions which the House of Lords had concurred in, and upon which the Prince had agreed to accept the Regency. By the resolutions, the Queen was to have the sole direction only of such a portion of the household as should be deemed requisite and suitable for the due attendance on His Majesty's person, and for the maintenance of his dignity; but by the Bill the whole of the household, with the exception of two offices, is placed under the direction of the Queen. Amongst others, there are placed under her direction the Master of the Horse and the Master of the Buck Hounds, which can have nothing to do with attendance on the King's person, and, in his melancholy situation, cannot contribute to the maintenance of his dignity. Upon the division, the numbers were, for the Bill as it had passed through the Committee, 212; for the amendment, 190.

The Bill passed.

Feb. 5th, *Tu.* The Royal Assent was this day given by commission, under the authority of the two Houses, to the Bill which they have passed for establishing a Regency.

The Regent sworn in.

6th, *Wed.* The Prince took the oaths as Regent before the Privy Council.

The Ministers continued in their offices.

The Prince had determined, the moment he should have entered upon his office, to have changed the administration; and a new Ministry had been arranged. Lord Grenville was to have been First Lord of the Treasury; Lord Holland, First Lord of the Admiralty; Lord Grey, Ponsonby, and Whitbread, Secretaries of State; Lord Erskine, Speaker of the House of Lords; and the Great Seal was to have been put in commission. Piggott and I were to have had our former offices of Attorney and Solicitor-General.*

In consequence, however, of an intrigue which has been carried on with great art, the Prince has determined not to make any change, but to proceed in the administration of the Government with

* It was at first intended that the chief Baron of the Exchequer should resign, that Piggott should succeed him, and that I should be Attorney-General; but Piggott declined accepting the office of Chief Baron.

the Ministers whom the King had appointed. He announced this intention in a letter sent yesterday to Perceval, which was so expressed as to give him to understand that he and his colleagues had not the Prince's confidence; and in the hope that they might be induced, from understanding this, voluntarily to resign. Perceval, however, in his answer, affects to understand the Prince, who speaks of the unconstitutional situation in which he shall be placed, to mean only that the restrictions imposed on him by the Bill will have that effect; and says that he has no doubt that the Ministers, who will enjoy his confidence, will find themselves possessed of power fully adequate to carry on the Government. Such has been represented to me to be the effect of the letters, but I have not seen them. The Prince has told his confidential friends Sheridan, Adam, &c., that he shall consult with them on all public matters; and they have had great difficulty in convincing him that this is impossible; that he cannot, without violating the principles of the Constitution, have any secret advisers; that his ostensible Ministers must be his only advisers. The principal instrument in effecting this change in the Prince's intentions has been * * * * *, one of the King's physicians. He was in the habit of waiting on the Prince from the beginning of the King's illness, and, as was at that time reported, of representing to the Prince that the King's illness was much more alarming than it appeared in the ostensible reports made to be seen by the public. Of late, however, he has represented to the Prince in the strongest manner, the probability of the King's recovery; has told him that the King frequently makes the most anxious inquiries after him; and has represented to the Prince that a change of Ministers would in all probability, as soon as it was communicated to the King, produce such an *exacerbation* (this is the very term he used) as might put an end to his life; and he has very strongly forced upon the Prince the reflection, that he might be considered as, or that he would in effect be, guilty of parricide. The Queen, too, wrote a letter to him to say that the King had been informed of all that had passed during his illness, and was in the highest degree gratified by the manner in which the Prince had conducted himself while these matters had been pending. The Queen has not seen the King, and consequently wrote only from Perceval's representation, or rather (as I know the Prince himself has observed) by Perceval's dictation; the word "pending" being (as the Prince has said) likely enough to have escaped from a man once accustomed to the language of lawyers, but which would never have occurred to the Queen.

Slave Trade.

I this day, 6th, attended a committee of the African Institution, of which I am a member, on the subject of a Bill which they have determined to have immediately brought into Parliament, to make the dealing in slaves or fitting out vessels for that purpose a felony, but with benefit of clergy.* Notwithstanding the Act for its abolition, the Slave Trade is still carried on to a considerable extent.

* This Bill was brought into the House by Brougham, March 5th, and it passed through both Houses without opposition.

10th, *Sun.* Clarkson and Brougham called on me by appointment on the same subject, and we discussed together the difficulties attending it, which are very considerable.

12th, *Tu.* The Regent did not come in person to the Parliament, but his speech was delivered by commissioners.

Returns of the number of convicts ordered.

13th, *Wed.* I moved in the House of Commons for the same returns of the number of convicts and their offences, as I had moved for in the last Session (May 4th), but which have never yet been made.

Cruel military punishments.

16th, *Sat.* I happened to-day at dinner at the Duke of Gloucester's, to sit next to Lord Hutchinson, and had a good deal of conversation with him on the subject of military punishments. He is a great enemy to those ignominious and cruel punishments which are now continually resorted to. He told me, that while he was at Gibraltar, a soldier, whose only offence was that he had come dirty upon the parade, was flogged with such severity that he died, a few days after, in consequence of the punishment. He mentioned, too, a very recent instance of a man who had been thirty years in the Guards; and, his conduct there having been irreproachable, (he not having, even in a single instance, incurred the displeasure of his officers,) had been removed into the veteran battalion in the Tower; and who there, because he had been absent a day, had, at the age of sixty, been sentenced to receive three hundred lashes, and had had the sentence actually inflicted on him.

Criminal Law.

21st, *Th.* Leave was given me, in the House

of Commons, to bring in the same three Bills as I brought in last Session. No opposition was made to the motion, though some conversation took place on the subject of them.[1]

22d, *Fri.* I published a second edition of my pamphlet on *Criminal Law*, of 500 copies. The first edition was of 1500.[2]

[1] In the course of his speech Sir S. Romilly said: "It is not from light motives that I have presumed to recommend an alteration in a matter so important as the Criminal Law of the land. I have always thought that it was the duty of every man to use the means which he possessed for the purpose of advancing the well-being of his fellow creatures; and I am not aware of any way in which I can advance that well-being so effectually as by adopting the course which I now pursue. Lord Coke used to say 'that he considered every man who was successful in his profession as under an obligation to benefit society;' and the works which that great and learned man produced, after a life of labour in the high situation in which he was placed, were his mode of paying the social debt. So, for myself, my success and my good fortune in my profession has laid me under a debt to the society amongst whom I live; and the way in which I intend to discharge that obligation is, by endeavouring to meliorate the law, and thus to increase the security and happiness of my country. It is not a little that will discourage me. I am not to be discouraged by the consideration that I have hitherto spent a great deal of time on this subject without doing much good."—Ed.

[2] The following letter from Doctor Parr, on the subject of this pamphlet, was received by Sir S. Romilly in January preceding:—Ed.

"Dear Sir, Hatton, Jan. 22. 1811.

"I have just been reading a book which contains some very sensible observations on criminal law, and as I am sure you would not dislike reading it, I subjoin the title.[a] If you cannot get it in London, I will send it to you in any way you may point out. The writer holds many opinions in common with you and myself, but evidently writes under restraint.

"I shall now say a word or two, which I have long wished to say, about one part of your inimitable book. If a man is condemned, has a bad character, and is executed, you state or seem to state, that he is hanged for that for which he was not condemned. I have heard many sensible men complain of this passage as sophistical; and even to me it appears incorrect. In the course of a trial, the law *wisely* permits general evidence to be given for a prisoner, and *humanely* forbids it to be given against him. The permission is wise, because, when the proofs of a particular action are doubtful, the presumption arising from general good character ought to give a leaning to our judgments in favour of the person's innocence. The prohibition is

[a] *Observationes quædam Juris tum criminalis tum publici, ad L. Quisquis 5 C. ad L. Jul. Majestatis. Auctore Fred. Barone van Leyden.*

Petitions of the owners of bleaching

27th, *Wed.* I presented two petitions to the House of Commons; one from the proprietors of

---

humane, because our common sense of human infirmity makes us content with the rigours of punishment assigned to an offence, because general reproach is vague, and because men are prompted by the most unsocial feelings to speak evil of their fellow creatures, and from personal prejudice to catch at any opportunity for destroying them. Thus far all is well; and the object, in these cases, is to secure as much proof as can be obtained in a doubtful cause, or to admit only the most direct proof, where the penalty after condemnation is severe. But when the sentence has been passed, I cannot help thinking that the execution of it may sometimes be governed by circumstances. Surely the 'salus publica' is less endangered when a man, generally good, experiences some mitigation of punishment, than when a man generally bad. Upon a principle of utility, even if our feelings of humanity were out of the question, there is less chance of a repetition in one case than in the other; and upon the principle of example, which if it be not the sole, certainly is the chief, justification of punishment, the mitigation of it will operate as an encouragement to that general goodness which is ascribed to the offender.

"There is, indeed, one consideration in the case of bad men which ought to have much greater weight than it usually has in the minds of Judges. Dislike from party, quarrels with servants or neighbours, offence justly or unjustly taken in a quarrel, jealousy about game, and twenty other matters of the same sort, frequently induce men to wish to get rid of a convicted person: and well does it behove every Judge to be sure that the person who recommends the execution of the sentence is a man of veracity, of sense, of impartiality and kindness of nature in the habitual character of his mind. I remember hearing from Sergeant Whitaker that, while he was trying a man for a capital offence at Norwich, a person brought him a message from the late Lord Suffield, 'that the prisoner was a good-for-nothing fellow, and he hoped the Judge would look to him;' and the Sergeant kindled with indignation, and exclaimed in the hearing of the Court, 'Zounds! would Sir Harbord Harbord have me condemn the man before I have tried him?' What Sir Harbord did during the trial, many squires and justices of the peace, upon other occasions, do after it; and were I a Judge, I should listen with great caution to all unfavourable representations. The rich, the proud, the irascible, and the vindictive are very unfit to estimate the value of life to their inferiors.

"But let us return to your position. The man is condemned for what he did, and is hanged because he is condemned. Now he suffers for that particular deed, *as well as* for that which he is accused of having done at other times. I therefore think your position incorrect. To be sure you may contend that accusations of this kind are often brought, not only from very bad motives, but with very slender proofs, and that the proofs ought to be very strong before they should be permitted to have any influence in the infliction of death. You may farther contend, that the particular offence which produces condemnation ought, in its own nature, to be such as will generally warrant the destruction of the offender; and then room will be be left open, as from

bleach-greens in the North of Ireland, and the other from the master calico printers in the vicinity

grounds against capital punishments.

---

the unalterable necessity of human affairs it sometimes will be, for a conflict between two general principles. I mean what is called the certainty of punishment on the one hand, and the possible consistency, *under all circumstances*, of a mitigated punishment with the public good. Circumstances of greater or less importance will belong to almost every case; and the judgments of men, as well as their feelings, will be less dissatisfied when mercy is refused to a man habitually and notoriously dangerous to society. As matters now stand, the offences of which a man is not convicted are often more dangerous to the community than that of which he is convicted. But, even in such a case, I should often be unwilling to let the law take its course, unless the crime which has been proved is of such magnitude as, considered by itself, requires, for the public safety, the destruction of the individual. If the offences imputed to him were ever so numerous, ever so flagrant, ever so notorious, I would not hang him unless I saw something like proportion on the ground of utility between the offence charged and the appointed punishment. My good friend, I myself could not help feeling something of dissatisfaction and perplexity in that part of your book to which I am adverting. I saw in it something of tartness and verbal cavil; and, as the subject is of very high importance, I could wish you to revise what you have written. Surely the laws are not unwise where they take notice of repetition; but then it is always assumed that the repetition has been legally proved; and it is obvious that, by repetition, the injury done to the public is greater, and the chance of future injury is increased, by future repetition. I am not looking to the probable incorrigibleness of the offender as it regards himself, but as it regards the community; and if example be of use in preventing one offence, it is also of use in preventing more than one. The whole business deserves your best consideration. I, at this moment, recollect with great pleasure your shyness in the use of the word *deserve;* and upon moral as well as legal questions, I have often observed the ambiguity and fallacy which lurk under it. Theologians are just as positive, and just as mistaken, and just as mischievous in the use of it as the lawyers. Pray let me ask whether you have ever read some admirable remarks of Mr. Hutcheson upon the word *merit.* I remember a controversy I had with Doctor Johnson upon this very term: we began with Theology fiercely, I gently carried the conversation onward to Philosophy, and after a dispute of more than three hours, he lost sight of my heresy, and came over to my opinion upon the metaphysical import of the term. Let me beg of you again and again to raise and to keep up doubts in the minds of your hearers by the peculiar, just, and most important hesitation which you, and you among our public speakers only, manifest in the use of this popular and delusive term. You know enough of the world not to be surprised that, from the particular passage in your book to which I allude, rash or shallow men take occasion to say generally that your publication abounds with cavils. I have challenged some of my acquaintance to produce instances, and the only one of any consequence is that on

of London, stating that their property, while lying out to be bleached, was subject to continual depredations, which the laws that punished the offence with death had been found ineffectual to restrain; that they had found that, from the lenity of prosecutors, and the unwillingness of juries to convict, the law, in its present state, generally secured impunity to offenders, and operated as an encouragement to the commission of crimes; and they prayed that the Acts which made these offences capital might be repealed. At the time of presenting the petitions, I gave notice of a motion to repeal the two Acts. The Irish petition was signed by 150 persons, being a very great majority, and consisting of all the principal houses concerned in this branch

---

which I am now writing to you. It seems to me that both you and your opponents pass by a part of the case, or at least undervalue it. You lay too little stress upon the offence which has been proved, and they lay too little stress upon the aggravations which are imputed, but have not been proved, or at least are attended, very frequently, with imperfect proof.

"Well, I hope that these Regency squabbles are nearly at an end. After all, dear Sir, some bold and mighty principles have found their way into your debates, and hereafter will turn to account. But what is to become of the country under the feeble and divided government which Lord Eldon and Mr. Perceval have provided for us? One of my comforts is, that men of all parties seem to be pleased with you. Pray give my best compliments to Lady Romilly, Sir Arthur Piggott, and Mr. Sergeant Lens. I beg of you not to give yourself the trouble of answering this letter, except as it relates to the Latin juridical book; and one little dozen of words, monosyllabic or dissyllabic, will be sufficient to let me know whether and how I am to send it to you. As Sergeant Lens retains, I suppose, a good deal of his old fondness for classical lore, I wrote him a long rigmarole letter about the word *calumnia*. Pray desire him not to give himself any trouble at all about answering it. But let him tell you, and do you tell me, in two or three words, whether he agrees with me. I may hear his reasons when I see him.

"I am, dear Sir, with the very greatest respect and greatest regard,
"Your admirer, friend, and obedient humble servant,
"S. Parr."

of trade. The English petition was signed by only 24 names; but the trade in the neighbourhood of London, that is, to the extent of fifteen miles, is in very few hands; not more than thirty, as I was informed by the gentleman who gave me the petition. More would have signed both petitions, but it was thought desirable not to wait for more signatures. Both these petitions were set on foot and promoted by Quakers.

Penitentiary houses.

March 4th, *Mon.* Leave was given me, in the House of Commons, to bring in Bills to repeal these two Acts. On the same day, Ryder (the Secretary of State) moved for a committee to inquire into the expediency of erecting penitentiary houses. I had myself given notice of a motion on this subject; and had intended to move an address to the Regent, to give directions for carrying the two Acts for building penitentiary houses into execution, as I had moved in the last Session. But, knowing that there would be no use in insisting on this against the wishes of the Ministry, I gave way to Ryder, and I contented myself with moving that it should be an instruction to the Committee to inquire into the effects which have been produced by the punishment of transportation to New South Wales, and of imprisonment on board the Hulks. This the Ministers agreed to. I am named on the Committee, but shall not be able to attend it, or at least very rarely.

The resolutions of the House were in these words: "That a committee be appointed to consider of the expediency of erecting a penitentiary house or penitentiary houses, under the Acts of the 34th and 19th of his present Majesty; and in case the adoption of the measure now referred to their consideration should appear to them to be for the advantage of the public, to report whether any additional legislative provisions will be wanted for that purpose; and what number of persons such penitentiary house or penitentiary houses should, in their judgment, be calculated to receive; together with any observations which they may deem material upon the subject of their inquiry;" and it was ordered, "That it be an instruction to the Committee to inquire into the effects which have been produced by the punishment of transportation to New South Wales, and of imprisonment on board the Hulks; and to report the matter, as it shall appear to them, to the House, together with their observations thereupon."

Delay in the hearing of causes in the House of Lords and Court of Chancery.

7th, *Th.* Mr. M. A. Taylor moved in the House of Commons that a committee should be appointed to inquire into the state of the appeals in the House of Lords, and of causes in the Court of Chancery. He founded his motion upon the fact of there being in both these Courts delays in the hearing of causes, which were intolerable to the suitors. I thought it impossible for me, who know how great an evil this is, not to speak upon such a motion. It was at the same time extremely unpleasant to me to take any part in it. My opinion is, that the Chancellor's hesitation and delays, and habits of procrastination are the principal, if not the only, causes of the evil; but it is impossible for me, who am constantly attending his Court as counsel, with any decency to state this to the House.* All that I thought I could do with any propriety (and which I did), was to state the extent of the mischief, and to impress upon the House how urgently it called for a remedy; and to observe that it appeared to me that the causes of the evil were merely temporary, and did not require any such remedy as a permanent increase of judicial offices. This I said, because it has been rumoured that some plan had been in agitation for appointing a second Master of the Rolls. I said of the Chancellor all the good that can be said of him, and I only hinted at his defects. I observed of him, that, in point of learning in every part of the profession, and in talents, he had hardly been surpassed by any of his predecessors; and that, in anxiety to do justice to the suitors of his Court, he had perhaps never been equalled; that he carried this merit to an excess, and that his fault was over anxiety to do justice in each particular case, without considering how many other causes are waiting to be decided. I spoke, too, of his great attention and kindness to the Bar. In

* Upon Whitbread's motion made last ——— [1] for an inquiry into Lord Eldon's conduct during the King's illness in 1804, I voted for the motion. There were indeed six of us who were all counsel attending in his court, and who upon that occasion voted against the Chancellor. Sir A. Piggott, H. Martin, Leach, Greenhill, Wrottesley, and myself. These, too, are all the counsel attending his Court who are members of Parliament, except Giffin Wilson, who voted for him, and Abercromby, who, having been made a Commissioner of Bankrupts by the Chancellor, through respect for his illustrious father Sir Ralph Abercromby, thought it right to be absent. Kenrick, who voted for the Chancellor, used indeed to attend the Court, but had no business, and now seldom attends. G. Wilson and Kenrick on all occasions vote with the Ministers.

---

[1] This motion was made on the 25th February, 1811, and was lost by a majority of 117; — the numbers being, for the motion 81, against it 198. — Ed.

stating these things, I can hardly be accused of flattery, for I sincerely think that he has these merits. I did not profess to give his character: I was not called upon to state his defects, and it would have been inexcusable in me to have done it. Perceval had said that the cause of the delay was to be found merely in the increased business of the Court, proceeding from the augmented commerce and wealth of the nation, which he said had outgrown its establishment. I stated that I could not concur in this opinion; and that, from the information I possessed, I doubted very much whether there had of late years been any great increase of the business of the Court, except the business respecting bankruptcies.* In that department there certainly had been a great increase, but I conceived that, too, to be merely temporary. In the last year, the number of commissions of bankruptcy had been double that of the preceding year,

* I have since caused a search to be made in the Six Clerks' office, and the comparative numbers of Bills filed in the first and in the last ten years of the present King's reign, are as follows:—

Year	Bills	Year	Bills
1760	1383	1800	1459
1761	1521	1801	1402
1762	1607	1802	1506
1763	1636	1803	1499
1764	1696	1804	1706
1765	1606	1805	1530
1766	1590	1806	1582
1767	1635	1807	1747
1768	1503	1808	1892
1769	1571	1809	1922
	15,748		16,245
			15,748

More Bills filed from 1800 to 1809 than from 1760 to 1769 — not one-thirtieth - - - - 497

The number in 1760 is not accurate; all the Bills filed in one letter of the alphabet being wanting.

but this arose entirely from accidental causes, which could not be expected to occur again.

Adam moved that the debate should be adjourned for three weeks. Even this Perceval opposed; and, upon a division, the numbers were, for the motion 47, against it 79.[1] The original motion was then got rid of by the previous question.

Lord Chancellor Eldon

8th, *Fri.* What has passed to-day in the Court of Chancery affords a strong exemplification of my assertion of yesterday, that the Lord Chancellor was over anxious to decide properly. He has, for a long time, had a great number of cases which have been argued before him, waiting for his judgment to be pronounced—some original causes, and many more motions and petitions. The distress which is occasioned to many parties by this is hardly to be conceived. On this day, three cases were, by his order, put into his paper, for him to deliver his judgment. Of two of them, he merely directed that they should stand over till the following Monday, without giving any reason: the third was a case of Foster *v.* Bellamy. It was a Bill filed by a pauper to redeem a very old mortgage, the plaintiff alleging that he was heir-at-law to the mortgager. The defendent disputed the fact of his being heir, and the plaintiff had gone into evidence to prove his title; but the evidence was so unsatisfactory, that all that I, who was counsel for the plaintiff, could do, was to ask that an issue might be directed to try the fact of his being heir. Of this case, which had been argued before the

[1] This number, as stated in the Journals of the House of Commons, is 78. — Ed.

long vacation, the Lord Chancellor said to-day, that he had read all the evidence over three several times, and that he did not think that there was sufficient proved to warrant his directing an issue, but that, as it was the case of a pauper, he would go over all the evidence once more; and for that purpose he directed the cause to stand over generally, without appointing any time for his final determination. He thus condemns all the other impatient suitors to continue waiting in anxious expectation of having their causes decided, till he shall have made himself quite sure, by another perusal of the depositions, that he has not been already three times mistaken.

Parish apprentices.

12th. Whitbread having put into my hands a Bill for the better regulation of parish apprentices, which it is proposed by Mr. Bootle to bring into the House*, I this day returned it to Whitbread, with a letter containing my observations on it. The principal evil which it is intended by the Bill to remedy is the binding children apprentices, by parish officers, to masters, residing at a very great distance from the parishes to which the children belong and where their parents are resident. This is an evil which has grown of late years to a very great magnitude. It is a very common practice with the great populous parishes in London to bind children in large numbers to the proprietors of cotton-mills in Lancashire and Yorkshire, at a distance of 200 miles. The children, who are sent off by waggon-loads at a time, are as much lost for

* The Bill was brought in by him on Tuesday, April 9th. *Vide infrà*, p. 398.

ever to their parents as if they were shipped off for the West Indies. The parishes that bind them, by procuring a settlement for the children at the end of forty days, get rid of them for ever; and the poor children have not a human being in the world to whom they can look up for redress against the wrongs they may be exposed to from these wholesale dealers in them, whose object it is to get every thing that they can possibly wring from their excessive labour and fatigue. Instances have come to my own knowledge of the anguish sustained by poor persons, on having their children thus for ever torn from them, which could not fail to excite a strong interest in their favour, if they were more generally known. Instances have recently occurred of masters, who, with 200 such apprentices, have become bankrupts and been obliged to send all their apprentices to the poorhouse of the parish in which their manufactory happened to be established, to be supported by strangers, and by strangers who consider them as fraudulently thrown upon them for relief. The objects of the Bill are to prohibit the binding of parish apprentices at a greater distance than forty miles; to oblige parish officers to visit and inquire into the treatment of the apprentices they bind out; and to shorten the period of parish apprenticeship, in all cases which the magistrates shall think proper, to five years.[1] All these objects appear to me to be very good, and I have only suggested some alterations in the Bill,

[1] Another provision of the Bill, as it was brought in, was to put a limit upon the number of apprentices who might be bound to one and the same master. — Ed.

and mentioned the propriety and expediency of repealing the statute of Queen Elizabeth, which makes the serving a seven years' apprenticeship necessary to the setting up any trade. I have also suggested the expediency of postponing the payment of the premiums which are usually given with parish apprentices, till after some part of the term for which they are bound shall have elapsed. Instances (and not very few) have occurred in our criminal tribunals, of wretches who have murdered their parish apprentices, that they might get fresh premiums with new apprentices. If the payment of the premium were postponed till the end of the whole, or a certain portion of the term; and if it were made necessary that the master should produce the child when he claims the premium, the premium would operate, not as it now does, as a motive for the destruction of the child, but as an insurance on his life. I suggested this in my letter to Whitbread. These are subjects to which many years ago I gave much attention, but I have never before met with any opportunity of doing any thing useful with respect to them.

Military punishments.

In the Mutiny Bill of this year, Sutton, the Judge-Advocate, has caused a clause to be inserted to *empower* military Courts Martial to imprison instead of inflicting corporal punishment. This is intended to prevent the inflicting of such severe corporal punishments as are now in use, to the extent sometimes of 1000 lashes. I entertain some doubt, however, whether it will have this effect.

Spilsby Poor Bill.

19th, *Tu.* I opposed, upon the second reading, a Bill for regulating the poor of Spilsby and nineteen adjoining parishes in the county of Lincoln, and erecting a house of industry, on account of some extraordinary penal clauses contained in it. One of these clauses empowered the master of the poor-house to punish any of the poor maintained in it for what he might deem misbehaviour, with solitary confinement, and that without limit; another made the offence of damaging the house, after it should be erected, or any of the fences about it, felony; a third enabled the directors of the poor to let out the paupers, by the day or the week, to any persons they might think proper, to labour for them; and a fourth empowered the overseers of the poor of any parish in the county of Lincoln to contract with the directors of the poor of Spilsby for the maintenance of their poor; and enacted that, upon such contract being entered into, the poor of all such parishes should be transferred to the house of industry at Spilsby, and be there subject to the same punishments and regulations as the poor of Spilsby.* No person in the House knew that there were any such clauses in the Bill, and the second reading was put off for a week. Lord Walsingham, the chairman of committees in the House of Lords, drew my attention

* By another clause in the Bill the directors have power to inflict corporal punishment on all the poor, of whatever age, in the house of industry. (See p. 18.) Another clause empowers the directors to compel all poor persons in the parishes, whom they shall find to want relief, whether they apply for it or not, to go into the house of industry. (p. 15.) Authority, too, is given to the directors to enter into the houses of poor persons, at any time in the day, to discover whether there are any persons there who are in want, or who are accustomed to beg, and to carry them to the House of Industry. (p. 17.)

to this Bill, in consequence of what I had said last Session on the Lambeth Poor Bill. But for this circumstance, the Bill would have passed as a matter of course, without any notice being taken of it; and I believe without any person, not even the member who brought it in, knowing what was contained in it.[1]

Spilsby Poor Bill.

26, *Tu.* The Spilsby Poor Bill came on again to-day, and Mr. Chaplin, one of the members for Lincolnshire, proposed that it should be postponed for a month, in order that the objectionable clauses might be omitted, and that the Bill might be new-modelled. Many members, however, thought that a Bill containing such highly objectionable clauses ought not to be entertained by the House at all. At their suggestion, therefore, I moved, in order to get rid of the Bill altogether, that, instead of being read on that day month, it should be read on that day six months, when the House would not be sitting: and that motion was carried without a division. The rejection of this Bill will probably have the good effect of preventing in future the bringing in Bills with similar clauses.* Some more effectual measure, however, is necessary to put a stop to this parochial legislation, which is rapidly spreading through every part of the kingdom. The

* Some strong observations on this Bill have been made in Cobbett's *Weekly Register* of Saturday, March 30th.

[1] The second reading of this Bill was moved by Sir James Graham, who, on Sir S. Romilly's resuming his seat, is reported to have said that he did not know such clauses were in the Bill, and that he believed the members for Boston and Derby (in whose absence he had taken charge of the Bill) were not acquainted with what had been stated by Sir S. Romilly. See Hans. *Parl. Deb.*, vol. xix. p. 433. — Ed.

powers of magistrates are transferred to parish officers; the necessity of proofs upon oath previous to punishment is dispensed with; and the means of vexation and oppression are placed at the entire disposal of a number of petty local tyrants, just at the pleasure of the attorney who draws, or the committee of the parish who give instructions for, these Bills, which generally pass through the House unnoticed by any one.* Even those who are disposed to watch such Bills most anxiously must find their vigilance continually eluded. In the very last Session a Bill was passed, which enables the assistant overseer of the parish of Brighthelmstone to punish any person, received into the workhouse, who shall be guilty of using any abusive or improper language, with solitary confinement for forty-eight hours; and which empowers any five of the directors or guardians, without any proof or examination on oath, to imprison and keep to hard labour for fourteen days any person who shall be found wandering or committing any act of vagrancy in the parish: and these clauses are in a very long Bill, the title of which makes no mention whatever of the poor. In its title it purports to be a Bill only for paving, lighting, and cleansing the town,

* In the spring of 1813, a Bill was brought into the House, amongst other things, to repeal all these clauses in local acts, by declaring that it should not be lawful for any master or any other person having the superintendence of a poor-house, or churchwarden, overseer, or other person having, under the authority of any local Act, the management of the poor, to confine any poor person longer than forty-eight hours, or to punish any adult person with corporal punishment. The Bill was put off, and Kenrick, who brought it in, undertook to bring in a similar Bill in the next Session. A similar Bill was brought in by Kenrick in 1814, and, with some alterations, passed. It is the statute 54 Geo. III. c. 170.; another Act on this subject passed in 1816, brought in by Sir Robert Heron, 56 Geo. III. c. [130.].

removing nuisances, regulating the market, regulating weights and measures, and building a town-hall (50 Geo. III. c. 38., see sections 161. and 165.).* In the same Session a Bill passed for regulating the poor in the parish of St. George the Martyr in Southwark (50 Geo. III. c. 45.), which empowers any one churchwarden or overseer to cause any children, under the age of fifteen, who shall be found wandering in the parish to be sent to the workhouse and detained there till he shall attain the age of fifteen; and to cause any person who shall be found wandering, begging, or committing any act of vagrancy or *riot*, to be sent to the workhouse and detained there as long as the churchwardens and overseers shall direct; and which, in case of misbehaviour, authorises the same methods of punishment to be used with them as with other poor kept in the workhouse. The contents of this clause are described in the marginal abbreviations of the Bill in these words, "for receiving distressed children." Another Bill, which passed in the same Session, with respect to the poor of St. Paul's, Shadwell (50 Geo. III. c. 208.), enables any seven of the trustees of the poor to send any children found wandering in the parish, whom they shall judge to be under the age of fourteen, to the workhouse, to be detained there till they (the trustees) shall judge that they are

* 13th Dec. 1813. The House of Commons came to a resolution, on the motion of Mr. Horner, that no Bill should be presented to the House relating to poor-rates or to the maintenance or employment of the poor, or to workhouses, containing any clause whereby the general law of settlement of the poor shall be departed from, or any power of corporal punishment given to any persons employed in the management of the poor.

of the age of twenty-one; and it enables the same number of trustees to send any person who shall be found to misbehave himself to the workhouse, there to be detained and employed as long as they shall think proper, and to be subject to the same punishment as other poor in the workhouse.

Abuses in charitable institutions.

On the same day, 26th of *March*, Mr. Lockhart moved for leave to bring in a Bill for registering charitable donations. I said that I thought the Bill would be of little use. That charitable institutions were very grossly abused, was that which admitted of no doubt; but the continuance of these abuses did not proceed from ignorance of the nature of the charitable institutions, for the nature of the institutions, and the abuses committed with respect to them, were notorious; but from the difficult and expensive nature of the remedy provided by the law, which deterred men from having recourse to it. The only remedy at present was by information filed by the Attorney-General in the Court of Chancery, which admitted (in the case of trustees who were desirous of resisting the interposition of the Court by wearying out their opponents) of such expedients of delay and multiplying expense (and that, too, by those who had in their hands the charity funds with which to carry on the litigation), that it was very wonderful that any persons had public spirit and perseverance enough to become the relators in such informations, and to prosecute them to a final decree. I said that the true remedy for this evil was to put an end to all this expense and delay, and to enable the Chancellor and the Master of the Rolls to act (as the Chancellor already does in cases where he has a visitatorial authority) in a summary way, upon petition and affidavits. If this mode of proceeding were adopted, I said, I had little doubt that these evils would soon be corrected.

Lord Folkestone's motion respecting informations for libel.

28th, *Th.* Lord Folkestone moved that there should be laid before the House of Commons an account of the informations which had been filed by the Attorney-General, *ex officio*, for libels, from the year 1800 to the present time; together with an account of the proceedings which had been had under such informations respectively. He stated that the number of such informations which had been filed by the present Attorney-General (Sir V. Gibbs) exceeded very greatly the number of those which had been filed by any preceding Attorney-General in the same period of time: that the yearly average, from the beginning of the present reign to within the last three years, had been two; but that in the last three years there had been filed forty informations, being at the rate of nearly fourteen a year: that the Attorney-General had shown great partiality, and had filed several informations which he never brought to trial, but kept suspended over the heads of the defendants. The Attorney-General entered into a long defence of his conduct, but opposed giving to the House the information required. I supported the motion, not on the ground of its appearing that the Attorney-General was censurable, but on the ground that it was extremely important that the information called fo should be laid before the House. I said, that as the information required respected prosecutions carried on by a public officer for the benefit of the public, and at the public expense, and related to a subject of such importance as the liberty of the press, it was necessary, in order to justify the withholding it, to show that some material detriment would ensue to the public service by producing it; that this, however, was not pretended. But it was said that the conduct of the Attorney-General was not only not culpable, but highly meritorious, and that the papers were called for only to ground a censure upon him. His conduct might be meritorious, but it should be recollected that the charge consisted only of a statement of facts; that the defence, too, consisted partly of denial and partly of a very different statement of facts. It would seem not a little extraordinary if, in such a state of the question, the House were to refuse to ascertain, as it might in the most authentic manner, what the facts really were. If there were any foundation for the charge, the information ought undoubtedly to be obtained: if there were no foundation for it, it was, if possible, more important that the information should be given, in order to convince every one that there was no foundation for it, and to remove those suspicions which certainly existed, and which it was most desirable should be completely removed. I said that it was extraordinary that the Attorney-General, having such an opportunity of justifying himself, and of showing that he was entitled to the approbation and applause which were claimed for him, should choose to forego it, and should prefer leaving hanging over him suspicions which it was said he could entirely dispel; that considering how often such a mode of proceeding was adopted, it was really surprising that persons in public situations should obtain the credit which they did, by declaring that they held themselves to be responsible; that this responsibility was become an unmeaning word, if no inquiry was ever to take place; that it was well known, that while a Minister was, as it were, boasting of his responsibility, and stating his anxiety to be judged by the public, the very men who loudly applauded the magnanimity of that sentiment were to be found the next day constituting a majority who resolved that there should be no inquiry, although without such inquiry no man could be responsible. In this I alluded to what had lately passed on the subject of the Regency, and of the inquiry proposed by Whitbread into Lord Eldon's conduct. I said that I was myself in some degree interested in the event of the motion; since it was not confined to the acts of the present Attorney-General, but extended to those of his predecessors in office for the last ten years; and that, while I was Solicitor-General, there had been no information filed, and none which it had been determined not to file, on which I had not been consulted; and that upon all of them I had concurred entirely with the then Attorney-General. I took notice of what had been said of the present extraordinary licentiousness of the press, and observed that there hardly ever was a time in which the press was not thought to be extraordinarily licentious by those who were in office, and by their near connexions; but that, if it were really true that the press was at present more than usually licentious, this fact seemed to afford the strongest argument in favour of leaving it free; since it must have become thus licentious in consequence of greater restraints having lately been imposed on it than had existed before for a century. I meant the restraints imposed on the publishers of newspapers by the Act of 38 Geo. III., and on printers of every description, by the Act of 39 Geo. III.[1]

Criminal Law.

29th, *Fri.* On the second reading of the Bills which I have brought in to take away capital punishments in several felonies, Perceval opposed them; but after a pretty long debate, they were carried by a majority of 26; for them 79, against them 53. This having been the division on the Bill relating to stealing in dwelling-houses, which Perceval said that he considered as the most objectionable, the others passed without a division.

In the course of the debate, Frankland produced some written answers, given by the Recorder of London and the Common Sergeant, to questions put to them by the Solicitor-General, and which the Solicitor-General, being obliged himself to be absent on his circuit as a Welsh Judge, had put into Frankland's hands to be used upon this occasion. The opinions of the Recorder and Common Sergeant were decidedly against the expediency of repealing the Acts which inflict capital punish-

[1] On a division the numbers were,—for Lord Folkestone's motion, 36, against it, 119. — Ed.

ments in these cases; and they stated that of late years these offences had very greatly increased. A better reason than this for altering the law could hardly be given, unless statutes were passed not to deter offenders and prevent crimes, but to encourage and to multiply them. If an alteration is to be made, it can only be by lessening the punishment and very seldom remitting it; for, in the way of severity, no alteration can be made, since no person would approve of a law to introduce the rack or breaking on the wheel.

Law relating to printers.

April 5th, *Fri.* In a committee of the whole House, upon a Bill brought in by H. Martin, to mitigate the severities of the Act of 39 Geo. III. relative to printers, I suggested the propriety of limiting the amount of penalties which might be exacted for printing any number of impressions of one paper, to some certain sum. The Attorney-General adopted this suggestion, and consented to limit them to 500*l.* As he had proposed originally to alter the Bill, justices would have had a power of mitigating, indeed, if they thought proper, but might also, if they thought proper, exact the penalty of 20*l.* for every copy; consequently, for a work of 1000 or 1500 copies, 20,000*l.* or 30,000*l.*, — a much greater punishment for disobeying a law (which was only intended as a measure of precaution to make it difficult for a person to publish libellous or seditious writings without exposing himself to punishment) than the Court of King's Bench could, consistently with the Bill of Rights, inflict for the most seditious and dangerous libel.

8th, *Mon.* On the third reading of the Bill

Criminal Law.

to take away the punishment of death for the offence of stealing to the value of 40*s.* in a dwelling house, the numbers on a division were, for it 50, against it 39. Ryder (the Secretary of State) and the Attorney-General both spoke against it; and Treasury letters had been sent out requiring an attendance. The Ministers, however, were not able to procure more than 39 members to vote against the Bill. The other four Bills to take away capital punishments passed without a division.[1]

21st, *Sun.* I passed the last week, being Easter Week, at Mrs. Fisher's at Ealing, with Anne and some of the children, and returned to-day. I have spent my time principally in answering some cases, and in reading as much as is printed of Bentham and Dumont's work on punishments (*Théorie des Peines Légales*). It begins by stating what are the qualities to be required in punishments, and then proceeds to analyse all the punishments which are now in use. It is executed admirably, and it never was attempted before. Penal legislation hitherto has resembled what the science of physic must have been when physicians did not

Bentham's work on punishments.

[1] On this occasion, Mr. Whitbread spoke in favour of the Bills and of the general principle of Sir S. Romilly's proposed alterations in the criminal law. He concluded his speech by saying that "the public opinion on the subject of this Bill might be seen from the rise of his honourable and learned friend even from the high eminence on which he formerly stood in public estimation. His finding time from his severe avocations to pursue this excellent and beneficent plan, after all the political feuds of this day were forgotten, would transmit his name with honour to posterity as the benefactor of his country. Some men, by their virtuous exertions, acquired fame after their death; but, of his honourable and learned friend, his country might, in his lifetime, say, 'Presenti tibi largimur honores.' Hans. *Parl. Deb.*, vol. xix. p. 744. — Ed.

know the properties and effects of the medicines they administered.*

May 15th, *Wed.* On the claim of the Earldom of Berkeley, I this day summed up the evidence in the Committee of Privileges in the House of Lords.

Delays in Chancery and in the House of Lords.

17th, *Fri.* Michael Angelo Taylor again brought the delays which prevail in Chancery and in the House of Lords under the notice of the House. His motion now was, that a committee be appointed to inquire into the causes which have retarded the decisions of suits in the Court of Chancery; and he said that, if that were carried, he should move for a committee to inspect the Lords' Journals, in order to ascertain the state of the appeals in their House. Perceval, as on the former occasion, so on this, moved the previous question. The reason he had before given was, that a committee was immediately to be appointed in the House of Lords to consider of a remedy for the evil; and he now said that such a committee had been appointed, and had prepared a report which would be immediately made. He afterwards, however, consented to waive the previous question, and to concur in a motion to adjourn the debate till next Thursday.[1] I opposed this motion, and pressed the House to consent to the immediate appointment of a committee. I said that, whether the Committee of the House of Lords or

* This work was published in July, 1811, in two volumes, octavo, under the title of *Théorie des Peines et des Récompenses.*

---

1 The motion for adjournment was carried by a majority of 40 to 19. —Ed.

Ministers were about to suggest a remedy or not, it was important that no time should be lost in ascertaining the causes of the evil, and particularly whether they were of a permanent or of a temporary nature: that, till this was done, it was impossible to determine what the nature of the remedy should be: that I understood that it was intended to propose the appointing a permanent additional Judge in the Court of Chancery, under the title of Vice-Chancellor, or second Master of the Rolls; who was, as well as the present Master of the Rolls, to hear all the original causes; and that the Chancellor was to be reserved to hear causes upon appeal and motions only, and petitions in Bankruptcy and Lunacy; in order that by such means he might have more time to devote, as Speaker of the House of Lords, to hearing appeals in that House: that, as I knew that when this project came in the form of a Bill, there would be little opportunity of discussing its merits, particularly at so late a period of the Session, I thought it right to avail myself of this occasion for stating my objections to it: that it appeared to me that such a plan would not only have the effect of altering the constitution of the Court, but that there would be great risk that it would totally alter the law which is administered in the Court: that it was in my opinion extremely important that the Lord Chancellor (on whose opinion the system of law there administered so much depended that it had in truth been the creation of former Chancellors, particularly of Lord Nottingham) should be a person to whose mind the doctrines of the

Court were familiar, by his being in the daily habit of applying them to the cases which came before him: that it would quite alter the nature of his office if he were to be merely a Judge of Appeal, — to be sitting ordinarily in another place, and to be paying occasional visits to the Court of Chancery, in order to decide on the doctrines of the Court, only when the suitors were dissatisfied with the decrees of the ordinary Judges there: that very different qualifications would be necessary to fill the office, if so altered, from those which were now thought requisite to a Chancellor: that the system of Equity had grown up to what we now find it, by being formed of the decisions of a single Judge; and that it was impossible to say what would be the effect of having two Judges sitting to decide original causes, and, according to the bias of the mind of each, gradually deviating in contrary directions from what were now supposed to be the doctrines of the Court: that if, as I supposed to be the case, the evil was temporary, and the arrears had been collecting only within the last ten years, it was probable that in a very few years after the appointment of this new Judge the evil would be completely removed; and that, as a plaintiff may set down his cause where he pleases, and as one Master of the Rolls would probably be, or might be, more a favourite with the profession than another, it might happen that, in a short time, one of the offices would become something very like a sinecure: that it was very objectionable (unless it were necessary in order to remedy a greater evil) to increase the patronage of the

Crown in the profession of the Law, and to hold out to its members new objects of ambition at the disposal of Ministers; that the additional expense, too, of the salary of this new Judge was not to be disregarded: that these were all matters which at least required very serious consideration, before the Legislature adopted any such plan as was in contemplation: and that, in order properly to consider these matters, it was necessary to be in possession of facts of which the House was at present wholly ignorant. I likewise intimated that, if the Committee were refused, I should probably move for returns of the state of the Court of Chancery now and at some former periods[1], which would produce some of the information which it was intended should be got through the medium of a committee. I stated that I believed that the arrear and delays complained of had all arisen within the last ten years, and that the evil, being temporary, might well be remedied by some temporary expedient; and that this great hazardous alteration in the law and constitution of the Court was by no means necessary.

The Poor Laws.

24th, *Fri.* I joined with many other members in opposing a Bill to prevent any person gaining a settlement a sa pauper, by renting a tenement of 10*l.* a year, unless the tenement was one entire tenement held under one landlord, and all in the same parish. The ground on which I opposed it, was the bad policy of increasing the difficulties of paupers acquiring settlements. (*Vide antè*, p. 343.) The Bill was thrown out.

[1] See *suprà*, p. 376. note. — Ed.

Criminal Law.

On the same day, in the House of Lords, three of the Bills which I had carried through the House of Commons (those relating to stealing in dwelling-houses and on vessels in navigable rivers, and privately stealing in shops) were thrown out on the opposition of Lord Ellenborough, the Lord Chancellor, Lord Redesdale, and Lord Liverpool. They were supported by the Lords Holland, Lauderdale, Erskine, and Lansdowne.* The numbers were, for the Bills 10, against them 27. The two other Bills relating to stealing from bleaching-grounds are to be allowed to pass.[2]

25th, *Sat.* In the Gazette of this night is announced the re-appointment by the Prince Regent of the *Duke of York* to be Commander-in-Chief.

June 2. Whitsunday. I pass these short holidays in town.

5th, *Wed.* The Committee of the House of Lords having made their report on the subject of adopting measures for the more expeditious hearing and decision of causes in their House, in which they had, amongst other things, resolved, "That it was expedient, in order to secure at the same time a sufficient attendance upon the House of Lords by the Lord Chancellor, and sufficient means for carrying on the business in the Court of

Delays in the Court of Chancery.

* The Duke of Gloucester, the Duke of Somerset, Lord Cowper, Lord King, Lord Stanhope, and ——[1] voted for them. Lord Grenville, in the debate on the Revenue Penal Law Bill, a short time back, declared his entire approbation of my Bills, and expressed his regret that he should not be in town on the second reading.

1 Left blank in the original. — Ed.
2 They are the 51 Geo. III. c. 39. and 41. — Ed.

Chancery, that an additional Judge in the Court of Chancery should be appointed." Mr. Taylor brought on again to-day his motion for appointing a committee to inquire into the causes which had retarded the decision of suits in the Court of Chancery, the debate on which had been adjourned. I supported the motion, on the grounds on which I before supported it.[1] On a division, the numbers were equal, 36 for, and 36 * against it. The Speaker decided for the motion, and a committee has accordingly been appointed. I am a member of it.

The Duke of York's restoration to office.

6th, *Th.* Lord Milton moved in the House of Commons a resolution which was in these words: — "That, upon a deliberate consideration of the recent circumstances under which his Royal Highness the Duke of York retired from the command of the army in March, 1809, it appears to this House that it has been highly improper and indecorous in the advisers of the Prince Regent to have recommended to his Royal Highness the re-appointment of the Duke of York to the office of Commander-in-Chief." I voted for the motion. The minority was a very small one, only 47 against 296. Several persons, whose votes I should have thought (judging from their past conduct) could not possibly have been influenced by any apprehension of displeasing the Prince, very prudently absented themselves. Some of my

* Perceval and all his adherents voted against the Committee; but yet I know that the Chancellor, in private, complained bitterly of Perceval for not making a greater exertion to resist this proceeding.

[1] See *suprà*, p. 392. — Ed.

friends were very anxious that I should do the same. I had no hesitation, however, in determining to attend and to vote. In the course of the debate I was several times tempted to say a few words. It is, however, perhaps as well that I did not. If I had spoken, I should have said that if, on a review of my conduct when the inquiry on the Duke of York took place, I could have discovered that I had been wrong, I should gladly have seized this opportunity of acknowledging my error; but that on reconsideration of the opinion I then delivered, I could not find any reason to alter it; and that what had passed since the inquiry had closed, had not, in my opinion, at all altered the case favourably for His Royal Highness. That, on the contrary, what had since passed had rather confirmed than weakened the opinion I had before entertained; because, although an open rupture had taken place between the accuser and the principal witness in support of the accusation, and each had appealed to the public, and had endeavoured to represent the other in the most odious point of view; yet, under circumstances so favourable for the party accused, though much had appeared highly discreditable to the witness and the accuser, not one single fact had transpired which had altered the state of the case when the House had to decide upon it, or which had cleared up any part of the mystery which hung over some of the transactions.

Parish apprentices.

7th, *Fri.* Mr. Bootle having given up, for the present Session, the Bill which he had brought in for the relief of parish apprentices, and having to-day moved for some returns of the number of apprentices bound out by the parishes in London*, I took this opportunity of expressing my concern that the Bill was given up, and of stating my view of the subject pretty much at large. Some conversation ensued; in the course of which Sir Robert Peel, a cotton manufacturer, expressed his disapprobation of the Bill. He said that it would be highly unjust to prevent a man from taking as many apprentices as he thought proper: that the children so bound from London were boys educated to picking pockets; and that it was the happiest thing possible for them to be removed from their former connexions. Mr. Wortley, who spoke on the same side, insisted that, although in the higher ranks of society it was true that to cultivate the affections of children for their family was the source of every virtue, yet that it was not so among the lower orders, and that it was a benefit to the children to take them away from their miserable and depraved parents. He said, too, that it would be highly injurious to the public to put a stop to the binding so many apprentices to the cotton manufacturers, as it must necessarily raise the price of labour and enhance the price of cotton manufactured goods. These are topics not to be forgotten when the subject comes again before Parliament. If Mr. Bootle does not bring in the Bill in the next Session, I think that I shall.†

* Mr. East has suggested to me the propriety of repealing the Act which enables parish officers to compel persons to take parish apprentices.

† Mr. Bootle (Wilbraham) did not bring in this Bill till 1815. It then passed the Commons without any opposition; but it was given up in the Lords, upon some very absurd objections made to it.

Returns of convicts.

12th, *Wed.* I moved for returns of all persons tried for different offences in England, Ireland, and Scotland, which were ordered.

Delays in the Court of Chancery.

18th, *Tu.* The Committee to inquire into the causes of delays in the Court of Chancery have made a Report. I attended the Committee a good deal, and suggested some things which are in the Report. We have only been able to state what arrear of business there is in Chancery and in the Appellate Court of the House of Lords, and what the amount of the Chancellor's emoluments are, and from what sources they are derived. With respect to other objects which we conceived we ought to have accomplished if the state of the Session had afforded us time; such as the inquiry into the causes of the delays, whether the evil required a temporary or a permanent remedy, and our opinion upon such remedies as had been or might be suggested,—we state that we have required information to enable us to pursue them, but have not yet been able to procure it. We have stated this in order to make it difficult to refuse the appointment of a committee for the same purposes in a future Session. The only opinion given in our Report was suggested by myself, and relates to a part of the Chancellor's fees. The passage as I suggested it was this:—"It appears that a considerable part of the emoluments of the office of Lord Chancellor [1] is derived from fees, nominally paid to his Secretary of Bankrupts, but who accounts for such fees to the Lord Chan-

[1] No part of the income of the Lord Chancellor is now derived from this source. The amount and application of the fees paid in Bankruptcy were regulated by 1 & 2 Will. IV. c. 56.—Ed.

cellor himself, and is allowed by his Lordship, in lieu of them, a certain fixed salary. Your Committee cannot see this without remarking that it appears to them highly inexpedient that the emoluments of any judicial officer should be constituted in part of fees ostensibly payable not to himself, but to a person in a subordinate situation. As any complaint of improper fees taken by an inferior and ministerial officer must be made to his superior, the Judge of the Court, it appears to be highly objectionable that such fees should be received for the use of the Judge himself; who must, in that case, have to sit in judgment on supposed or alleged abuses, from which, if they existed, he would himself derive a benefit. If it should be thought that any alteration should be made in this respect, your Committee suggest the propriety of abolishing these fees altogether; which, though they are but of small amount in each commission, can be considered in no other light than as a tax upon distress and insolvency." The Committee adopted this suggestion of mine, but not exactly in these words. We speak only of the mischief which would result from complaints to be made to a Chancellor, a judge in his own cause. The fact is, that such a complaint was actually made to the present Lord Chancellor some years ago by a solicitor of the name of Lowe.* The Chancellor

* This petition came on to be heard in ———— [1]; it stated Lord Hardwicke's order of the 28th of November, 1743, and complained that the table of fees was not stuck up in the office; that the Deputy-Secretary, upon issuing a commission, claimed a fee of *5s.*, not warranted

[1] Left blank in the original. — Ed.

desired the Master of the Rolls to assist him in hearing it. I was counsel for Lowe; the petition was heard; it stood over for judgment, but no judgment was ever given; and the fees were taken by the Lord Chancellor as before. These fees have, by the late increase of commissions of bankruptcy, become very considerable. In the last year they amounted to no less than 4900*l.* The fact of Lowe having made his complaint appeared to the Committee on the evidence of the Secretary of Bankrupts; but it was thought proper, and indeed suggested by myself, to strike that statement out of his deposition before we reported the evidence; because the passage in the body of the Report, coupled with the fact, might be thought to establish a very serious charge against the Chancellor; which, if to be made at all, ought to be made upon a fuller investigation of all the facts than we had, at the present advanced period of the Session, an opportunity of making. It was expected, indeed, that Parliament would be prorogued immediately, and that not a day was to be lost to enable us to make our Report.

---

by Lord Hardwicke's order; that the Secretary of Bankrupts claimed a fee for copying, under the denomination of stationery (but in the latter part of the petition this fee was stated to have been discontinued); that the charge for office copies of affidavits was made by the folio, and not by the sides, as directed by Lord Hardwicke's order, and was stamped with a less stamp than it ought to be, according to the folios charged: that two guineas were charged for a docket; but that the petitioner was unable to state how the Secretary could make out his claim to more than two shillings and sixpence: that a charge of one guinea for preparing the commission was charged, and was an imposition; but the petition states that charge, at least as to the petitioner, to have been discontinued.

The project of making a third Judge to sit in the Court of Chancery has, for the present Session at least, been abandoned: and in my opinion this is a great good which has resulted from appointing this Committee. I prepared some observations on this subject to have been submitted to the Committee, if we had proceeded so far as to have given an opinion on this scheme. It may be of use to me to recollect them hereafter, and I therefore insert them here: —

"It is stated in the Report of the Select Committee of the Lords that the view with which it is suggested that an additional Judge in the Court of Chancery should be appointed, is, 'that there may be secured at the same time a sufficient attendance upon the House of Lords by the Lord Chancellor, and sufficient means for carrying on the business in the Court of Chancery.' To accomplish this object, therefore, it must be made the province of such additional Judge to do a great part of the business of the Court of Chancery, which is now done by the Lord Chancellor. That business may be classed under three heads: — 1st, The hearing causes, whether coming before the Lord Chancellor as original causes, or for further directions on pleas and demurrers, or on exceptions to the Reports of Masters. 2d, The interlocutory proceedings of motions and petitions. And, 3d, The review of the decrees of the Master of the Rolls upon appeal. The last of these has hitherto occupied but a very inconsiderable portion of the time of the Lord Chancellor. It appears by the Report of the Lords' Committee, that in the ten last years of the Chancellorship of Lord Hardwicke, he had decided only fifty-eight causes on rehearings and appeals, being an average of less than six a year, including rehearings of decrees originally pronounced by himself. The number is greater in the last ten years; but even in that period the average number does not exceed nine a year.

"The hearing of motions and petitions in causes occupies but a small portion of the Lord Chancellor's time, compared with that which he gives to the decision of causes. The appointment of an additional Judge, therefore, would not enable the Lord Chancellor to attend much more assiduously in the House of Lords than he does at present, unless such Judge were to relieve the Lord Chancellor from all the duties which fall under the first of the heads, before enumerated; perhaps from those which fall under the two first of these heads, but certainly from those which fall under the first of them. This, however, would be an alteration in the constitution of the Court which appears to be open to the strongest objections. It would be, in effect, to separate from the office of Lord Chancellor those functions which have been hitherto considered as the most essential to it, and as constituting its nature and character; and to leave the person who may hold the Great Seal in name still a Chancellor, but in truth a magistrate of a very different description. He would have a variety of great and important duties to discharge, but the least of them would be to transact the business of the Court of Chancery; and, in the mean time, the ancient office of Lord Chancellor would, in effect, be divided between two Masters of the Rolls (or whatever name they are to be called by), neither of them subject to the control of the other, but each in his own hall exercising an original and independent jurisdiction.

"This seems the more objectionable, on account of the nature of that peculiar system of jurisprudence which is known in this country by the name of Equity. The rules of this system are not laid down in any statutes, but are to be collected solely from decisions, very few of which took place more than a century and a half ago; from decisions, too, of Judges, of whom some were in a great degree the authors of the system they were administering, and who were applying to the particular cases before them the rules which they had themselves established.

"It appears to be most essential to the due administration of such a system of jurisprudence, that the person administering it should be intimately acquainted with the whole of the system, and should have the general rules and doctrines of the Court constantly present to his mind, and the memory of them kept alive by habitual and almost daily use. It is very obvious that, if, of the three Judges who are to preside in the same Court of Equity, two are to have the law of the Court in all its branches familiar to them, and kept constantly in their view by a regular and uninterrupted attendance in Court; and the third is only, as an occasional visitor, to refresh his memory by looking back into the Records of the Court on particular heads, just so as to enable him to decide nine or ten causes, or twice that number, which may happen to be brought before him for decision on appeals in the course of a year; this effect must in process of time be produced. The appeal will be from a Judge, a perfect master of the law of the Court, to one who has only a defective recollection of it; from one who has never absented himself from that which may be considered as his native court, to one who has migrated into another place, and returns as a kind of foreigner. Or, if that effect be not really produced, there will always be a prevailing idea that it has been produced. The suitor who, having had a decree in his favour, sees it reversed on appeal, will be apt to observe that the Judge of the most experience must be the most likely to have understood the case, and to have decided it properly; and the disappointed appellant, whose appeal has been fruitless, will be well disposed to remark, that it is not surprising that the appellate Judge should have had so much deference for his superior in experience and ability, though his inferior in rank, as to have submitted to him his own opinion and to have affirmed his decree from deference, not to the reasons of the judgment, but to the character and authority of the Judge.

"In a system of jurisprudence that is founded on no positive rules laid down by the Legislature, which may at all times be referred to, it must necessarily happen, with respect to some of its doctrines, that they are gradually and insensibly departed from by successive decisions. It may be sufficient to refer to such matters as fraud and breach of trust, and the acts which are considered as part performances of parol agreements, to illusory appointments, and the circumstances which convert executors into trustees of a residue undisposed of, to bring to the recollection of those who are well acquainted with the history of the Court, examples of what is here alluded to. In such a system, decisions may be considerably influenced by the peculiar notions and particular habits of thinking of each Judge; and when two original Judges differently constituted, as they must necessarily be, by nature and by education, are sitting at the same time, it can hardly be avoided that, with respect to the same rules, there should sometimes be deviations in quite opposite directions, and that there should come to be gradually established two different laws administered at the same time, on the same subject, and by the same Court.

"Another very great evil attendant on this project is its necessary tendency to add greatly to the expense of suits in Equity, and permanently to increase the business of the Court and to protract the final decision of causes. It has already been observed, that appeals from the decrees of the Master of the Rolls to the Lord Chancellor were till lately very few in number, and that in Lord Hardwicke's time they were still fewer. A plaintiff has a right to set down his cause wherever he pleases; and till of late years it was never usual to set down causes of much difficulty or importance before the Master of the Rolls. Such causes were, by reason of the probability that the party against whom the decree was pronounced would appeal, and to avoid the expense of a second hearing, generally set down in the first instance before the Lord Chancellor. From his decree there only lies an immediate appeal to the Lords; but from a decree at the Rolls, the cause can very rarely be carried into the House of Lords till it has first gone by appeal to the Lord Chancellor. Of late, however, this has been considerably altered; the alteration occasioned in a great degree by the difficulty there is to obtain any decision from the Lord Chancellor. Not only has the number of causes set down before the present Master of the Rolls very greatly increased, but they are for the most part causes very different in their nature, and of much greater difficulty and importance, than those which used to be set down before him. If the plan of appointing an additional Judge should be adopted, it will not be in the power of the parties to prevent those intermediate appeals; and no doubt can be entertained that such appeals will become much more numerous as long as a high opinion shall be entertained of the person who is appointed to the office of Lord Chancellor. If ever, indeed, a time should come when the learning and talents of the persons appointed to the two subordinate judicial offices in Chancery, or, indeed, if either of them shall be more highly estimated by the public than those of the person who is selected for the high office of Lord Chancellor, and that this opinion should even be entertained and acknowledged by the Lord Chancellor himself, so that he shall come to sit in his Court of Appeal only to acknowledge the superiority of the Judge who is appealed from; whenever this happens, there will probably be few appeals, and the expense and delay of such proceedings will be avoided; but the evil will be of another character, and of a much greater magnitude.

"The alteration proposed may be described in a few words, but it should seem with great accuracy, to be a division of the Chancery into two courts, and the creation of an intermediate court of appeal between the Chancery and the House of Lords.

"In the preceding observations, nothing is said of the expense which will attend the creation of this new office, or of the increase of the patronage to be exercised by the Ministers of the Crown in the profession of the law, although these are considerations which ought not to be disregarded."

The Regent's festival.

19th, *Wed.* The Regent gave a grand festival, probably the most splendid and the most expensive that ever was given in this country. About 3000 persons were entertained at supper. I was present; the Regent spoke to me in his usual way, and my recent vote against the Duke of York does not seem to be at all resented. A reason given for this festival was, that it might give employment to the manufacturers; and it was desired that the dresses of all the guests should be of British manufacture. It does not seem likely, however, to gain the Regent much popularity. The great expense of this entertainment has been contrasted with the misery of the starving weavers of Lancashire and Glasgow. Among the higher orders, great offence has been given by the omission of invitations, either through neglect or design.

The French Prince, who calls himself Louis XVIII., and the other Princes of the House of Bourbon, were among the company, and were received with great distinction. The policy of this is not easy to be discovered.

Insolvent Debtors' Bill.

24th, *Mon.* A Bill for the relief of insolvent debtors having passed the Lords, and having been read twice in the Commons, I observed, on the House going into a Committee upon it, "that such Bills were, in my opinion, in the highest degree objectionable; that it was impossible, on any principles of law or justice, to support an *ex post facto* law, which took away, merely because such was the pleasure of the legislature, the stipulated effect of contracts entered into under the sanction of law; that nothing could palliate such measures but the intolerable mischiefs of the law as it at present stood; that a stronger declaration of the defect of our law on the subject of debtor and creditor, and of the imperative necessity of a change in it, could not be made than these insolvent bills, which now passed, as it were, periodically at the end of every two or three years; the legislature thus proclaiming its own reproach and disgrace, in leaving the law in such a state."

Lord Stanhope's Bill to prevent the sale of bank notes for less than their nominal value.

July 19th, *Fri.* The Session of Parliament has been protracted much beyond the period that was expected and originally intended by Ministers: first, in consequence of the determination of the Lords to decide upon the claim to the Earldom of Berkeley; and since, by a Bill which Lord Stanhope brought into the House of Lords to prevent the sale of bank notes for less than their ostensible value. The Ministers at first expressed their disapprobation of this foolish and mischievous Bill; but it having appeared, in the course of the debates upon it, that Lord King had given a notice to his tenants to pay their rent in gold, and that conduct having been defended by Lord Grenville and Lord Lauderdale, the Ministers determined to adopt the Bill; and they have prolonged the Session for the mere purpose of carrying it through. On the second reading of the Bill in the Lords, the Ministers had not determined what course they should take; but after consultations between Perceval, Lord Liverpool, and others of the Ministers while the debate was going on, they resolved to support it; and in the committee, they added a clause to take away from every person having a right to distrain for rent or any other debt, his power of distress, if the amount of his rent were tendered to him in bank notes. The third reading of this Bill in the House of Commons was on this day. I had voted against it on the first reading, and on going into a committee; and on this day I both spoke and voted against it. The minorities were all very small.[1] All the Regent's personal friends made a point, by his direction, of supporting the Bill in every stage of it, such as Lord Yarmouth, Tyrwhitt, and M'Mahon. Sheridan, too, attended and spoke in support of it.

24th, *Wed.* Parliament prorogued.

The Lord Chancellor.

Aug. 23d, *Fri.* The Chancellor ended his sittings. In the last fortnight, he has done more busi-

[1] On this occasion 95 voted in favour of the Bill, 20 against it.—Ed.

ness than in all the rest of the year. He has heard nearly three hundred petitions in Bankruptcy, and has decided as well as heard them. In the last week he sat every morning from nine to four; and in the evening, from half after five till ten; and he has not only done the business expeditiously, but with very great ability. It should seem as if his object had been to exhibit the most striking contrast imaginable to his usual mode of administering justice.

25th, *Sun.* Left town. Slept at Winchester, and the next day,

26th, passed over to the Isle of Wight to East Cowes.

30th, *Fri.* Set out for Durham.

Sept. 10th, *Tu.* Returned to Cowes in the Isle of Wight.

Prospect of an approaching election.

The King, whose insanity seems now to admit scarcely of any hope of recovery, was thought, a few weeks ago, to be in a state of health so alarming as to forebode a speedy termination of his sufferings. As his death must be soon followed by calling a new Parliament, a great deal of canvassing for seats has been going on throughout the kingdom. It has been intimated to me that it was proposed, in several places where the electors are very numerous, to put me up as a candidate; particularly at Liverpool, at Bristol, and in the county of Middlesex. Liverpool, however, affords the prospect of a violent contest, carried on with all the tumult which has so often disgraced that place at times of elections: I have, therefore, on the first intimation of the matter to me, expressed my determination not to consent to become the cause or the subject of any such contest. With respect, however, to Bristol, or to Middlesex, the case might be very different; and my sentiments respecting them are fully expressed in the correspondence which follows. The first letter was written to me by Lord Grenville. I received it just as I was leaving town, and did not answer it till I got to the Isle of Wight.

"My dear Sir, Dropmore, Aug. 23. 1811.

"It was mentioned to me a short time since, that there was a disposition among the same persons who had supported my election as Steward of Bristol, to look to you as a proper person to represent that city in a new Parliament. My answer could contain little more than expressions of that sincere regard and esteem which I feel towards you, and of the satisfaction I should derive from any public testimony of those feelings towards you, from so respectable and considerable a body as the electors of Bristol. A stranger myself to that place, I have very little pretensions to any interest there; and even the little I have, I felt I could not honourably pledge, until I had had the opportunity of communicating on the subject with the Duke of Norfolk, in concert with whom I had acted in all that regarded Bristol. I have this day seen him; and on the result of our conversation I think myself authorised to say on his part, as I most readily do on my own, that, if this object should be one in which you are willing to engage, you have every right to command whatever feeble

Lord Grenville's letter respecting Bristol.

assistance can be derived from the expression of my best wishes for your success, in every quarter in which they can by possibility be useful to it. If, when the business of your Court will admit of it, you can find a leisure day or two to give me the pleasure of your company here, I could in conversation better than by letter explain to you the little I know about Bristol and its interests.

"I am, dear Sir, with the most sincere regard, most truly yours, &c.

"GRENVILLE."

To this letter I returned the following answer :—

"My dear Lord, Cowes, Aug. 27. 1811.

My answer.

"I cannot too much thank your Lordship for your kind letter. Such a testimony of your good opinion I feel to be in the highest degree honourable, as it certainly is most flattering to me. It is proper, however, that I should fully explain to your Lordship what my views and sentiments respecting Bristol are. It had never entered my mind to offer myself as a candidate for it; but it has lately been suggested to me, that I might probably have a proposal made to me on behalf of the electors to represent them. In truth, however, to this moment, no direct communication with me on the subject has taken place. However much I might be flattered with the honour of representing such a body of constituents, yet nothing can be less suited to my inclination than to engage in a contest to obtain it. I certainly would not incur the expense of it; and I would still less expose myself to the trouble and vexation which must attend it. I am told, however, by the only gentleman who has ever talked with me on the subject, that the proposal would never be made to me, unless it could first be ascertained that I could come in without any contest, and consequently without any expense. The only difficulty that had occurred to that gentleman as likely to occasion me to hesitate at accepting the offer, was, that I might find the business which a Member for Bristol has necessarily to do for his constituents, incompatible with my other numerous occupations. Such an addition, however, to my labours I would cheerfully submit to, for what I own would be so highly gratifying to me, as to receive so strong and so honourable a proof of approbation of my public conduct, as that of being returned to Parliament by a numerous body of electors, to every one of whom I am personally a total stranger. That I shall receive such an honour, is that however of which I do not entertain any sanguine expectations. It would give me very great pleasure to be able to avail myself of your Lordship's obliging invitation, but I must leave this place in a few days for Durham, and I am afraid that, after that, my other engagements will take me very far from Dropmore. I write by this day's post to the Duke of Norfolk, to thank him for the interest which your Lordship says he is so kind as to take for me."

The idea of electing me for Middlesex, it seems, had been mentioned in a club, which is called the

Middlesex Freeholders' Club. Some of the members related this to my friend Basil Montagu, who told them he thought it very probable that I might have formed some engagements, which would make it impossible for me to accept such an offer if it were made to me; and he immediately afterwards wrote to me on the subject.

On the 10th of September, I sent him an answer from Cowes, where I then was, in these words:—

Letters respecting Middlesex election.

"My answer to your question is, that I am under no engagement to offer myself as a candidate to sit in Parliament for any place. I have not, indeed, had any direct application whatever made to me on the subject; and all that has passed with respect to the place you mention is, that it has been intimated to me, that such an application would very probably be made to me. With respect to the offer which you say I possibly may receive from a considerable number of the freeholders of Middlesex, I have no difficulty in explaining to you what I feel on that subject. I should think it the height of folly and presumption in me to offer myself as a candidate to represent the county. I feel that I have no kind of pretensions to it; but if the freeholders should be so well satisfied with my past conduct in parliament as to wish that I should represent them; and if, unsolicited on my part, they should be disposed to elect me, I certainly should consider it as the highest honour that could be conferred on me. I never have made, and I never will make, popular applause the object of my pursuit; but yet I have always felt that, next to the satisfaction which arises from the consciousness of having faithfully discharged one's duty, the best reward, in this life, of public services is the approbation of the public. With all this, however, I should feel great alarm at any proposal of the kind you mention being hastily made by too warm and sanguine friends. It would mortify me, I own, to a very great degree, to be put in nomination as a candidate and not to be returned; and yet I would not, in any event, put myself to any expense beyond that of the hustings which every candidate must bear, nor would I solicit a single vote. I cannot think that, under such circumstances, I should have the smallest chance of success."

I meant this letter to be shown to the persons who had applied to Montagu; and thinking I had not been sufficiently explicit, three days afterwards I wrote to him again.*

"My dear Sir, Cowes, Sept. 13. 1811.

"I answered your letter so quickly after I had read it, that I am afraid I did not explain myself so clearly as the importance of the occasion required, and I therefore trouble you with a second letter. Proud as I should be of so flattering a testimony in favour of my conduct in Parliament as that of being elected to represent the county of Middlesex, yet there are many circumstances

* I afterwards understood from Montagu that he did not show either of my letters to any one.

which, the more I reflect upon them, the more they convince me that it is hardly possible that I ever should obtain it. The popular representative, and much more the popular candidate, for a great county, is expected, I believe, to attend public dinners, and to make speeches at taverns, and give patriotic toasts. For such occupations I have neither time, capacity, nor inclination; and if, without these, the honour of representing Middlesex cannot be gained, I certainly never shall gain it. I do not presume to censure those who adopt such a line of conduct, but it would not suit me; and I am convinced that such a complete change of conduct and of character would entirely take away the chance, whatever it may be, which I may now have of doing any public good. Upon reading your letter again, I think I observe that this has struck you as forcibly as it does me. I have no expectation of ever being in a judicial station; but, without the expectation of it, I certainly do not pretend that there are no circumstances in which I might not think it greatly to be desired, and I never will act a part unbecoming the dignity of a station which, though I do not aspire to it, and though there is no probability, yet there is a possibility that I may at some time fill. It would be to entertain a very false and a ridiculously vain opinion of myself, to suppose that I stand so high in public estimation that I have any the remotest chance of being returned to Parliament without some exertion on my part; and I certainly have formed no such opinion: and yet, unless that were the case, I do not see how it would be possible for me to represent the county. Pray excuse the trouble of this second letter; but I should be extremely sorry if, by not being sufficiently explicit, I should have been the cause, to those who think well of me, of inconvenience which they never would have put themselves to, if they had known my real sentiments."

About a fortnight after this, I received a letter from Mr. Cartwright, who is generally called Major Cartwright, inclosing certain resolutions, as follows:—

"James Street, Buckingham Gate, Oct. 1. 1811.

"Dear Sir,

"I have thought it due to you to apprise you of a deputation which is appointed to wait on you, and the object of it. By the inclosed you will see that a beginning has been made towards a Middlesex election, propitious to public freedom. The Middlesex Freeholders' Club have thought it due to the constitution, as well as to their own consistency, to make such an explicit declaration of their opinion touching parliamentary reform as comes within their conception of the people's rights; and they of course are anxious that the representatives of their county should be chosen from among men holding, on a matter so infinitely important, the same opinions with themselves. It made likewise a part of their consideration, that their declarations may have a good effect in the way of example to other electors, besides promoting discussion which is ever favourable to political liberty. To Sir Samuel Romilly, more I believe

Mr. Cartwright's letter.

than to any other man of the present day, the parties would gladly have dispensed with asking a specific declaration of opinion, as a ground for entering into a positive resolution of proposing him. But, considering that, in times like the present, to propose to their county the election of a particular man involves in it a serious responsibility, they ought to be able to state that they have not so done on mere presumption, but on full knowledge of his holding correct opinions on points essential to the constitution. And this line of conduct seems the more advisable, when the declaration is to manifest how the party making it is to be classed; that is, whether as a real and rational reformist, or as one of those who style themselves moderate reformists; for under the respective leaders of these classes the mass of the people seem ripe for arranging themselves. Nothing having been settled as to the mode of making the wished-for declaration, my own idea of the matter is, that the most eligible way would be, not to give an individual signature, but one in common among several; and I shall make it my business to collect some, of persons every way respectable, in readiness for such a purpose. In the desperate situation in which public liberty stands, my own judgment tells me that, by making an honest and manly appeal to public reason and public spirit, we hazard nothing. It cannot make things worse. It may bring salvation. The power of truth, although proverbial, does not prevent its lying sometimes for ages dormant, while at critical periods, and issuing from the lips of men revered for their virtue and wisdom, its influence is rapid and resistless. We seem to be in a political crisis favourable to such an influence. After a thirty years' discussion on representation, sound argument must ever be at hand for putting down shallow sophistry or unprincipled cavil; and, as the public is not likely to prefer a shadow to a substance, or ignorance to knowledge, I am perfectly at ease on the part likely to be taken by the mass of the nation between the class of reformists I have already named. Although one of the deputation appointed to wait on you, I may very possibly be out of the way at the proper time, as I am now only detained in town by a life-boat experiment, and expect, in a week or less, to go into the North for two months or more.

"With the greatest respect and esteem, I remain, dear Sir, truly yours,

"J. CARTWRIGHT.

"To Sir S. Romilly."

Resolutions of the Middlesex Freeholders' Club.

At a meeting of the Middlesex Freeholders' Club, held at the Crown and Anchor Tavern, in the Strand, on Tuesday, September 24th, 1811, J. Cartwright in the chair, Resolved, "That it be earnestly recommended to the Freeholders of Middlesex, and to electors throughout the kingdom, not only to follow the example of Westminster, in sending to Parliament a representative free of personal expense, but never at any future election to vote for any person to serve in Parliament who shall not first have subscribed a declaration as follows:— 'I declare it to be my opinion that representation ought to have at least as wide an extent as taxation in support of the poor, the Church, and the State;

that such representation as a common right ought to be fairly distributed throughout the community; and that Parliaments ought to be brought back to a constitutional duration, that is, not exceeding one year.'" Resolved, "That provided the foregoing resolution shall express the opinion of Sir Samuel Romilly, and he shall signify the same by his signature, that gentleman shall at the next election be put in nomination for Middlesex, when a subscription shall be immediately opened for defraying all legal and unavoidable expense, that his election may be secured." Resolved, "That our chairman, together with Mr. Brooks and Mr. Adams, be a deputation to wait on Sir Samuel Romilly with the foregoing resolutions."

"N.B. The last resolution written from memory."

My answer was as follows: —

"TO JOHN CARTWRIGHT, ESQ.

"Dear Sir, "Cowes, Oct. 3.

"I am very much obliged to you for apprizing me of the resolutions come to at the meeting of the Middlesex Freeholders' Club, held on the 24th of last month, and of the application intended in consequence of them to be made to me. Whenever that application is made, I shall think myself obliged to decline the honour intended me; not, however, that I have any wish to retire from Parliament, or that I do not justly estimate the value of public opinion on the conduct of public men. To be returned by a numerous body of independent electors, to represent them in Parliament, without any solicitation on my part, and without using those arts which are often practised of making high professions and specious promises, and on no other ground than that I had by my past conduct appeared faithfully to discharge the duty which I owe to my country, would have been an honour of which I should have been prouder than of any that could be conferred upon me from any other quarter. But to put myself forward, though upon the invitation of a most respectable body of freeholders, as a candidate, and to subscribe an article of political faith, as a condition upon which a subscription was to be set on foot to defray the expense of a contest in my favour, is that which, though I shall not presume to censure it in others, would neither suit my inclination nor agree with those rules by which I have determined always to govern my conduct. I am very shortly about to leave this place, and shall be afterwards in Glamorganshire, and then in Herefordshire; but my stay in those places is so unfixed that I hardly know with certainty where I shall be on any particular day till the end of the month, when I shall return to London. I take the liberty of mentioning this to you, because I am very anxious to prevent the gentlemen who have done me the honour to undertake to communicate the resolutions to me having the trouble of making a useless journey; and you are perfectly at liberty, if you think proper, to communicate this letter to them."

A few days afterwards I received another and a very long letter from Mr. Cartwright, in which he seemed anxious that I should be prevailed on to give my opinion on the proposition contained in the resolution; and, if I approved it, that I should sign it; and that, after I had done so, a proposal should be made to me to stand for the county. The letter, however, was not so framed as to require an answer. But, on the 2d of November, he wrote to me again, and suggested some alteration which had been proposed in the resolution, and used many arguments to induce me to sign it. My answer to him was in these words: —

"Dear Sir, "Lincoln's Inn, Nov. 6. 1811.

"Your letter of the 5th of last month was received by me in the Isle of Wight, and I yesterday was honoured with yours of the 2d instant. I am very much obliged by the interest which you take on my behalf. I cannot say, however, after having very maturely considered your arguments, that I am convinced by them. If I were offering myself as a candidate to represent the county, I could well understand that the freeholders might say, 'Before we give you our votes, we desire to have an explicit declaration of your opinion on the subject of a reform in Parliament, and, to remove all misunderstanding, we desire to have it in writing.' But I am no candidate; I have not asked, and I will not ask, any man for his vote. If I were elected to represent the county, which I have never supposed in the least probable, the value of that honour, which I should consider as the highest that I could have received, would in my estimation consist principally in its having been conferred upon me without any solicitation, profession, or interference on my part. You will not, I am sure, suppose that I have the vanity to imagine that I have deserved any such honour; I know very well that I have not, and I am well contented to remain without it."

A little time after this, I received another letter from Mr. Cartwright, telling me that a case would be laid before me which he wished me to answer; and accordingly, in a few days, a case, with a fee of three guineas, was left at my chambers. The case was in these words: —

"Whereas A., B., and C. are anxious that, in matters touching the election of representatives to serve in Parliament, their own conduct should be in strict conformity with their public duty, and rightly directed to the advancement of the public service: And whereas they believe that the legislature hath not authority to violate the constitution, or to invade the rights and liberties of the nation: And whereas they also assent to that maxim which says, that Acts of Parliament which should be contrary to the constitution, and subversive of those rights and liberties, would not be statutes but corruptions: Wherefore, for their satisfaction, in respect of the proper constitutional securities of public liberty, and in aid of their judgment on the important point of their choosing representatives, they desire the opinion of Sir Samuel Romilly in answer to each of the three following queries:—

"1st. Doth not constitutional law require that Parliamentary representation should have at least as wide an extent as direct taxation, in support of the poor, the church, and the state?

"2dly. Doth not constitutional law require that such representation, as a common right, be fairly distributed throughout the community?

"3dly. Is it not required by the constitution, and by the rights and liberties of the nation, that the duration of Parliament should not exceed one year?

"Sir Samuel Romilly is requested to leave his answer with his clerk, sealed, and to be delivered to either of the persons who left the case."

This case I sealed up, and left out for the persons who should call for it, with this note: —

"Sir Samuel Romilly cannot consider the enclosed case as being laid before him, in the regular course of his profession, for his opinion on any question of law, and therefore he must decline answering it. He has directed his clerk to return the fee which was left with it.

"Lincoln's Inn, Nov. 18. 1811."

Thus, I presume, ends the scheme which had been formed of putting me up as a candidate for the county. I have placed all the preceding letters together, and now return to my journal.

I stayed in the Isle of Wight till the 12th of October, and then set out for Herefordshire, meaning to pass through Glamorganshire, that I might look at an estate which I have contracted to purchase.

29th. *Tu.* Arrived in town.

30th. *Wed.* The Lord Chancellor sat at Lincoln's-Inn Hall, and held the first seal.

The Lord Chancellor and the Master of the Rolls.

Nov. 28th. The Lord Chancellor has, in the course of this Michaelmas Term, been prevented from attending the Court for above a week by ill health. His place was supplied as usual by the Master of the Rolls, who heard so many causes, and made such progress in the Chancellor's paper, that, after striking out many causes, because the solicitors had not delivered briefs in them, he discontinued his sitting, in order to give the parties in the remaining causes time to prepare themselves to have their causes heard. If, among the expedients which have been thought of for clearing the present arrear of business, one should suggest that of the Chancellor's staying away entirely from his Court, it would be considered as a jest. The truth, however, is, that this would be so effectual an expedient, that, if the Lord Chancellor were only confined to his room by illness for two successive terms, there is no doubt that all the arrear of business, except the Bankrupt and Lunatic Petitions, and the Appeals (which the Master of the Rolls cannot hear), would be entirely got rid of. Application was made to-day to the Lord Chancellor, to restore to the paper two causes which had been struck out, when the Master of the Rolls sat for him, on the ground that they stood so low down that the solicitors had no reason to suppose that they would be called on, and had omitted to deliver their briefs to counsel. The Chancellor refused the application; and availed himself of this, as he has of several former opportunities, to complain from the Bench that great injustice had been done him, in representing him as the cause of the delays which existed in the Court; when it was manifest that the blame lay with the solicitors alone, who, though they charged their clients for their attendance every day that a cause was in the paper, neglected, it seems, to prepare and deliver their briefs. It would not quite follow of necessity, if the solicitors were the cause of delay in this instance, that the Chancellor might not be the cause of it in a great many others. The truth, however, is, that in this very instance much more blame is imputable to the Chancellor than to the solicitors. It is because the progress which he is accustomed to make is so very slow, that a solicitor never thinks of delivering briefs in causes which in the beginning of a Term stand, as these did, thirty or forty down in the cause book; and, indeed, that, with a due regard to economy on behalf of his client, he ought not to deliver them; since, by doing so, he will run the risk of having to pay (as has often happened) refreshing fees to counsel for seven or eight terms before the cause comes on to be heard.

Bristol election.

The gentlemen who have thought of proposing me as a candidate at Bristol have caused the following letter to be written to me: —

"Sir,

"Mr. Baillie, who for the last three Parliaments has been returned by the Whig interest of this city, having signified to his friends that ill health will prevent him again offering himself for our representation, several gentlemen, who are members of the Independent and Constitutional Club established in this city for the avowed purpose of preserving the freedom of election, and who have viewed with great satisfaction the uniform integrity and independence of your political conduct, are desirous of putting you in nomination in the club for that important trust, provided they have your sanction so to do. At the same time, they feel it their duty to apprize you that the large commercial interests of this city frequently impose considerable trouble on its representatives, in numerous applications which must necessarily be made to the Board of Treasury, and other public offices. In the multiplicity of your professional engagements, they have conceived that it is possible you may not wish to be burthened with the trouble of representing us; but some of them, who know your systematic and indefatigable exertions in business, indulge a confident hope that you will accede to their request; and they desire me to say that on their parts no pains shall be spared to accomplish the object of their most anxious wishes. I feel, Sir, that I ought to apologise to you, on behalf of my friends and myself, for taking this freedom with a gentleman personally unknown to every one of us; but our sole

Mr. Harris's letter.

object in requesting you to become a candidate, whenever the vacancy shall occur, is with a view to the public service; and, in the present critical state of affairs, we have thought that your opinions in Parliament might possibly derive some additional weight from being the representative of the second city in the kingdom: and this must be our apology. It is important for us to learn your sentiments as early as possible; and, if you will have the goodness to favour me with them at your earliest possible convenience, I will immediately communicate them to your other friends.

"I have the honour to be, Sir, your most obedient and faithful humble servant,

"Wintour Harris, Jun.

"Bristol, Dec. 14. 1811."

I returned the following answer: —

"Sir, "Lincoln's Inn, Dec. 17. 1811.

My answer.

"I have received the honour of your letter of the 14th instant, apprizing me that several gentlemen who are members of the Independent and Constitutional Club, established in Bristol for the avowed purpose of preserving the freedom of election, are desirous of putting me in nomination to represent the city in Parliament, provided they have my sanction to do so. Nothing, Sir, could be more gratifying to me than to be returned to Parliament by the city of Bristol. To receive such a testimonial of approbation of my public conduct from so numerous and so highly respectable a body of electors, would be considered by me as the highest honour I could attain, and as the noblest reward I could receive for my humble but anxious endeavours faithfully to discharge my duty to the public. It would afford me, too, the most lively satisfaction to find the opinions I have maintained, and the principles I have acted on, strengthened and supported by such authority. As I have scarcely the honour of a personal acquaintance with any individual in Bristol, it is those principles and opinions alone which can possibly have recommended me to their notice; and I can hardly express to you how very grateful it would be to me, to owe a seat in Parliament, and as the representative of such a city, to no personal favour, even with respect to a single vote, to no promises, to no professions, to no local interest, to no solicitation on my part, but solely to the favourable opinion which the electors entertained of my past conduct. But, favourably as some gentlemen may be disposed to think of me, it may perhaps be impossible that I should be elected to represent your city, without engaging personally in a contest, or canvassing for votes. You, Sir, who undoubtedly know what is likely to be expected by the electors, must be well able to judge of this. For myself, I can only say that, highly as I should prize the honour of representing Bristol, it is that which I should not a moment hesitate to forego, if, in order to obtain it, it were necessary for me to engage in a personal contest, or to enter upon a canvass of the voters, or even to take any step which could be considered as announcing myself as a candidate previous to a dissolution of Parliament or to a vacancy in the representation of the city. A stranger, personally, to every elector, I know not on what pretence I could put myself forward as a candidate, or ask them for their votes. It would be unnecessary to do so if my past services in Parliament have, in their opinion, rendered me worthy of the honour of representing them; and if they have not, it would be a very foolish presumption in me to aspire to that honour. I observe what you are pleased to suggest respecting the applications necessary to be made by a representative of Bristol to the Treasury and other public boards. With the extent and nature of those applications I am unacquainted; it is quite impossible for me, therefore, to judge how far they may be compatible with my present unavoidable occupations; and I would not, for any consideration, hold out to the electors expectations which I could not fulfil. Though I would most cheerfully devote to the performance of such services all the time that I could properly withdraw from my other labours, yet I am bound to say that, as long as I continue in the profession which I now follow, I am afraid that it will be scarcely possible for me to give any very considerable portion of time to applications and attendances upon public boards, and at the same time keep the engagements which I have entered into with those who have entrusted to my hands interests which to them are highly important. I have thought it right to be thus frank and explicit; for, proportioned to the satisfaction which I should feel at being one of the representatives of Bristol, would be the mortification I should experience, if, after having been raised to that honourable station, I should be found to disappoint the expectations of those who had placed me there. Let me beg of you, Sir, to accept my best thanks for the very kind and flattering terms in which you have been pleased to make this communication to me.

"I have the honour to be, Sir,

"Your most obedient and faithful Servant,

"SAMUEL ROMILLY."

END OF THE SECOND VOLUME.

LONDON:
Printed by A. SPOTTISWOODE,
New-Street-Square.